The Collected Works of
William Howard Taft

The Collected Works of
William Howard Taft

David H. Burton, General Editor

VOLUME IV

PRESIDENTIAL MESSAGES TO CONGRESS

Edited with Commentary by
David H. Burton

OHIO UNIVERSITY PRESS

ATHENS

Ohio University Press, Athens, Ohio 45701
© 2002 by Ohio University Press
Printed in the United States of America
All rights reserved

Ohio University Press books are printed on acid-free paper ♾ ™

09 08 07 06 05 04 03 02   5 4 3 2 1

Publication of *The Collected Works of William Howard Taft* has been made possible in part through the generous support of the Earhart Foundation of Ann Arbor, Michigan, and the Louisa Taft Semple Foundation of Cincinnati, Ohio.

Frontispiece: Photograph of William Howard Taft courtesy of
William Howard Taft National Historic Site

Library of Congress Cataloging-in-Publication Data
(Revised for volume 4)

Taft, William H. (William Howard), 1857–1930.
Presidential messages to congress / edited with commentary by David H. Burton.
   p.   cm.—(The collected works of William Howard Taft ; v. 4)
Includes bibliographical references.
ISBN 0-8214-1435-6 (acid-free paper)
   1. Citizenship—United States. 2. United States—Politics and government—1910–1913. 3. United States—Foreign relations—1910–1913. I. Burton, David Henry, 1925– . II. Taft, William H. (William Howard), 1857–1930. Presidential messages to congress. III. Title. IV. Series: Taft, Willam H. (William Howard), 1857–1930. Selections. 2002 ; v. 4.

JK1759.T27 2002
323.6'5'0973—dc21   00-055807

Dedicated to
the Taft family,
for five generations serving
Ohio and the nation

The Collected Works of
William Howard Taft

David H. Burton, General Editor

VOLUME ONE
Four Aspects of Civic Duty and *Present Day Problems*
Edited with commentary by David H. Burton and A. E. Campbell

VOLUME TWO
Political Issues and Outlooks
Edited with commentary by David H. Burton

VOLUME THREE
Presidential Addresses and State Papers
Edited with commentary by David H. Burton

VOLUME FOUR
Presidential Messages to Congress
Edited with commentary by David H. Burton

VOLUME FIVE
Popular Government and *The Anti-trust Act and the Supreme Court*
Edited with commentary by David Potash and Donald F. Anderson

VOLUME SIX
The President and His Powers and *The United States and Peace*
Edited with commentary by Wilson Carey McWilliams and Frank X. Gerrity

VOLUME SEVEN
Taft Papers on League of Nations
Edited with commentary by Frank X. Gerrity

VOLUME EIGHT
"Liberty under Law" and Selected Supreme Court Opinions
Edited with commentary by Francis Graham Lee
Cumulative Index

Contents

Commentary

————

David H. Burton

M ost of the interaction between the executive and the legislative branches of the federal government—or, to personalize it, between Taft and the leaders in Congress—occurred between December 1910 and March 1913. This is exactly the period which volume four covers, and the speeches presented here demonstrate the president's well-thought-out advice to the law-making body. And of course it provided the public with a window on Taft's leadership. To put it another way, Taft was not shy about using his veto power from time to time, however exceptional this proved to be. He displayed leadership in his 1910 message when he went out of his way, if not out on a limb, to recommend a federal law to protect resident aliens against denial of the civil rights guaranteed them by treaty. In his book *United States and Peace,* written some years later, he reiterated his plea because no action had been taken by Congress to address the issue.

As a rule his annual messages demonstrated the president's wide-ranging concern for issues as diverse as Alaskan railroads, Panama Canal tolls, national parks, and the Bureau of Lighthouses, as a sampling of the Congressional Record testifies. Taft's reputation as a detail man is borne out, yet he put such particulars in the larger framework of constitutional/political reality. His special message on Canadian reciprocity, that is free trade between the countries, is a good example of Taft buffeted by the winds of domestic politics: the fierce opposition of corporate-minded congressmen. He sought what he considered a worthwhile move, international in character, with our nearest and dearest neighbor. He went so far as to recommend this trade proposal on two occasions. The Canadian Reciprocity Treaty, when it was finally drafted, was rejected by the United States Senate as a danger to, among other industries, the New England fisheries. Not to be outdone, the Canadian government resisted the treaty on the grounds that it was a devious attempt to bring about economic domination by the United States. Taft was ahead of his time in this undertaking.

President Taft's resort to the veto power was never more abundantly in evidence than in his rejection of a joint Congressional resolution for the admission of New Mexico and Arizona to statehood. Pointing out in his August 22, 1911, veto message that he had approved the constitution of New Mexico beforehand, he interpreted the joint resolution as a political ploy, a *ruse de guerre*. He strongly opposed the Arizona constitution because it provided for the recall of elected judges. He deemed this "pernicious in its effects . . . destructive of the independence of judges . . . injurious to the cause of free government." Tough language indeed—and effective. Arizona altered its constitution to meet Taft's objection and thereupon became the forty-eighth state to enter the Union.

In a post-presidential book, *The President and His Powers,* Taft, writing as someone who had occupied that high office, offered the judgment that a president should be as strong an executive as the Constitution allowed. It should be noted in this respect that he conceived of his responsibilities as including the conduct of diplomacy as the United States entered into its place among the world powers. His prior experience—he was civil governor in the Philippines and then Secretary of War in Theodore Roosevelt's cabinet—was vital as he undertook his program of Dollar Diplomacy. During Taft's administration the State Department was reorganized and greatly expanded, but admittedly his ideas on trade and diplomacy were not always accepted by the Senate. He did not allow the so-called "big picture" to distract him from some prosaic matters which affected the people at large, as borne out in his concern for improved service by the Post Office: rural free delivery, parcel post, and, most people-sensitive, a postal savings bank for the plain people. And there is this recurring note discoverable in his messages: a concern for economy and efficiency in all Federal government services.

In 1912, the last full year of his presidency, Taft advocated two reforms which were remarkably "progressive" in character. His special message of February 20, 1912, called on the Congress to pass an Employers' Workmen's Liability Act. Partway through his message he extolled its benefits to workers: "I sincerely hope that this act will pass. I deem it one of the great steps of progress toward a satisfactory solution of an important phase of the controversies between employer and employee." The other reform of 1912 dealt with international peace. In proposing to enter into treaties of arbitration with Great Britain and France, Taft argued the proposition that there should be no disagreement between the parties which could not be submitted to binding arbitration. It was an offer of far-reaching significance, and the president was especially eager to see the treaties through to completion. As he told his military aide and good friend Archie Butt, passage of the treaties would be the capstone of his presidency, or, if he should fail in his efforts, the bitterest of defeats. Unfortunately, the Senate so revised the terms of the treaty that Taft was unwilling to send it on to London or Paris. The president's dream of international accord had died aborning.

One final observation is in order. Throughout these many messages Taft reveals in himself a certain kind of paternalism. It is not a variation of "father knows best." Rather there is exhibited time after time concern for the American people, for men and women from different walks of life. He comes across less as the judge he had been or the chief justice he was to become and more as a sitting president of all the people. He never forgot his friends in the Philippines or the ordinary folks who needed a safe place to invest their modest savings. He was very much an American in the historic sense—witness his zealous concern for the civil rights of aliens living in his native land. Legend has it that William Howard Taft was a wonderful grandfather. History reveals the political Taft in much the same light.

1

Second Annual Message

The White House, December 6, 1910

To the Senate and House of Representatives:
During the past year the foreign relations of the United States have continued upon a basis of friendship and good understanding.

Arbitration

The year has been notable as witnessing the pacific settlement of two important international controversies before the Permanent Court of The Hague.

The arbitration of the fisheries dispute between the United States and Great Britain, which has been the source of nearly continuous diplomatic correspondence since the Fisheries Convention of 1818, has given an award which is satisfactory to both parties. This arbitration is particularly noteworthy not only because of the eminently just results secured, but also because it is the first arbitration held under the general arbitration treaty of April 4, 1908, between the United States and Great Britain, and disposes of a controversy the settlement of which has resisted every other resource of diplomacy, and which for nearly ninety years has been the cause of friction between two countries whose common interest lies in maintaining the most friendly and cordial relations with each other.

The United States was ably represented before the tribunal. The complicated history of the questions arising made the issue depend, more than ordinarily in such cases, upon the care and skill with which our case was presented, and I should be wanting in proper recognition of a great patriotic service if I did not refer to the lucid historical analysis of the facts and the signal ability and force of the argument—six days in length—presented to the Court in support of our case by Mr. Elihu Root. As Secretary of State, Mr. Root had given close study to the intricate facts bearing on the controversy, and by diplomatic correspondence had helped to frame the issues. At the solicitation of the Secretary of State and myself, Mr. Root, though burdened by his duties as Senator from New York, undertook the preparation of the case as leading counsel, with the condition imposed by himself that, in view of his position as Senator, he should not receive any compensation.

The tribunal constituted at The Hague by the Governments of the United States and Venezuela has completed its deliberations and has rendered an award in the case of the Orinoco Steamship Company against Venezuela. The award may be regarded as satisfactory since it has, pursuant to the contentions of the United States, recognized a number of important principles making for a judicial attitude in the determining of international disputes.

In view of grave doubts which had been raised as to the constitutionality of The Hague Convention for the Establishment of an International Prize Court, now before the Senate for ratification, because of that provision of the Convention which provides that there may be an appeal to the proposed Court from the decisions of national courts, this government proposed in an Identic Circular Note addressed to those Powers who had taken part in the London Maritime Conference, that the powers signatory to the Convention, if confronted with such difficulty, might insert a reservation to the effect that appeals to the International Prize Court in respect to decisions of its national tribunals, should take the form of a direct claim for compensation; that the proceedings thereupon to be taken should be in the form of a trial *de novo,* and that judgment of the Court should consist of compensation for the illegal capture, irrespective of the decision of the national court whose judgment had thus been internationally involved. As the result of an informal discussion it was decided to provide such procedure by means of a separate protocol which should be ratified at the same time as the Prize Court Convention itself.

Accordingly, the Government of the Netherlands, at the request of this Government, proposed under date of May 24, 1910, to the powers signatory to The Hague Convention, the negotiation of a supplemental protocol embodying stipulations providing for this alternative procedure. It is gratifying to observe that this additional protocol is being signed without objection, by the powers signatory to the original convention, and there is every reason to believe that the International Prize Court will be soon established.

The Identic Circular Note also proposed that the International Prize Court when established should be endowed with the functions of an Arbitral Court of Justice under and pursuant to the recommendation adopted by the last Hague Conference. The replies received from the various powers to this proposal inspire the hope that this also may be accomplished within the reasonably near future.

It is believed that the establishment of these two tribunals will go a long way toward securing the arbitration of many questions which have heretofore threatened and, at times, destroyed the peace of nations.

Peace Commission

Appreciating these enlightened tendencies of modern times, the Congress at its last session passed a law providing for the appointment of a commission of five members "to be appointed by the President of the United States to consider the expediency of utilizing existing international agencies for the purpose of limiting the armaments of the nations of the world by international agreement, and of constituting the combined navies of the world an international force for the preservation of universal peace, and to consider and report upon any other means to diminish the expenditures of government for military purposes and to lessen the probabilities of war."

I have not as yet made appointments to this Commission because I have invited and am awaiting the expressions of foreign governments as to their willingness to cooperate with us in the appointment of similar commissions or representatives who would meet with our commissioners and by joint action seek to make their work effective.

Great Britain and Canada

Several important treaties have been negotiated with Great Britain in the past twelve months. A preliminary diplomatic agreement has been reached regarding the arbitration of pecuniary claims which each Government has against the other. This agreement, with the schedules of claims annexed, will, as soon as the schedules are arranged, be submitted to the Senate for approval.

An agreement between the United States and Great Britain with regard to the location of the international boundary line between the United States and Canada in Passamaquoddy Bay and to the middle of Grand Manan Channel was reached in a Treaty concluded May 21, 1910, which has been ratified by both Governments and proclaimed, thus making unnecessary the arbitration provided for in the previous treaty of April 11, 1908.

The Convention concluded January 11, 1909, between the United States and Great Britain providing for the settlement of international differences between the United States and Canada including the apportionment between the two countries of certain of the boundary waters and the appointment of Commissioners to adjust certain other questions has been ratified by both Governments and proclaimed.

The work of the International Fisheries Commission appointed in 1908, under the treaty of April 11, 1908, between Great Britain and the United States, has resulted in the formulation and recommendation of uniform regulations governing the fisheries of the boundary waters of Canada and the United States for the purpose of protecting and increasing the supply of food fish in such waters. In completion of this work, the regulations agreed upon require congressional legislation to make them effective and for their enforcement in fulfillment of the treaty stipulations.

Portugal

In October last the monarchy in Portugal was overthrown, a provisional Republic was proclaimed, and there was set up a de facto Government which was promptly recognized by the Government of the United States for purposes of ordinary intercourse pending formal recognition by this and other Powers of the Governmental entity to be duly established by the national sovereignty.

Liberia

A disturbance among the native tribes of Liberia in a portion of the Republic during the early part of this year resulted in the sending, under the Treaty of 1862, of an American vessel of war to the disaffected district, and the Liberian authorities, assisted by the good offices of the American Naval Officers, were able to restore order. The negotiations which have been undertaken for the amelioration of the conditions found in Liberia by the American Commission, whose report I transmitted to Congress on March 25 last, are being brought to conclusion, and it is thought that within a short time practical measures of relief may be put into effect through the good offices of this Government and the cordial cooperation of other governments interested in Liberia's welfare.

The Near East

Turkey

To return the visit of the Special Embassy announcing the accession of His Majesty Mehemet V, Emperor of the Ottomans, I sent to Constantinople a Special Ambassador who, in addition to this mission of ceremony, was charged with the duty of expressing to the Ottoman Government the value attached by the Government of the United States to increased and more important relations between the countries and the desire of the United States to contribute to the larger economic and commercial development due to the new régime in Turkey.

The rapid development now beginning in that ancient empire and the marked progress and increased commercial importance of Bulgaria, Rumania, and Serbia make it particularly opportune that the possibilities of American commerce in the Near East should receive due attention.

Montenegro

The National Skoupchtina having expressed its will that the Principality of Montenegro be raised to the rank of Kingdom, the Prince of Montenegro on August 15 last assumed the title of King of Montenegro. It gave me pleasure to accord to the new kingdom the recognition of the United States.

The Far East

The center of interest in Far Eastern affairs during the past year has again been China.

It is gratifying to note that the negotiations for a loan to the Chinese Government for the construction of the trunk railway lines from Hankow southward to Canton and westward through the Yangtse Valley, known as the Hukuang Loan, were concluded by the representatives of the various financial groups in May last and the results approved by their respective governments. The agreement, already initialed by the Chinese Government, is now awaiting formal ratification. The basis of the settlement of the terms of this loan was one of exact equality between America, Great Britain, France, and Germany in respect to financing the loan and supplying materials for the proposed railways and their future branches.

The application of the principle underlying the policy of the United States in regard to the Hukuang Loan, viz., that of the internationalization of the foreign interest in such of the railways of China as may be financed by foreign countries, was suggested on a broader scale by the Secretary of State in a proposal for internationalization and commercial neutralization of all the railways of Manchuria. While the principle which led to the proposal of this Government was generally admitted by the powers to whom it was addressed, the Governments of Russia and Japan apprehended practical difficulties in the execution of the larger plan which prevented their ready adherence. The question of constructing the Chinchow-Aigun railway by means of an international loan to China is, however, still the subject of friendly discussion by the interested parties.

The policy of this Government in these matters has been directed by a desire to make the use American capital in the development of China an instrument in the promotion of China's welfare and material prosperity without prejudice to her legitimate rights as an independent political power.

This policy has recently found further exemplification in the assistance given by this Government to the negotiations between China and a group of American bankers for a loan of $50,000,000 to be employed chiefly in currency reform. The confusion which has from ancient times existed in the monetary usages of the Chinese has been one of the principal obstacles to commercial intercourse with that people. The United States in its Treaty of 1903 with China obtained a pledge from the latter to introduce a uniform national coinage, and the following year, at the request of China, this Government sent to Peking a member of the International Exchange Commission, to discuss with the Chinese Government the best methods of introducing the reform. In 1908 China sent a Commissioner to the United States to consult with American financiers as to the possibility of securing a large loan with which to inaugurate the new currency system, but the death of Their Majesties, the Empress Dowager and the Emperor of China, interrupted the negotiations, which were not resumed until a few months ago, when this Government was asked to communicate to the bankers concerned the request of China for a loan of $50,000,000 for the purpose under review. A preliminary agreement between the American group and China has been made covering the loan.

For the success of this loan and the contemplated reforms which are of the greatest importance to the commercial interests of the United States and the civilized world at large, it is realized that an expert will be necessary, and this Government has received assurances from China that such an adviser, who shall be an American, will be engaged.

It is a matter of interest to Americans to note the success which is attending the efforts of China to establish gradually a system of representative government. The provincial assemblies were opened in October, 1909, and in October of the present year a consultative body, the nucleus of the future national parliament, held its first session at Peking.

The year has further been marked by two important international agreements relating to Far Eastern affairs. In the Russo-Japanese Agreement relating to Manchuria, signed July 4, 1910, this Government was gratified to note an assurance of continued peaceful conditions in that region and the reaffirmation of the policies with respect to China to which the United States together with all other interested powers are alike solemnly committed.

The treaty annexing Korea to the Empire of Japan, promulgated August 29, 1910, marks the final step in a process of control of the ancient empire by her powerful neighbor that has been in progress for several years past. In communicating the fact of annexation the Japanese Government gave to the Government of the United States assurances of the full protection of the rights of American citizens in Korea under the changed conditions.

Friendly visits of many distinguished persons from the Far East have been made during the year. Chief among these were Their Imperial Highnesses Princes Tsai-tao and Tsai-Hsun of China; and His Imperial Highness Prince Higashi Fushimi, and Prince Tokugawa, President of the House of Peers of Japan. The Secretary of War has recently visited Japan and China in connection with his tour to the Philippines, and a large delegation of American business men are at present traveling in China. This exchange of friendly visits has had the happy effect of even further strengthening our friendly international relations.

Latin America

During the past year several of our southern sister Republics celebrated the one hundredth anniversary of their independence. In honor of these events, special embassies were sent from this country to Argentina, Chile, and Mexico, where the gracious reception and splendid hospitality extended them manifested the cordial relations and friendship existing between those countries and the United States, relations which I am happy to believe have never before been upon so high a plane and so solid a basis as at present.

The Congressional commission appointed under a concurrent resolution to attend the festivities celebrating the centennial anniversary of Mexican independence, together with a special ambassador, were received with the highest honors and with the greatest cordiality, and returned with the report of the bounteous hospitality and warm reception of President Diaz and the Mexican people, which left no doubt of the desire of the immediately neighboring Republic to continue the mutually beneficial and intimate relations which I feel sure the two governments will ever cherish.

At the Fourth Pan-American Conference which met in Buenos Aires during July and August last, after seven weeks of harmonious deliberation, three conventions were signed providing for the regulation of trade-marks, patents, and copyrights, which when ratified by the different Governments, will go far toward furnishing to American authors, patentees, and owners of trade-marks the protection needed in localities where heretofore it has been either lacking or inadequate. Further, a convention for the arbitration of pecuniary claims was signed and a number of important resolutions passed. The Conventions will in due course be transmitted to the Senate, and the report of the Delegation of the United States will be communicated to the Congress for its information. The special cordiality between representative men from all parts of America which was shown at this Conference cannot fail to react upon and draw still closer the relations between the countries which took part in it.

The International Bureau of American Republics is doing a broad and useful work for Pan American commerce and comity. Its duties were much enlarged by the International Conference of American States at Buenos Aires and its name was shortened to the more practical and expressive term of Pan American Union. Located now in its new building, which was specially dedicated April 26 of this year to the development of friendship, trade and peace among the American nations, it has improved instrumentalities to serve the twenty-two republics of this hemisphere.

I am glad to say that the action of the United States in its desire to remove imminent danger of war between Peru and Ecuador growing out of a boundary dispute, with the cooperation of Brazil and the Argentine Republic as joint mediators with this Government, has already resulted successfully in preventing war. The Government of Chile, while not one of the mediators, lent effective aid in furtherance of a preliminary agreement likely to lead on to an amicable settlement, and it is not doubted that the good offices of the mediating Powers and the conciliatory cooperation of the Governments directly interested will finally lead to a removal of this perennial cause of friction between Ecuador and Peru. The inestimable value of cordial cooperation between the sister republics of America for the maintenance of peace in this hemisphere has never been more clearly shown than in this mediation, by which three American Governments have given to this hemisphere the honor of first invoking the most far-reaching provisions of The Hague Convention for the pacific settlement of international disputes.

There has been signed by the representatives of the United States and Mexico a protocol submitting to the United States-Mexican Boundary Commission (whose membership for the purpose of this case is to be increased by the addition of a citizen of Canada) the question of sovereignty over the Chamizal Tract which lies within the present physical boundaries of the city of El Paso, Texas. The determination of this question will remove a source of no little annoyance to the two Governments.

The Republic of Honduras has for many years been burdened with a heavy bonded debt held in Europe, the interest on which long ago fell in arrears. Finally conditions were such that it became imperative to refund the debt and place the finances of the Republic upon a sound basis. Last year a group of American bankers undertook to do this and to advance funds for railway and other improvements contributing directly to the country's prosperity and commerce—an arrangement which has long been desired by this Government. Negotiations to this end have been under way for more than a year and it is now confidently believed that a short time will suffice to conclude an arrangement which will be satisfactory to the foreign creditors, eminently advantageous to Honduras, and highly creditable to the judgment and foresight of the Honduran Government. This is much to be desired since, as recognized by the Washington Conventions, a strong Honduras would tend immensely to the progress and prosperity of Central America.

During the past year the Republic of Nicaragua has been the scene of internecine struggle. General Zelaya, for seventeen years the absolute ruler of Nicaragua, was throughout his career the disturber of Central America and opposed every plan for the promotion of peace and friendly relations between the five republics. When the people of Nicaragua were finally driven into rebellion by his lawless exactions, he violated the laws of war by the unwarranted execution of two American citizens who had regularly enlisted in the ranks of the revolutionists. This and other offenses made it the duty of the American Government to take measures with a view to ultimate reparation and for the safeguarding of its interests. This involved the breaking off of all diplomatic relations with the Zelaya Government for the reasons laid down in a communication from the Secretary of State, which also notified the contending factions in Nicaragua that this Government would hold each to strict accountability for outrages on the rights of American citizens. American forces were sent to both coasts of Nicaragua to be in readiness should occasion arise to protect Americans and their interests, and remained there until the war was over and peace had returned to that unfortunate country. These events, together with Zelaya's continued exactions, brought him so clearly to the bar of public opinion that he was forced to resign and to take refuge abroad.

In the above-mentioned communication of the Secretary of State to the Chargé d'Affaires of the Zelaya Government, the opinion was expressed that the revolution represented the wishes of the majority of the Nicaraguan people. This has now been proved beyond doubt by the fact that since the complete overthrow of the Madriz Government and the occupation of the capital by the forces of the revolution, all factions have united to maintain public order and as a result of discussion with an Agent of this Government, sent to Managua at the request of the Provisional Government, comprehensive plans are being made for the future welfare of Nicaragua, including the rehabilitation of public credit. The moderation and conciliatory spirit shown by the various factions give ground for the confident hope that Nicaragua will soon take its rightful place among the law-abiding and progressive countries of the world.

It gratifies me exceedingly to announce that the Argentine Republic some months ago placed with American manufacturers a contract for the construction of two battle-ships and certain additional naval equipment. The extent of this work and its importance to the Argentine Republic make the placing of the bid an earnest of friendly feeling toward the United States.

Tariff Negotiations

The new tariff law, in section 2, respecting the maximum and minimum tariffs of the United States, which provisions came into effect on April 1,

1910, imposed upon the President the responsibility of determining prior to that date whether or not any undue discrimination existed against the United States and its products in any country of the world with which we sustained commercial relations.

In the case of several countries, instances of apparent undue discrimination against American commerce were found to exist. These discriminations were removed by negotiation. Prior to April 1, 1910, when the maximum tariff was to come into operation with respect to importations from all those countries in whose favor no proclamation applying the minimum tariff should be issued by the President, one hundred and thirty-four such proclamations were issued. This series of proclamations embraced the entire commercial world, and hence the minimum tariff of the United States has been given universal application, thus testifying to the satisfactory character of our trade relations with foreign countries.

Marked advantages to the commerce of the United States were obtained through these tariff settlements. Foreign nations are fully cognizant of the fact that under section 2 of the tariff act the President is required, whenever he is satisfied that the treatment accorded by them to the products of the United States is not such as to entitle them to the benefits of the minimum tariff of the United States, to withdraw those benefits by proclamation giving ninety days' notice, after which the maximum tariff will apply to their dutiable products entering the United States. In its general operation this section of the tariff law has thus far proved a guaranty of continued commercial peace, although there are unfortunately instances where foreign governments deal arbitrarily with American interests within their jurisdiction in a manner injurious and inequitable.

The policy of broader and closer trade relations with the Dominion of Canada which was initiated in the adjustment of the maximum and minimum provisions of the Tariff Act of August, 1909, has proved mutually beneficial. It justifies further efforts for the readjustment of the commercial relations of the two countries so that their commerce may follow the channels natural to contiguous countries and be commensurate with the steady expansion of trade and industry on both sides of the boundary line. The reciprocation on the part of the Dominion Government of the sentiment which was expressed by this Government was followed in October by the suggestion that it would be glad to have the negotiations, which had been temporarily suspended during the summer, resumed. In accordance with this suggestion the Secretary of State, by my direction, dispatched two representatives of the Department of State as special commissioners to Ottawa to confer with representatives of the Dominion Government. They were authorized to take such steps for formulating a reciprocal trade agreement as might be necessary and to receive and consider any propositions which the Dominion Government might care to submit.

Pursuant to the instructions issued conferences were held by these commissioners with officials of the Dominion Government at Ottawa in the early part of November.

The negotiations were conducted on both sides in a spirit of mutual accommodation. The discussion of the common commercial interests of the two countries had for its object a satisfactory basis for a trade arrangement which offers the prospect of a freer interchange for the products of the United States and of Canada. The conferences were adjourned to be resumed in Washington in January, when it is hoped that the aspiration of both Governments for a mutually advantageous measure of reciprocity will be realized.

Fostering Foreign Trade

All these tariff negotiations, so vital to our commerce and industry, and the duty of jealously guarding the equitable and just treatment of our products, capital, and industry abroad devolve upon the Department of State.

The Argentine battle-ship contracts, like the subsequent important one for Argentine railway equipment, and those for Cuban Government vessels, were secured for our manufacturers largely through the good offices of the Department of State.

The efforts of that Department to secure for citizens of the United States equal opportunities in the markets of the world and to expand American commerce have been most successful. The volume of business obtained in new fields of competition and upon new lines is already very great and Congress is urged to continue to support the Department of State in its endeavors for further trade expansion.

Our foreign trade merits the best support of the Government and the most earnest endeavor of our manufacturers and merchants, who, if they do not already in all cases need a foreign market, are certain soon to become dependent on it. Therefore, now is the time to secure a strong position in this field.

American Branch Banks Abroad

I cannot leave this subject without emphasizing the necessity of such legislation as will make possible and convenient the establishment of American banks and branches of American banks in foreign countries. Only by such means can our foreign trade be favorably financed, necessary credits be arranged, and proper avail be made of commercial opportunities in foreign countries, and most especially in Latin America.

Aid to Our Foreign Merchant Marine

Another instrumentality indispensable to the unhampered and natural development of American commerce is merchant marine. All maritime and commercial nations recognize the importance of this factor. The greatest commercial nations, our competitors, jealously foster their merchant marine. Perhaps nowhere is the need for rapid and direct mail, passenger and freight communication quite so urgent as between the United States and Latin America. We can secure in no other quarter of the world such immediate benefits in friendship and commerce as would flow from the establishment of direct lines of communication with the countries of Latin America adequate to meet the requirements of a rapidly increasing appreciation of the reciprocal dependence of the countries of the Western Hemisphere upon each other's products, sympathies and assistance.

I alluded to this most important subject in my last annual message; it has often been before you and I need not recapitulate the reasons for its recommendation. Unless prompt action be taken, the completion of the Panama Canal will find this the only great commercial nation unable to avail in international maritime business of this great improvement in the means of the world's commercial intercourse.

Quite aside from the commercial aspect, unless we create a merchant marine, where can we find the seafaring population necessary as a natural naval reserve and where could we find, in case of war, the transports and subsidiary vessels without which a naval fleet is arms without a body? For many reasons I cannot too strongly urge upon the Congress the passage of a measure by mail subsidy or other subvention adequate to guarantee the establishment and rapid development of an American merchant marine, and the restoration of the American flag to its ancient place upon the seas.

Of course such aid ought only to be given under conditions of publicity of each beneficiary's business and accounts which would show that the aid received was needed to maintain the trade and was properly used for that purpose.

Federal Protection to Aliens

With our increasing international intercourse, it becomes incumbent upon me to repeat more emphatically than ever the recommendation which I made in my Inaugural Address that Congress shall at once give to the Courts of the United States jurisdiction to punish as a crime the violation of the rights of aliens secured by treaty with the United States, in order that the general government of the United States shall be able, when called upon by a friendly nation, to redeem its solemn promise by treaty to secure to the citizens or subjects of that nation resident in the United States, freedom from violence and due process of law in respect to their life, liberty and property.

Merit System for Diplomatic and Consular Service

I also strongly commend to the favorable action of the Congress the enactment of a law applying to the diplomatic and consular service the principles embodied in Section 1753 of the Revised Statutes of the United States, in the Civil Service Act of January 16, 1883, and the Executive Orders of June 27, 1906, and of November 26, 1909. The excellent results which have attended the partial application of Civil Service principles to the diplomatic and consular services are an earnest of the benefit to be wrought by a wider and more permanent extension of those principles to both branches of the foreign service. The marked improvement in the consular service during the four years since the principles of the Civil Service Act were applied to that service in a limited way, and the good results already noticeable from a similar application of civil service principles to the diplomatic service a year ago, convince me that the enactment into law of the general principles of the existing executive regulations could not fail to effect further improvement of both branches of the foreign service, offering as it would by its assurance of permanency of tenure and promotion on merit, an inducement for the entry of capable young men into the service and an incentive to those already in to put forth their best efforts to attain and maintain that degree of efficiency which the interests of our international relations and commerce demand.

Government Ownership of Our Embassy and Legation Premises

During many years past appeals have been made from time to time to Congress in favor of Government ownership of embassy and legation premises abroad. The arguments in favor of such ownership have been many and oft repeated and are well known to the Congress. The acquisition by the Government of suitable residences and offices for its diplomatic officers, especially in the capitals of the Latin-American States and of Europe, is so important and necessary to an improved diplomatic service that I have no hesitation in urging upon the Congress the passage of some measure similar to that favorably reported by the House Committee on Foreign Affairs on February 14, 1910 (Report No. 438), that would authorize the gradual and annual acquisition of premises for diplomatic use.

The work of the Diplomatic Service is devoid of partisanship; its importance should appeal to every American citizen and should receive the generous consideration of the Congress.

Treasury Department

Estimates for Next Year's Expenses

Every effort has been made by each department chief to reduce the estimated cost of his department for the ensuing fiscal year ending June 30, 1912. I say this in order that Congress may understand that these estimates thus made present the smallest sum which will maintain the departments, bureaus, and offices of the Government and meet its other obligations under existing law, and that a cut of these estimates would result in embarrassing the executive branch of the Government in the performance of its duties. This remark does not apply to the river and harbor estimates, except to those for expenses of maintenance and the meeting of obligations under authorized contracts, nor does it apply to the public building bill nor to the navy building program. Of course, as to these Congress could withhold any part or all of the estimates for them without interfering with the discharge of the ordinary obligations of the Government or the performance of the functions of its departments, bureaus, and offices.

A Fifty-Two Million Cut

The final estimates for the year ending June 30, 1912, as they have been sent to the Treasury, on November 29 of this year, for the ordinary expenses of the Government, including those for public buildings, rivers and harbors, and the navy building program, amount to $630,494,013.12. This is $52,964,887.36 less than the appropriations for the fiscal year ending June 30, 1911. It is $16,883,153.44 less than the total estimates, including supplemental estimates submitted to Congress by the Treasury for the year 1911, and is $5,574,659.39 less than the original estimates submitted by the Treasury for 1911.

These figures do not include the appropriations for the Panama Canal, the policy in respect to which ought to be, and is, to spend as much each year as can be economically and effectively expended in order to complete the Canal as promptly as possible, and, therefore, the ordinary motive for cutting down the expense of the Government does not apply to appropriations for this purpose. It will be noted that the estimates for the Panama Canal for the ensuing year are more than fifty-six millions of dollars, an increase of twenty millions over the amount appropriated for this year—a difference due to the fact that the estimates for 1912 include something over nineteen millions for the fortification of the Canal. Against the estimated expenditures of $630,494,013.12, the Treasury has estimated receipts for next year $680,000,000, making a probable surplus of ordinary receipts over ordinary expenditures of about $50,000,000.

Typical Economies

The Treasury Department is one of the original departments of the Government. With the changes in the monetary system made from time to time and with the creation of national banks, it was thought necessary to organize new bureaus and divisions which were added in a somewhat haphazard way and resulted in a duplication of duties which might well now be ended. This lack of system and economic coordination has attracted the attention of the head of that Department who has been giving his time for the last two years, with the aid of experts and by consulting his bureau chiefs, to its reformation. He has abolished four hundred places in the civil service without at all injuring its efficiency. Merely to illustrate the character of the reforms that are possible, I shall comment on some of the specific changes that are being made, or ought to be made by legislative aid.

Auditing System

The auditing system in vogue is as old as the Government and the methods used are antiquated. There are six Auditors and seven Assistant Auditors for the nine departments, and under the present system the only function which the Auditor of a department exercises is to determine, on accounts presented by disbursing officers, that the object of the expenditure was within the law and the appropriation made by Congress for the purpose on its face, and that the calculations in the accounts are correct. He does not examine the merits of the transaction or determine the reasonableness of the price paid for the articles purchased, nor does he furnish any substantial check upon disbursing officers and the heads of departments or bureaus with sufficient promptness to enable the Government to recoup itself in full measure for unlawful expenditure. A careful plan is being devised and will be presented to Congress with the recommendation that the force of auditors and employees under them be greatly reduced, thereby effecting substantial economy. But this economy will be small compared with the larger economy that can be effected by consolidation and change of methods. The possibilities in this regard have been shown in the reduction of expenses and the importance of methods and efficiency in the office of the Auditor for the Post Office Department, who, without in the slightest degree impairing the comprehensiveness and efficiency of his work, has cut down the expenses of his office $120,000 a year.

Customs Collection

Again, in the collection of the revenues, especially the customs revenues, a very great improvement has been effected, and further improvements are contemplated. By the detection of frauds in weighing sugar, upwards of $3,400,000 have been recovered from the beneficiaries of the fraud, and an entirely new system free from the possibilities of such abuse has been devised. The Department has perfected the method of collecting duties at the Port of New York so as to save the Government upwards of ten or eleven million dollars; and the same spirit of change and reform has been infused into the other customs offices of the country.

The methods used at many places are archaic. There would seem to be no reason at all why the Surveyor of the Port, who really acts for the Collector, should not be a subordinate of the Collector at a less salary and directly under his control, and there is but little reason for the existence of the Naval Officer, who is a kind of local auditor. His work is mainly an examination of accounts which is conducted again in Washington and which results in no greater security to the Government. The Naval Officers in the various ports are Presidential appointees, many of them drawing good salaries, and those offices should be abolished or with reduced force made part of the central auditing system.

There are entirely too many customs districts and too many customs collectors. These districts should be consolidated and the collectors in charge of them, who draw good salaries, many of them out of proportion to the collections made, should be abolished or treated as mere branch offices, in accordance with the plan of the Treasury Department, which will be presented for the consideration of Congress. As an illustration, the cost of collecting $1 of revenue at typical small ports like the port of York, Me., was $50.04. At the port of Annapolis, Md., it cost $309.41 to collect $1 of revenue; at Natchez, $52.76; at Alexandria, Va., $122.49.

It is not essential to the preventing of smuggling that customs districts should be increased in number. The violation of the customs laws can be quite as easily prevented, and much more economically, by the revenue-cutter service and by the use of the special agent traveling force of the Treasury Department. A reorganization of the special customs agents has been perfected with a view to retaining only those who have special knowledge of the customs laws, regulations, and usual methods of evasion, and with this improvement, there will be no danger to the Government from the recommended consolidation and abolition of customs districts.

An investigation of the appraising system now in vogue in New York, New York has shown a sacrifice of the interests of the Government by under-appraisement, which is in the course of being remedied by reorganization and the employment of competent experts. Prosecutions have been instituted growing out of the frauds there discovered and are now awaiting hearing in the Federal Courts.

Very great improvements have been made in respect to the mints and assay offices. Diminished appropriations have been asked for those whose continuance is unnecessary, and this year's estimate of expenses is $326,000 less than two years ago. There is an opportunity for further saving in the abolition of several mints and assay offices that have now become unnecessary. Modern machinery has been installed there, more and better work has been done, and the appropriations have been consequently diminished.

In the Bureau of Engraving and Printing, great economies have been effected. Useless divisions have been abolished with the result of saving $440,000 this year in the total expenses of the Bureau despite increased business.

The Treasurer's office and that of the Division of Public Moneys in part cover the same functions and this is also true of the office of the Register and the Division of Loans and Currency. Plans for the elimination of the duplication in these offices will be presented to Congress.

Comptroller of the Currency

The office of the Comptroller of the Currency is one most important in the preservation of proper banking methods in the national banking system of the United States, and the present Comptroller has impressed his subordinates with the necessity of so conducting their investigations as to establish the principle that every bank failure is unnecessary because proper inspection and notice of threatening conditions to the responsible directors and officers can prevent it.

Public Buildings

In our public buildings we still suffer from the method of appropriation, which has been so much criticised in connection with our rivers and harbors. Some method should be devised for controlling the supply of public buildings, so that they will harmonize with the actual needs of the Government. Then, when it comes to the actual construction, there has been in the past too little study of the building plans and sites with a view to the actual needs of the Government. Post-Office buildings which are in effect warehouses for the economical handling of transportation of thousands of tons of mail have been made monumental structures, and often located far from the convenient and economical spot. In the actual construction of the buildings, a closer scrutiny of the methods employed by the Government architects or by architects employed by the Government have resulted in decided economies. It is hoped that more time will give opportunity for a more thorough reorganization. The last public building bill carried authorization for the ultimate expenditure of $33,011,500 and I approved it because of the many good features it contained, just as I approved the river and harbor bill, but it was drawn upon a principle that ought to be abandoned. It seems to me that the wiser method of preparing a public building bill would be the preparation of a report by a commission of Government experts whose duty it should be to report to Congress the Government's needs in the way of the construction of public buildings in every part of the country, just as the Army Engineers make report with reference to the utility of proposed improvements in rivers and harbors, with the added function which I have recommended for the Army Engineers of including in their recommendation the relative importance of the various projects found to be worthy of approval and execution.

Revenues

As the Treasury Department is the one through which the income of the Government is collected and its expenditures are disbursed, this seems a proper place to consider the operation of the existing tariff bill, which became a law August 6, 1909 As an income-producing measure, the existing tariff bill has never been exceeded by any customs bill in the history of the country.

The corporation excise tax, proportioned to the net income of every business corporation in the country, has worked well. The tax has been easily collected. Its prompt payment indicates that the incidence of the tax has not been heavy. It offers, moreover, an opportunity for knowledge by the Government of the general condition and business of all corporations, and that means by far the most important part of the business of the country. In the original act provision was made for the publication of returns. This provision was subsequently amended by Congress, and the matter left to the regulation of the President. I have directed the issue of the needed regulations, and have made it possible for the public generally to know from an examination of the record, the returns of all corporations, the stock of which is listed on any public stock exchange or is offered for sale to the general public by advertisement or otherwise. The returns of those corporations whose stock is not so listed or offered for sale are directed to be open to the inspection and examination of creditors and stockholders of the corporation whose record is sought. The returns of all corporations are subject to the inspection of any government officer or to the examination of any court, in which the return made by the corporation is relevant and competent evidence.

The Payne Tariff Act

The schedules of the rates of duty in the Payne tariff act have been subjected to a great deal of criticism, some of it just, more of it unfounded, and to much misrepresentation. The act was adopted in pursuance of a declaration by the party which is responsible for it that a customs bill should be a tariff for the protection of home industries, the measure of the protection to be the difference between the cost of producing the imported article abroad and the cost of producing it at home, together with such addition to that difference as might give a reasonable profit to the home producer. The chief criticism of this tariff is a charge that in respect to a number of the schedules the declared measure was not followed, but a higher difference retained or inserted by way of undue discrimination in favor of certain industries and manufactures. Little, if any, of the criticism of the tariff has been directed against the protective principle above stated.

Tariff Board

The time in which the tariff was prepared undoubtedly was so short as to make it impossible for the Congress and its experts to acquire all the information necessary strictly to conform to the declared measure. In order to avoid criticism of this kind in the future and for the purpose of more nearly conforming to the party promise, Congress at its last session made provision at my request for the continuance of a board created under the authority of the maximum and minimum clause of the tariff bill, and authorized this board to expend the money appropriated under my direction for the ascertainment of the cost of production at home and abroad of the various articles included in the schedules of the tariff. The tariff board thus appointed and authorized has been diligent in preparing itself for the necessary investigations. The hope of those who have advocated the use of this board for tariff purposes is that the question of the rate of a duty imposed shall become more of a business question and less of a political question, to be ascertained by experts of long training and accurate knowledge. The halt in business and the shock to business, due to the announcement that a new tariff bill is to be prepared and put in operation, will be avoided by treating the schedules one by one as occasion shall arise for a change in the rates of each, and only after a report upon the schedule by the tariff board competent to make such report. It is not likely that the board will be able to make a report during the present session of Congress on any of the schedules, because a proper examination involves an enormous amount of detail and a great deal of care; but I hope to be able at the opening of the new Congress, or at least during the session of that Congress, to bring to its attention the facts in regard to those schedules in the present tariff that may prove to need amendment. The carrying out of this plan, of course, involves the full cooperation of Congress in limiting the consideration in tariff matters to one schedule at a time, because if a proposed amendment to a tariff bill is to involve a complete consideration of all the schedules and another revision, then we shall only repeat the evil from which the business of this country has in times past suffered most grievously by stagnation and uncertainty, pending a resettlement of a law affecting all business directly or indirectly. I can not too much emphasize the importance and benefit of the plan above proposed for the treatment of the tariff. It facilitates the removal of noteworthy defects in an important law without a disturbance of business prosperity, which is even more important to the happiness and the comfort of the people than the elimination of instances of injustice in the tariff.

The inquiries which the members of the Tariff Board made during the last summer into the methods pursued by other Governments with reference to the fixing of tariffs and the determination of their effect upon trade, show that each Government maintains an office or bureau, the officers and employees of which have made their life work the study of tariff matters, of foreign and home prices and cost of articles imported, and the effect of the tariff upon trade, so that whenever a change is thought to be necessary in the tariff law this office is the source of the most reliable information as to the propriety of the change and its effect. I am strongly convinced that we need in this Government just such an office, and that it can be secured by making the Tariff Board already appointed a permanent tariff commission, with such duties, powers, and emoluments as it may seem wise to Congress to give. It has been proposed to enlarge the board from three to five. The present number is convenient, but I do not know that an increase of two members would be objectionable.

Whether or not the protective policy is to be continued, and the degree of protection to be accorded to our home industries, are questions which the people must decide through their chosen representatives; but whatever policy is adopted, it is clear that the necessary legislation should be based on an impartial, thorough, and continuous study of the facts.

Banking and Currency Reform

The method of impartial scientific study by experts as a preliminary to legislation, which I hope to see ultimately adopted as our fixed national policy with respect to the tariff, rivers and harbors, waterways, and public buildings, is also being pursued by the nonpartisan Monetary Commission of Congress. An exhaustive and most valuable study of the banking and currency systems of foreign countries has been completed.

A comparison of the business methods and institutions of our powerful and successful commercial rivals with our own is sure to be of immense value. I urge upon Congress the importance of a nonpartisan and disinterested study and consideration of our banking and currency system. It is idle to dream of commercial expansion, and of the development of our national trade on a scale that measures up to our matchless opportunities, unless we can lay a solid foundation in a sound and enduring banking and currency system. The problem is not partisan, is not sectional—it is national.

War Department

The War Department has within its jurisdiction the management of the Army, and, in connection therewith, the coast defenses; the government of the dependencies of the Philippines and of Puerto Rico; the recommendation of plans for the improvement of harbors and waterways, and their execution when adopted; and, by virtue of an executive order, the supervision of the construction of the Panama Canal.

The Army of the United States is a small body compared with the total number of people for the preservation of whose peace and good order it is a last resource. The Army now numbers about 80,000 men, of whom about 18,000 are engaged in the Coast Artillery and detailed to the management and use of the guns in the forts and batteries that protect our coasts. The rest of the Army, or about 60,000, is the mobile part of our national forces and is divided into 31 regiments of infantry, including the Puerto Rican regiment, 15 regiments of cavalry, 6 regiments of field artillery, a corps of ordnance, of engineers, and of signal, a quartermaster's department, a commissary department, and a medical corps.

The general plan for an army of the United States at peace should be that of a skeleton organization with an excess of trained officers and thus capable of rapid enlargement by enlistments, to be supplemented in emergency by the national militia and a volunteer force. In some measure this plan has been adopted in the very large proportion of cavalry and field artillery as compared with infantry in the present army and on a peace basis. An infantry force can be trained in six months; a cavalry or a light artillery force not under one and one-half or two years; hence the importance of having ready a larger number of the more skilled soldiers.

The militia system, for which Congress by the Constitution is authorized to provide, was developed by the so-called Dick law, under which the discipline, the tactics, the drill, the rank, the uniform, and the various branches of the militia are assimilated as far as possible to those of the Regular Army. Under the militia law, as the Constitution provides, the Governors of the States appoint the militia officers, but, by appropriations from Congress, States have been induced to comply with the rules of assimilation between the Regular Army and the militia, so that now there is a force, the efficiency of which differs in different States, which could be incorporated under a single command with the Regular Army, and which for some time each year receives the benefit of drill and maneuvers with conditions approximating actual military service, under the supervision of Regular Army officers.

In the Army of the United States, in addition to the regular forces and the militia forces which may be summoned to the defense of the Nation by the President, there is also the volunteer force, which made up a very large part of the army in the Civil War, and which in any war of long continuance would become its most important constituent. There is an act which dates from the Civil War, known as the Volunteer Act, which makes provision for the enlistment of volunteers in the Army of the United States in time of war. This was found to be so defective in the Philippine War that a special act for the organization of volunteer regiments to take part in that war was adopted, and it was much better adapted to the necessities of the case. There is now pending in Congress a bill repealing the present Volunteer Act and making provision for the organization of volunteer forces in time of war, which is admirably adapted to meet the exigencies which would be then presented. The passage of the bill would not entail a dollar's expense upon the Government at this time, or in the future, until war comes, but when war does come the methods therein directed are in accordance with the best military judgment as to what they ought to be, and the act would prevent the necessity for the discussion of new legislation and the delays incident to its consideration and adoption. I earnestly urge the passage of this Volunteer Bill.

I further recommend that Congress establish a commission to determine as early as practicable a comprehensive policy for the organization, mobilization and administration of the Regular Army, the organized militia, and the volunteer forces in the event of war.

Need for Additional Officers

One of the great difficulties in the prompt organization and mobilization of militia and volunteer forces is the absence of competent officers of the rank of captain to teach the new army, by the unit of the company, the business of being soldiers and of taking care of themselves so as to render effective service. This need of army officers can only be supplied by provisions of law authorizing the appointment of a greater number of army officers than are needed to supply the commands of regular army troops now enlisted in the service. There are enough regular army officers to command the troops now enlisted, but Congress has authorized, and the Department has followed the example of Congress and exercised the authority conferred by detailing these army officers to duty other than that of the command of troops. For instance, there are a large number of army officers assigned to duty with military colleges or in colleges in which military training is given. Then a large number of officers are assigned to General Staff duty, and there are various other places to which army officers can be and are legally assigned, which take them away from their regiments and companies. In order that the militia of each State should be properly drilled and made more like the regular army, regular army officers should be detailed to assist the Adjutant-General of each State in the supervision of the state militia; but this is impossible unless provision is made by Congress for a very considerable increase in the number of company and field officers of the Army. A bill is pending in Congress for this purpose, and I earnestly hope that, in the interest of the proper development of a republican army, an army, small in the time of peace but possible of prompt and adequate enlargement in time of war, shall become possible under the laws of the United States.

Proposed Increase in Army Engineers

A bill, the strong argument for which can be based on the ground quite similar to that of the increased officers bill, is a bill for the increase of sixty in the Army Engineers. The Army Engineers are largely employed in the expenditure of the moneys appropriated for the improvement of rivers and harbors and in the construction of the Panama Canal. This, in addition to their military duties, which include the building of fortifications both on our coasts and in our dependencies, requires many more engineers than the Army has, and public works, civil and military, are, therefore, much delayed. I earnestly recommend the passage of this bill, which passed the House at the last session and is now pending in the Senate.

Fortifications

I have directed that the estimates for appropriation for the improvement of coast defenses in the United States should be reduced to a minimum, while those for the completion of the needed fortifications at Corregidor in the Philippine Islands and at Pearl Harbor in the Hawaiian Islands should be expedited as much as possible. The proposition to make Olongapo and Subig Bay the naval base for the Pacific was given up, and it is to be treated merely as a supply station, while the fortifications in the Philippines are to be largely confined to Corregidor Island and the adjacent islands which command entrance to Manila Bay and which are being rendered impregnable from land and sea attack. The Pacific Naval base has been transferred to Pearl Harbor in the Hawaiian Islands. This necessitates the heavy fortification of the harbor and the establishment of an important military station near Honolulu. I urge that all the estimates made by the War Department for these purposes be approved by Congressional appropriation.

Philippine Islands

During the last summer, at my request, the Secretary of War visited the Philippine Islands and has described his trip in his report. He found the Islands in a state of tranquility and growing prosperity, due largely to the change in the tariff laws, which has opened the markets of America to the products of the Philippines, and has opened the Philippine markets to American manufactures. The rapid increase in the trade between the two countries is shown in the following table:

Philippine exports, fiscal years 1908–1910
[Exclusive of gold and silver]

Fiscal year	To U.S.	To Other Countries	Total
1908	$10,323,233	$22,493,334	$32,816,567
1909	10,215,331	20,778,232	30,993,563
1910	18,741,771	21,122,398	39,864,169

Note: Latest monthly returns show exports for the year ending August, 1910, to the United States $20,035,902, or 49 percent of the $41,075,738 total, against $11,031,275 to the United States, or 34 percent of the $32,183,871 total for the year ending August, 1909.

Philippine imports, fiscal years 1908–1910
[Exclusive of gold and silver and government supplies]

Fiscal year	From U.S.	From Other Countries	Total
1908	$5,079,487	$25,838,870	$30,918,357
1909	4,691,770	23,100,627	27,792,397
1910	10,775,301	26,292,329	37,067,630

Note: Latest monthly returns show imports for the year ending August, 1910, from the United States $11,615,982, or 30 percent of the $39,025,667 total, against $5,193,419 from the United States, or 18 percent of the $28,948,011 total for the year ending August, 1909.

Puerto Rico

The year has been one of prosperity and progress in Puerto Rico. Certain political changes are embodied in the bill "To Provide a Civil Government for Puerto Rico and for other Purposes," which passed the House of Representatives on June 15, 1910, at the last session of Congress, and is now awaiting the action of the Senate.

The importance of those features of this bill relating to public health and sanitation can not be overestimated.

The removal from politics of the judiciary by providing for the appointment of the municipal judges is excellent, and I recommend that a step further be taken by providing therein for the appointment of secretaries and marshals of these courts.

The provision in the bill for a partially elective senate, the number of elective members being progressively increased, is of doubtful wisdom, and the composition of the senate as provided in the bill when introduced in the House, seems better to meet conditions existing in Puerto Rico. This is an important measure, and I recommend its early consideration and passage.

Rivers and Harbors

I have already expressed my opinion to Congress in respect to the character of the river and harbor bills which should be enacted into law; and I have exercised as much power as I could under the law in directing the Chief of Engineers to make his report to Congress conform to the needs of the committee framing such a bill in determining which of the proposed improvements is the more important and ought to be completed first, and promptly.

Panama Canal

At the instance of Colonel Goethals, the Army Engineer officer in charge of the work on the Panama Canal, I have just made a visit to the Isthmus to inspect the work done and to consult with him on the ground as to certain problems which are likely to arise in the near future. The progress of the work is most satisfactory. If no unexpected obstacle presents itself, the canal will be completed well within the time fixed by Colonel Goethals, to wit, January 1, 1915, and within the estimate of cost, $375,000,000.

Press reports have reached the United States from time to time giving accounts of slides of earth of very large yardage in the Culebra Cut and elsewhere along the line, from which it might be inferred that the work has been much retarded and that the time of completion has been necessarily postponed.

The report of Doctor Hayes, of the Geological Survey, whom I sent within the last month to the Isthmus to make an investigation, shows that this section of the Canal Zone is composed of sedimentary rocks of rather weak structure and subject to almost immediate disintegration when exposed to the air. Subsequent to the deposition of these sediments, igneous rocks, harder and more durable, have been thrust into them, and being cold at the time of their intrusion united but indifferently with the sedimentary rock at the contacts. The result of these conditions is that as the cut is deepened, causing unbalanced pressures, slides from the sides of the cut have occurred. These are in part due to the flowing of surface soil and decomposed sedimentary rocks upon inclined surfaces of the underlying undecomposed rock and in part by the crushing of structurally weak beds under excessive pressure. These slides occur on one side or the other of the cut through a distance of 4 or 5 miles, and now that their character is understood, allowance has been made in the calculations of yardage for the amount of slides which will have to be removed and the greater slope that will have to be given to the bank in many places in order to prevent their recurrence. Such allowance does not exceed ten millions of yards. Considering that the number of yards removed from this cut on an average of each month through the year is 1,300,000, and that the total remaining to be excavated, including slides, is about 30,000,000 yards, it is seen that this addition to the excavation does not offer any great reason for delay.

While this feature of the material to be excavated in the cut will not seriously delay or obstruct the construction of a canal of the lock type, the increase of excavation due to such slides in the cut made 85 feet deeper for a sea-level canal would certainly have been so great as to delay its completion to a time beyond the patience of the American people.

Fortify the Canal

Among questions arising for present solution is whether the Canal shall be fortified. I have already stated to the Congress that I strongly favor fortification and I now reiterate this opinion and ask your consideration of the subject in the light of the report already before you made by a competent board.

If, in our discretion, we believe modern fortifications to be necessary to the adequate protection and policing of the Canal, then it is our duty to construct them. We have built the Canal. It is our property. By convention we have indicated our desire for, and indeed undertaken, its universal and equal use. It is also well known that one of the chief objects in the construction of the Canal has been to increase the military effectiveness of our Navy.

Failure to fortify the Canal would make the attainment of both these aims depend upon the mere moral obligations of the whole international public—obligations which we would be powerless to enforce and which could never in any other way be absolutely safeguarded against a desperate and irresponsible enemy.

Canal Tolls

Another question which arises for consideration and possible legislation is the question of tolls in the Canal. This question is necessarily affected by the probable tonnage which will go through the Canal. It is all a matter of estimate, but one of the government commission in 1900 investigated the question and made a report. He concluded that the total tonnage of the vessels employed in commerce that could use the Isthmian Canal in 1914 would amount to 6,843,805 tons net register, and that this traffic would increase 25.1 percent per decade; that it was not probable that all the commerce included in the totals would at once abandon the routes at present followed and make use of the new Canal, and that it might take some time, perhaps two years, to readjust trade with reference to the new conditions which the Canal would establish. He did not include, moreover, the tonnage of war vessels, although it is to be inferred that such vessels would make considerable use of the Canal. In the matter of tolls he reached the conclusion that a dollar a net ton would not drive business away from the Canal, but that a higher rate would do so.

In determining what the tolls should be we certainly ought not to insist that they should at once amount to enough to pay the interest on the investment of $400,000,000 which the United States has made in the construction of the Canal. We ought not to do this, first, because the benefit to be derived by the United States from this expenditure is not to be measured solely by a return upon the investment. If it were, then the construction might well have been left to private enterprise. It was because an adequate return upon the money invested could not be expected immediately, or in the near future, and because there were peculiar political advantages to be derived from the construction of the Canal that it fell to the Government to advance the money and perform the work.

In addition to the benefit to our naval strength, the Canal greatly increases the trade facilities of the United States. It will undoubtedly cheapen the rates of transportation in all freight between the Eastern and Western seaboard. Then, if we are to have a world canal, and if we are anxious that the world's trade shall use it, we must recognize that we have an active competitor in the Suez Canal and that there are other means of carriage between the two oceans—by the Tehuantepec Railroad and by other railroads and freight routes in Central America.

In all these cases the question whether the Panama Canal is to be used and its tonnage increased will be determined mainly by the charge for its use. My own impression is that the tolls ought not to exceed $1 per net ton. On January 1, 1911, the tolls in the Suez Canal are to be 7 francs and 25 centimes for 1 net ton by Suez Canal measurement, which is a modification of Danube measurement. A dollar a ton will secure under the figures above a gross income from the Panama Canal of nearly $7,000,000. The cost of maintenance and operation is estimated to exceed $3,000,000. Ultimately, of course, with the normal increase in trade, we hope the income will approximate the interest charges upon the investment. The inquiries already made of the Chief Engineer of the Canal show that the present consideration of this question is necessary in order that the commerce of the world may have time to adjust itself to the new conditions resulting from the opening of this new highway. On the whole I should recommend that within certain limits the President be authorized to fix the tolls of the Canal and adjust them to what seems to be commercial necessity.

Maintenance of Canal

The next question that arises is as to the maintenance, management, and general control of the canal after its completion. It should be premised that it is an essential part of our navy establishment to have the coal, oil and other ship supplies, a dry dock, and repair shops, conveniently located with reference to naval vessels passing through the canal. Now, if the Government, for naval purposes, is to undertake to furnish these conveniences to the navy, and they are conveniences equally required by commercial vessels, there would seem to be strong reasons why the Government should take over and include in its management the furnishing, not only to the navy but to the public, dry-dock and repair-shop facilities, and the sale of coal, oil, and other ship supplies.

The maintenance of a lock canal of this enormous size in a sparsely populated country and in the tropics, where the danger from disease is always present, requires a large and complete and well-trained organization with full police powers, exercising the utmost care. The visitor to the canal who is impressed with the wonderful freedom from tropical diseases on the Isthmus must not be misled as to the constant vigilance that is needed to preserve this condition. The vast machinery of the locks, the necessary amount of dredging, the preservation of the banks of the canal from slides, the operation and the maintenance of the equipment of the railway—will all require a force, not, of course, to be likened in any way to the present organization for construction, but a skilled body of men who can keep in a state of usefulness this great instrument of commerce. Such an organization makes it easy to include within its functions the furnishing of dry-dock, fuel, repairs and supply facilities to the trade of the world. These will be more essential at the Isthmus of Panama than they are at Port Said or Suez, because there are no depots for coal, supplies, and other commercial necessities within thousands of miles of the Isthmus.

Another important reason why these ancillary duties may well be undertaken by the Government is the opportunity for discrimination between patrons of the canal that is offered where private concessions are granted for the furnishing of these facilities. Nothing would create greater prejudice against the canal than the suspicion that certain lines of traffic were favored in the furnishing of supplies or that the supplies were controlled by any large interest that might have a motive for increasing the cost of the use of the canal. It may be added that the termini are not ample enough to permit the fullest competition in respect to the furnishing of these facilities and necessities to the world's trade even if it were wise to invite such competition and the granting of the concession would necessarily, under these circumstances, take on the appearance of privilege or monopoly.

Prohibition of Railroad Ownership of Canal Steamers

I can not close this reference to the canal without suggesting as a wise amendment to the interstate commerce law a provision prohibiting interstate commerce railroads from owning or controlling ships engaged in the trade through the Panama Canal. I believe such a provision may be needed to save to the people of the United States the benefits of the competition in trade between the eastern and western seaboards which this canal was constructed to secure.

Department of Justice

The duties of the Department of Justice have been greatly increased by legislation of Congress enacted in the interest of the general welfare of the people and extending its activities into avenues plainly within its constitutional jurisdiction, but which it has not been thought wise or necessary for the General Government heretofore to occupy.

I am glad to say that under the appropriations made for the Department, the Attorney-General has so improved its organization that a vast amount of litigation of a civil and criminal character has been disposed of during the current year. This will explain the necessity for slightly increasing the estimates for the expenses of the Department. His report shows the recoveries made on behalf of the Government, of duties fraudulently withheld, public lands improperly patented, fines and penalties for trespass, prosecutions and convictions under the antitrust law, and prosecutions under the interstate-commerce law. I invite especial attention to the prosecutions under the Federal law of the so-called "bucket shops," and of those schemes to defraud in which the use of the mail is an essential part of the fraudulent conspiracy, prosecutions which have saved ignorant and weak members of the public and are saving them hundreds of millions of dollars. The violations of the antitrust law present perhaps the most important litigation before the Department, and the number of cases filed shows the activity of the Government in enforcing that statute.

National Incorporation

In a special message last year I brought to the attention of Congress the propriety and wisdom of enacting a general law providing for the incorporation of industrial and other companies engaged in interstate commerce, and I renew my recommendation in that behalf.

Payment of Just Claims

I invite the attention of Congress to the great number of claims which, at the instance of Congress, have been considered by the Court of Claims and decided to be valid claims against the Government. The delay that occurs in the payment of the money due under the claims injures the reputation of the Government as an honest debtor, and I earnestly recommend that those claims which come to Congress with the judgment and approval of the Court of Claims should be promptly paid.

Reform in Judicial Procedure

One great crying need in the United States is cheapening the cost of litigation by simplifying judicial procedure and expediting final judgment. Under present conditions the poor man is at a woeful disadvantage in a legal contest with a corporation or a rich opponent. The necessity for the reform exists both in the United States courts and in all State courts. In order to bring it about, however, it naturally falls to the General Government by its example to furnish a model to all States. A legislative commission appointed by joint resolution of Congress to revise the procedure in the United States courts has as yet made no report.

Under the law the Supreme Court of the United States has the power and is given the duty to frame the equity rules of procedure which are to obtain in the Federal courts of first instance. In view of the heavy burden of pressing litigation which that Court has had to carry, with one or two of its members incapacitated through ill health, it has not been able to take up problems of improving the equity procedure, which has practically remained the same since the organization of the Court in 1789. It is reasonable to expect that with all the vacancies upon the Court filled, it will take up the question of cheapening and simplifying the procedure in equity in the courts of the United States. The equity business is much the more important in the Federal courts, and I may add much the more expensive. I am strongly convinced that the best method of improving judicial procedure at law is to empower the Supreme Court to do it through the medium of the rules of the court, as in equity. This is the way in which it has been done in England, and thoroughly done. The simplicity and expedition of procedure in the English courts today make a model for the reform of other systems.

Several of the Lord Chancellors of England and of the Chief Justices have left their lasting impress upon the history of their country by their constructive ability in proposing and securing the passage of remedial legislation effecting law reforms. I can not conceive any higher duty that the Supreme Court could perform than in leading the way to a simplification of procedure in the United States courts.

Relief of Supreme Court from Unnecessary Appeals

No man ought to have, as a matter of right, a review of his case by the Supreme Court. He should be satisfied by one hearing before a court of first instance and one review by a court of appeals. The proper and chief usefulness of a Supreme Court, and especially of the Supreme Court of the United States, is, in the cases which come before it, so to expound the law, and especially the fundamental law—the Constitution—as to furnish precedents for the inferior courts in future litigation and for the executive officers in the construction of statutes and the performance of their legal duties. Therefore, any provisions for review of cases by the Supreme Court that cast upon that Court the duty of passing on questions of evidence and the construction of particular forms of instruments, like indictments, or wills, or contracts, decisions not of general application or importance, merely clog and burden the Court and render more difficult its higher function, which makes it so important a part of the framework of our Government. The Supreme Court is now carrying an unnecessary burden of appeals of this kind, and I earnestly urge that it be removed.

The statutes respecting the review by the Supreme Court of the United States of decisions of the Court of Appeals of the District of Columbia ought to be so amended as to place that court in the same position with respect to the review of its decisions as that of the various United States Circuit Courts of Appeals. The act of March 2, 1907, authorizing appeals by the Government from certain judgments in criminal cases where the defendant has not been put in jeopardy, within the meaning of the Constitution, should be amended so that such appeals should be taken to the Circuit Courts of Appeals instead of to the Supreme Court in all cases except those involving the construction of the Constitution or the constitutionality of a statute, with the same power in the Supreme Court to review on *certiorari* as is now exercised by that court over determinations of the several Circuit Courts of Appeals. Appeals in copyright cases should reach final judgment in the courts of appeals instead of the Supreme Court as now. The decision of the courts of appeals should be made final also in all cases wherein jurisdiction rests on both diverse citizenship and the existence of a federal question, and not as now be reviewable in the Supreme Court when the case involves more than one thousand dollars. Appeals from the United States Court in Puerto Rico should run to the Circuit Court of Appeals of the third circuit instead of to the Supreme Court. These suggested changes would, I am advised, relieve the Supreme Court of the consideration of about 100 cases annually.

The American Bar Association has had before it the question of reducing the burden of litigation involved in reversals on review and new trials or re-hearings and in frivolous appeals in habeas corpus and criminal cases. Their recommendations have been embodied in bills now pending in Congress. The recommendations are not radical, but they will accomplish much if adopted into law, and I earnestly recommend the passage of the bills embodying them.

Injunction Bill

I wish to renew my urgent recommendation made in my last Annual Message in favor of the passage of a law which shall regulate the issuing of injunctions in equity without notice in accordance with the best practice now in vogue in the courts of the United States. I regard this of especial importance, first because it has been promised, and second because it will deprive those who now complain of certain alleged abuses in the improper issuing of injunctions without notice of any real ground for further amendment and will take away all semblance of support for the extremely radical legislation they propose, which will be most pernicious if adopted, will sap the foundations of judicial power, and legalize that cruel social instrument, the secondary boycott.

Judicial Salaries

I further recommend to Congress the passage of the bill now pending for the increase in the salaries of the Federal Judges, by which the Chief Justice of the United States shall receive $17,500 and the Associate Justices of the Supreme Court $17,000; the Circuit Judges constituting the Circuit Court of Appeals shall receive $10,000, and the District Judges $9,000. These judges exercise a wise jurisdiction and their duties require of them a profound knowledge of the law, great ability in the dispatch of business, and care and delicacy in the exercise of their jurisdiction so as to avoid conflict whenever possible between the Federal and the State courts. The positions they occupy ought to be filled by men who have shown the greatest ability in their professional work at the bar, and it is the poorest economy possible for the Government to pay salaries so low for judicial service as not to be able to command the best talent of the legal profession in every part of the country. The cost of living is such, especially in the large cities, that even the salaries fixed in the proposed bill will enable the incumbents to accumulate little, if anything, to support their families after their death. Nothing is so important to the preservation of our country and its beloved institutions as the maintenance of the independence of the judiciary, and next to the life tenure an adequate salary is the most material contribution to the maintenance of independence on the part of our Judges.

Post-Office Department

Postal Savings Banks

At its last session Congress made provision for the establishment of savings banks by the Post-Office Department of this Government, by which, under the general control of trustees, consisting of the Postmaster-General, the Secretary of the Treasury and the Attorney-General, the system could be begun in a few cities and towns, and enlarged to cover within its operations as many cities and towns and as large a part of the country as seemed wise. The initiation and establishment of such a system has required a great deal of study on the part of the experts in the Post-Office and Treasury Departments, but a system has now been devised which is believed to be more economical and simpler in its operation than any similar system abroad. Arrangements have been perfected so that savings banks will be opened in some cities and towns on the first of January, and there will be a gradual extension of the benefits of the plan to the rest of the country.

Wiping Out of Postal Deficit

As I have said, the Post-Office Department is a great business department, and I am glad to note the fact that under its present management principles of business economy and efficiency are being applied. For many years there has been a deficit in the operations of the Post-Office Department which has been met by appropriation from the Treasury. The appropriation estimated for last year from the Treasury over and above the receipts of the Department was $17,500,000. I am glad to record the fact that of that $17,500,000 estimated for, $11,500,000 were saved and returned to the Treasury. The personal efforts of the Postmaster-General secured the effective cooperation of the thousands of postmasters and other postal officers throughout the country in carrying out his plans of reorganization and retrenchment. The result is that the Postmaster-General has been able to make his estimate of expenses for the present year so low as to keep within the amount the postal service is expected to earn. It is gratifying to report that the reduction in the deficit has been accomplished without any curtailment of postal facilities. On the contrary the service has been greatly extended during the year in all its branches. A principle which the Postmaster-General has recommended and sought to have enforced in respect to all appointments has been that those appointees who have rendered good service should be reappointed. This has greatly strengthened the interest of postmasters throughout the country in maintaining efficiency and economy in their offices, because they believed generally that this would secure for them a further tenure.

Extension of the Classified Service

Upon the recommendation of the Postmaster-General, I have included in the classified service all assistant postmasters, and I believe that this giving a secure tenure to those who are the most important subordinates of Postmasters will add much to the efficiency of their offices and an economical administration. A large number of the fourth-class postmasters are now in the classified service. I think it would be wise to put in the classified service the first, second, and third class postmasters. It is more logical to do this than to classify the fourth-class postmasters, for the reason that the fourth-class post-offices are invariably small, and the postmasters are necessarily men who must combine some other business with the postmastership, whereas the first, second, and third class postmasters are paid a sufficient amount to justify the requirement that they shall have no other business and that they shall devote their attention to their post-office duties. To classify first, second, and third class postmasters would require the passage of an act changing the method of their appointment so as to take away the necessity for the advice and consent of the Senate. I am aware that this is inviting from the Senate a concession in respect to its quasi executive power that is considerable, but I believe it to be in the interest of good administration and efficiency of service. To make this change would take the postmasters out of politics; would relieve Congressmen who now are burdened with the necessity of making recommendations for these places of a responsibility that must be irksome and can create nothing but trouble; and it would result in securing from postmasters greater attention to business, greater fidelity, and consequently greater economy and efficiency in the post-offices which they conduct.

The Franking Privilege

The unrestricted manner in which the franking privilege is now being used by the several branches of the Federal service and by Congress has laid it open to serious abuses, a fact clearly established through investigations recently instituted by the Department. While it has been impossible without a better control of franking to determine the exact expense to the Government of this practice, there can be no doubt that it annually reaches into the millions. It is believed that many abuses of the franking system could be prevented, and consequently a marked economy effected, by supplying through the agencies of the postal service special official envelopes and stamps for the free mail of the Government, all such envelopes and stamps to be issued on requisition to the various branches of the Federal service requiring them, and such records to be kept of all official stamp supplies as will enable the Post-Office Department to maintain a proper postage account covering the entire volume of free Government mail. As the first step in the direction of this reform, special stamps and stamped envelopes have been provided for use instead of franks in the free transmission of the official mail resulting from the business of the new postal savings system. By properly recording the issuance of such stamps and envelopes accurate records can be kept of the cost to the Government of handling the postal savings mail, which is certain to become an important item of expense and one that should be separately determined. In keeping with this plan it is hoped that Congress will authorize the substitution of special official stamps and stamped envelopes for the various forms of franks now used to carry free of postage the vast volume of Departmental and Congressional mail matter. During the past year methods of accounting similar to those employed in the most progressive of our business establishments have been introduced in the postal service and nothing has so impeded the Department's plan in this regard as the impossibility of determining with any exactness how far the various expenses of the postal service are increased by the present unrestricted use of the franking privilege. It is believed that the adoption of a more exact method of dealing with this problem as proposed will prove to be of tremendous advantage in the work of placing the postal service on a strictly businesslike basis.

Second-Class Mail Matter

In my last Annual Message I invited the attention of Congress to the inadequacy of the postal rate imposed upon second-class mail matter in so far as that includes magazines, and showed by figures prepared by experts of the Post-Office Department that the Government was rendering a service to the magazines, costing many millions in excess of the compensation paid. An answer was attempted to this by the representatives of the magazines, and a reply was filed to this answer by the Post-Office Department. The utter inadequacy of the answer, considered in the light of the reply of the Post-Office Department, I think must appeal to any fair-minded person. Whether the answer was all that could be said in behalf of the magazines is another question. I agree that the question is one of fact; but I insist that if the fact is as the experts of the Post-Office Department show, that we are furnishing to the owners of magazines a service worth millions more than they pay for it, then justice requires that the rate should be increased. The increase in the receipts of the Department resulting from this change may be devoted to increasing the usefulness of the Department in establishing a parcels post and in reducing the cost of first-class postage to one cent. It has been said by the Postmaster-General that a fair adjustment might be made under which the advertising part of the magazine should be charged for at a different and higher rate from that of the reading matter. This would relieve many useful magazines that are not circulated at a profit, and would not shut them out from the use of the mails by a prohibitory rate.

Parcels Post

With respect to the parcels post, I respectfully recommend its adoption on all rural-delivery routes, and that 11 pounds—the international limit—be made the limit of carriage in such post, and this, with a view to its general extension when the income of the Post-Office will permit it and the Postal Savings Banks shall have been fully established. The same argument is made against the parcels post that was made against the postal savings bank—that it is introducing the Government into a business which ought to be conducted by private persons, and is paternalism. The Post-Office Department has a great plant and a great organization, reaching into the most remote hamlet of the United States, and with this machinery it is able to do a great many things economically that if a new organization were necessary it would be impossible to do without extravagant expenditure. That is the reason why the postal savings bank can be carried on at a small additional cost, and why it is possible to incorporate at a very inconsiderable expense a parcels post in the rural-delivery system. A general parcels post will involve a much greater outlay.

Navy Department

Reorganization

In the last annual report of the Secretary of the Navy and in my Annual Message, attention was called to the new detail of officers in the Navy Department by which officers of flag rank were assigned to duty as Aides to the Secretary in respect to naval operations, personnel, inspection, and material. This change was a substantial compliance with the recommendation of the Commission on Naval Reorganization, headed by Mr. Justice Moody, and submitted to President Roosevelt on February 26, 1909. Through the advice of this committee of line officers, the Secretary is able to bring about a proper coordination of all the branches of the naval department with greater military efficiency. The Secretary of the Navy recommends that this new organization be recognized by legislation and thus made permanent. I concur in the recommendation.

Legislative Recommendations

The Secretary, in view of the conclusions of a recent Court of Inquiry on certain phases of Marine Corps administration, recommends that the Major-General Commandant of the Marine Corps be appointed for a four years' term, and that officers of the Adjutant and Inspector's department be detailed from the line. He also asks for legislation to improve the conditions now existing in the personnel of officers of the Navy, particularly with regard to the age and experience of flag officers and captains, and points out that it is essential to the highest efficiency of the Navy that the age of our officers be reduced and that flag officers, particularly, should gain proper experience as flag officers, in order to enable them to properly command fleets. I concur in the Secretary's recommendations.

Covering of Naval Supply Fund into Treasury

I commend to your attention the report of the Secretary on the change in the system of cost accounting in navy-yards, and also to the history of the naval supply fund and the present conditions existing in regard to that matter. Under previous practice and what now seems to have been an erroneous construction of the law, the supply fund of the navy was increased from $2,700,000 to something over $14,000,000, and a system of accounting was introduced which prevented the striking of a proper balance and a knowledge of the exact cost of maintaining the naval establishment. The system has now been abandoned and a Naval Supply Account established by law July 1, 1910. The Naval Supply fund of $2,700,000 is now on deposit in the Treasury to the credit of the Department. The Secretary recommends that the Naval Supply Account be made permanent by law and that the $2,700,000 of the naval supply fund be covered into the Treasury as unnecessary, and I ask for legislative authority to do this. This sum when covered into the Treasury will be really a reduction in the recorded Naval cost for this year.

Estimates and Building Program

The estimates of the Navy Department are $5,000,000 less than the appropriations for the same purpose last year, and included in this is the building program of the same amount as that submitted for your consideration last year. It is merely carrying out the plan of building two battleships a year, with a few needed auxiliary vessels. I earnestly hope that this program will be adopted.

Abolition of Navy-Yards

The Secretary of the Navy has given personal examination to every navy-yard and has studied the uses of the navy-yards with reference to the necessities of our fleet. With a fleet considerably less than half the size of that of the British navy, we have shipyards more than double the number, and there are several of these shipyards, expensively equipped with modern machinery, which after investigation the Secretary of the Navy believes to be entirely useless for naval purposes. He asks authority to abandon certain of them and to move their machinery to other places where it can be made of use.

In making these recommendations the Secretary is following directly along progressive lines which have been adopted in our great commercial and manufacturing consolidations in this country; that is, of dismantling unnecessary and inadequate plants and discontinuing their existence where it has been demonstrated that it is unprofitable to continue their maintenance at an expense not commensurate to their product.

Guantanamo Proper Naval Base

The Secretary points out that the most important naval base in the West Indies is Guantanamo, in the southeastern part of Cuba. Its geographical situation is admirably adapted to protect the commercial paths to the Panama Canal, and he shows that by the expenditure of less than half a million dollars, with the machinery which he shall take from other navy-yards, he can create a naval station at Guantanamo of sufficient size and equipment to serve the purpose of an emergency naval base. I earnestly join in the recommendation that he be given the authority which he asks. I am quite aware that such action is likely to arouse local opposition; but I conceive it to be axiomatic that in legislating in the interest of the Navy, and for the general protection of the country by the Navy, mere local pride or pecuniary interest in the establishment of a navy-yard or station ought to play no part. The recommendation of the Secretary is based upon the judgment of impartial naval officers, entirely uninfluenced by any geographical or sectional considerations.

John Paul Jones

I unite with the Secretary in the recommendation that an appropriation be made to construct a suitable crypt at Annapolis for the custody of the remains of John Paul Jones.

Peary

The complete success of our country in Arctic exploration should not remain unnoticed. For centuries there has been friendly rivalry in this field of effort between the foremost nations and between the bravest and most accomplished men. Expeditions to the unknown North have been encouraged by enlightened governments and deserved honors have been granted to the daring men who have conducted them. The unparalleled accomplishment of an American in reaching the North Pole, April 6, 1909, approved by critical examination of the most expert scientists, has added to the distinction of our navy, to which he belongs, and reflects credit upon his country. His unique success has received generous acknowledgment from scientific bodies and institutions of learning in Europe and America. I recommend fitting recognition by Congress of the great achievement of Robert Edwin Peary.

Department of the Interior

Appeals to Court in Land Cases

The Secretary of the Interior recommends a change of the law in respect to the procedure in adjudicating claims for lands, by which appeals can be taken from the decisions of the Department to the Court of Appeals of the District of Columbia for a judicial consideration of the rights of the claimant. This change finds complete analogy in the present provision for appeals from the decisions of the Commissioner of Patents. The judgments of the court in such cases would be of decisive value to land claimants generally and to the Department of the Interior in the administration of the law, would enable claimants to bring into Court the final consideration of issues as to the title to Government land and would, I think, obviate a good deal of the subsequent litigation that now arises in our Western courts. The bill is pending, I believe, in the House, having been favorably reported from the Committee on Public Lands, and I recommend its enactment.

Arrears Wiped Out

One of the difficulties in the Interior Department and in the Land Office has been the delays attendant upon the consideration by the Land Office and the Secretary of the Interior of claims for patents of public lands to individuals. I am glad to say that under the recent appropriations of the Congress and the earnest efforts of the Secretary and his subordinates, these arrears have been disposed of, and the work of the Department has been brought more nearly up to date in respect to the pending business than ever before in its history. Economies have been effected where possible without legislative assistance, and these are shown in the reduced estimates for the expenses of the Department during the current fiscal year and during the year to come.

Conservation

The subject of the conservation of the public domain has commanded the attention of the people within the last two or three years.

Agricultural Lands

There is no need for radical reform in the methods of disposing of what are really agricultural lands. The present laws have worked well. The enlarged homestead law has encouraged the successful farming of lands in the semi-arid regions.

Reclamation

The total sum already accumulated in the fund provided by the act for the reclamation of arid lands is about $69,449,058.76, and of this, all but $6,241,058.76 has been allotted to the various projects, of which there are thirty. Congress at its last session provided for the issuing of certificates of indebtedness not exceeding twenty millions of dollars, to be redeemed from the reclamation fund when the proceeds of lands sold and from the water-rents should be sufficient. Meantime, in accordance with the provisions of the law, I appointed a board of army engineers to examine the projects and to ascertain which are feasible and worthy of completion. That board has made a report upon the subject, which I shall transmit in a separate message within a few days.

Conservation Address

In September last a conservation Congress was held at St. Paul, at which I delivered an address on the subject of conservation so far as it was within the jurisdiction and possible action of the Federal Government. In that address I assembled from the official records the statistics and facts as to what had been done in this behalf in the administration of my predecessor and in my own, and indicated the legislative measures which I believed to be wise in order to secure the best use, in the public interest, of what remains of our National domain. There was in this address a very full discussion of the reasons which led me to the conclusions stated. For the purpose of saving in an official record a comprehensive résumé of the statistics and facts gathered with some difficulty in that address, and to avoid their repetition in the body of this message, I venture to make the address an accompanying appendix. The statistics are corrected to November fifteenth last.

Specific Recommendations

For the reasons stated in the conservation address, I recommend:

First, that the limitation now imposed upon the Executive which forbids his reserving more forest lands in Oregon, Washington, Idaho, Montana, Colorado, and Wyoming, be repealed.

Second, that the coal deposits of the Government be leased after advertisement inviting competitive bids, for terms not exceeding fifty years, with a minimum rental and royalties upon the coal mined, to be readjusted every ten or twelve years, and with conditions as to maintenance which will secure proper mining, and as to assignment which will prevent combinations to monopolize control of the coal in any one district or market. I do not think that coal measures under 2,500 acres of surface would be too large an amount to lease to any one lessee.

The Secretary of the Interior thinks there are difficulties in the way of leasing public coal lands, which objections he has set forth in his report, the force of which I freely concede. I entirely approved his stating at length in his report the objections in order that the whole subject may be presented to Congress, but after a full consideration I favor a leasing system and recommend it.

Third, that the law should provide the same separation in respect to government phosphate lands of surface and mineral rights that now obtains in coal lands and that power to lease such lands upon terms and limitations similar to those above recommended for coal leases, with an added condition enabling the Government to regulate, and if need be to prohibit, the export to foreign countries of the product.

Fourth, that the law should allow a prospector for oil or gas to have the right to prospect for two years over a certain tract of government land, the right to be evidenced by a license for which he shall pay a small sum;

and that upon discovery, a lease may be granted upon terms securing a minimum rental and proper royalties to the Government, and also the conduct of the oil or gas well in accord with the best method for husbanding the supply of oil in the district. The period of the leases should not be as long as those of coal, but they should contain similar provisions as to assignment to prevent monopolistic combinations.

Fifth, that water-power sites be directly leased by the Federal Government, after advertisement and bidding, for not exceeding fifty years upon a proper rental and with a condition fixing rates charged to the public for units of electric power, both rental and rates to be readjusted equitably every ten years by arbitration or otherwise, with suitable provisions against assignment to prevent monopolistic combinations. Or, that the law shall provide that upon application made by the authorities of the State where the water-power site is situated, it may be patented to the State on condition that the State shall dispose of it under terms like those just described, and shall enforce those terms, or upon failure to comply with the condition the water-power site and all the plant and improvement on the site shall be forfeited and revert to the United States, the President being given the power to declare the forfeiture and to direct legal proceedings for its enforcement. Either of these methods would, I think, accomplish the proper public purpose in respect to water-power sites, but one or the other should be promptly adopted.

Necessity for Prompt Action

I earnestly urge upon Congress that at this session general conservation legislation of the character indicated be adopted. At its last session this Congress took most useful and proper steps in the cause of conservation by allowing the Executive, through withdrawals, to suspend the action of the existing laws in respect to much of the public domain. I have not thought that the danger of disposing of coal lands in the United States under the present laws in large quantities was so great as to call for their withdrawal, because under the present provisions it is reasonably certain that the Government will receive the real value of the land. But, in respect to oil lands, or phosphate lands, and of gas lands in the United States, and in respect to coal lands in Alaska, I have exercised the full power of withdrawal with the hope that the action of Congress would follow promptly and prevent that tying up of the resources of the country in the western and less settled portion and in Alaska, which means stagnation and retrogression.

The question of conservation is not a partisan one, and I sincerely hope that even in the short time of the present session consideration may be given to those questions which have now been much discussed, and that action may be taken upon them.

Alaska

With reference to the government of Alaska, I have nothing to add to the recommendations I made in my last message on the subject. I am convinced that the migratory character of the population, its unequal distribution, and its smallness of number, which the new census shows to be about 50,000, in relation to the enormous expanse of the territory, make it altogether impracticable to give to those people who are in Alaska today and may not be there a year hence, the power to elect a legislature to govern an immense territory to which they have a relation so little permanent. It is far better for the development of the territory that it be committed to a commission to be appointed by the Executive, with limited legislative powers sufficiently broad to meet the local needs, than to continue the present insufficient government with few remedial powers, or to make a popular government where there is not proper foundation upon which to rest it.

The suggestion that the appointment of a commission will lead to the control of the government by corporate or selfish and exploiting interests has not the slightest foundation in fact. Such a government worked well in the Philippines, and would work well in Alaska, and those who are really interested in the proper development of that territory for the benefit of the people who live in it and the benefit of the people of the United States, who own it, should support the institution of such a government.

Alaskan Railways

I have been asked to recommend that the credit of the Government be extended to aid the construction of railroads in Alaska. I am not ready now to do so. A great many millions of dollars have already been expended in the construction of at least two railroads, and if laws be passed providing for the proper development of the resources of Alaska, especially for the opening up of the coal lands, I believe that the capital already invested will induce the investment of more capital, sufficient to complete the railroads building, and to furnish cheap coal not only to Alaska but to the whole Pacific coast. The passage of a law permitting the leasing of government coal lands in Alaska after public competition, and the appointment of a commission for the government of the territory, with enabling powers to meet the local needs, will lead to an improvement in Alaska and the development of her resources that is likely to surprise the country.

National Parks

Our national parks have become so extensive and involve so much detail of action in their control that it seems to me there ought to be legislation creating a bureau for their care and control. The greatest natural wonder of this country and the surrounding territory should be included in another national park. I refer to the Grand Canyon of the Colorado.

Pensions

The uniform policy of the Government in the matter of granting pensions to those gallant and devoted men who fought to save the life of the Nation in the perilous days of the great Civil War, has always been of the most liberal character. Those men are now rapidly passing away. The best obtainable official statistics show that they are dying at the rate of something over three thousand a month, and, in view of their advancing years, this rate must inevitably, in proportion, rapidly increase. To the man who risked everything on the field of battle to save the Nation in the hour of its direst need, we owe a debt which has not been and should not be computed in a begrudging or parsimonious spirit. But while we should be actuated by this spirit to the soldier himself, care should be exercised not to go to absurd lengths, or distribute the bounty of the Government to classes of persons who may, at this late day, from a mere mercenary motive, seek to obtain some legal relation with an old veteran now tottering on the brink of the grave. The true spirit of the pension laws is to be found in the noble sentiments expressed by Mr. Lincoln in his last inaugural address, wherein, in speaking of the Nation's duty to its soldiers when the struggle should be over, he said we should "care for him who shall have borne the battle, and for his widow and orphans."

Department of Agriculture

Value of this Year's Crops

The report of the Secretary of Agriculture invites attention to the stupendous value of the agricultural products of this country, amounting in all to $8,926,000,000 for this year. This amount is larger than that of 1909 by $305,000,000. The existence of such a crop indicates a good prospect for business throughout the country. A notable change for the better is commented upon by the Secretary in the fact that the South, especially in those regions where the boll weevil has interfered with the growth of cotton, has given more attention to the cultivation of corn and other cereals, so that there is a greater diversification of crops in the South than ever before—and all to the great advantage of that section.

Department Activities

The report contains a most interesting account of the activities of the Department in its various bureaus, showing how closely the agricultural progress in this country is following along the lines of improvement recommended by the Department through its publications and the results of its experiment stations in every State, and by the instructions given through the agricultural schools aided by the Federal Government and following the general curriculum urged by the head and bureau chiefs of the Department.

The activities of the Department have been greatly increased by the enactment of recent legislation, by the pure-food act, the meat-inspection act, the cattle-transportation act, and the act concerning the interstate shipment of game. This department is one of those the scope of whose action is constantly widening, and therefore it is impossible under existing legislation to reduce the cost and their estimates below those of preceding years.

Farmers' Income and Cost of Living

An interesting review of the results of an examination made by the Department into statistics and prices, shows that on the average since 1891, farm products have increased in value 72 percent while the things which the farmer buys for use have increased but 12 percent, an indication that present conditions are favorable to the farming community.

Forest Service

I have already referred to the forests of the United States and their extent, and have urged, as I do again, the removal of the limitation upon the power of the Executive to reserve other tracts of land in six Western States in which withdrawal for this purpose is now forbidden. The Secretary of Agriculture gives a very full description of the disastrous fires that occurred during the last summer in the national forests. A drought more intense than any recorded in the history of the West had introduced a condition into the forests which made fires almost inevitable, and locomotive sparks, negligent campers, and in some cases incendiaries furnished the needed immediate cause. At one time the fires were so extended that they covered a range of a hundred miles, and the Secretary estimates that standing timber of the value of 25 millions of dollars was destroyed. Seventy-six persons in the employ of the Forest Service were killed and many more injured and I regret to say that there is no provision in the law by which the expenses for their hospital treatment or of their interment could be met out of public funds. The Red Cross contributed a thousand dollars, and the remainder of the necessary expenses was made up by private contribution, chiefly from the force of the Forest Service and its officials. I recommend that suitable legislation be adopted to enable the Secretary of Agriculture to meet the moral obligations of the Government in this respect.

Appropriation for Fire Fighting

The specific fund for fighting fires was only about $135,000, but there existed discretion in the Secretary in case of an emergency to apply other funds in his control to this purpose, and he did so to the extent of nearly a million of dollars, which will involve the presentation of a deficiency estimate for the current fiscal year of over $900,000. The damage done was not therefore due to the lack of an appropriation by Congress available to meet the emergency, but the difficulty of fighting it lay in the remote points where the fires began and where it was impossible with the roads and trails as they now exist promptly to reach them. Proper protection necessitates, as the Secretary points out, the expenditure of a good deal more money in the development of roads and trails in the forests, the establishment of lookout stations, and telephone connection between them and places where assistance can be secured.

Reforestation

The amount of reforestation shown in the report of the Forest Service— only about 15,000 acres as compared with the 150 millions of acres of national forests—seems small, and I am glad to note that in this regard the Secretary of Agriculture and the chief of the Forest Service are looking forward to far greater activity in the use of available Government land for this purpose. Progress has been made in learning by experiment the best methods of reforesting. Congress is appealed to now by the Secretary of Agriculture to make the appropriations needed for enlarging the usefulness of the Forest Service in this regard. I hope that Congress will approve and adopt the estimate of the Secretary for this purpose.

Department of Commerce and Labor

The Secretary of the Department of Commerce and Labor has had under his immediate supervision the application of the merit system of promotion to a large number of employees, and his discussion of this method of promotions based on actual experience, I commend to the attention of Congress.

The Census Bureau

The taking of the census has proceeded with promptness and efficiency. The Secretary believes, and I concur, that it will be more thorough and accurate than any census which has heretofore been taken, but it is not perfect. The motive that prompts men with a false civic pride to induce the padding of census returns in order to increase the population of a particular city has been strong enough to lead to fraud in respect to a few cities in this country, and I have directed the Attorney-General to proceed with all the vigor possible against those who are responsible for these frauds. They have been discovered and they will not interfere with the accuracy of the census, but it is of the highest importance that official inquiry of this sort should not be embarrassed by fraudulent conspiracies in some private or local interest.

Bureau of Light-Houses

The reorganization of the Light-House Board has affected a very considerable saving in the administration, and the estimates for that service for the present year are $428,000 less than for the preceding year. In addition, three tenders, for which appropriations were made, are not being built because they are not at present needed for the service. The Secretary is now asking for a large sum for the addition of lights and other aids to the commerce of the seas, including a number in Alaska. The trade along that coast is becoming so important that I respectfully urge the necessity for following his recommendation.

Bureau of Corporations

The Commissioner of Corporations has just completed the first part of a report on the lumber industry in the United States. This part does not find the existence of a trust or combination in the manufacture of lumber. The Commissioner does find, however, a condition in the ownership of the standing timber of the United States, other than the Government timber, that calls for serious attention. The direct investigation made by the Commissioner covered an area which contains 80 percent of the privately owned timber of the country. His report shows that one-half of the timber in this area is owned by 200 individuals and corporations; that 14 percent is owned by 3 corporations, and that there is very extensive interownership of stock, as well as other circumstances, all pointing to friendly relations among those who own a majority of this timber, a relationship which might lead to a combination for the maintenance of a price that would be very detrimental to the public interest, and would create the necessity of removing all tariff obstacles to the free importations of lumber from other countries.

Bureau of Fisheries

I am glad to note in the Secretary's report the satisfactory progress which is being made in respect to the preservation of the seals of the Pribiloff Islands. Very active steps are being taken by the Department of State to secure an arrangement which shall protect the Pribiloff herd from the losses due to pelagic sealing. Meantime the Government has secured seal pelts of the bachelor seals (the killing of which does not interfere with the maintenance of the herd), from the sale of which next month it is expected to realize about $450,000, a sum largely in excess of the rental paid by the lessee of the Government under the previous contract.

Coast and Geodetic Survey

The Coast and Geodetic Survey has been engaged in surveying the coasts of the Philippine archipelago. This is a heavy work, because of the extended character of the coast line in those Islands, but I am glad to note that about half of the needed survey has been completed. So large a part of the coast line of the archipelago has been unsurveyed as to make navigation in the neighborhood of a number of the islands, and especially on the east side, particularly dangerous.

Bureau of Labor

The Commissioner of Labor has been actively engaged in composing the differences between employers and employees engaged in interstate transportation, under the Erdman Act, jointly with the Chairman of the Interstate Commerce Commission. I can not speak in too high terms of the success of these two officers in conciliation and settlement of controversies which, but for their interposition, would have resulted disastrously to all interests.

Tax on Phosphorous Matches

I invite attention to the very serious injury caused to all those who are engaged in the manufacture of phosphorous matches. The diseases incident to this are frightful, and as matches can be made from other materials entirely innocuous, I believe that the injurious manufacture could be discouraged and ought to be discouraged by the imposition of a heavy federal tax. I recommend the adoption of this method of stamping out a very serious abuse.

Eight-Hour Law

Since 1868 it has been the declared purpose of this Government to favor the movement for an eight-hour day by a provision of law that none of the employees employed by or *on behalf* of the Government should work longer than eight hours in every twenty-four. The first declaration of this view was not accompanied with any penal clause or with any provision for its enforcement, and, though President Grant by a proclamation twice attempted to give it his sanction and to require the officers of the Government to carry it out, the purpose of the framers of the law was ultimately defeated by a decision of the Supreme Court holding that the statute as drawn was merely a direction of the Government to its agents and did not invalidate a contract made in behalf of the Government which provided in the contract for labor for a day of longer hours than eight. Thereafter, in 1892, the present eight-hour law was passed, which provides that the services and employment of all laborers and mechanics who are now or may hereafter be employed by the Government of the United States, by the District of Columbia, or by any contractor or subcontractor on any of the public works of the United States and of the said District of Columbia is hereby restricted to eight hours in any one calendar day. This law has been construed to limit the application of the requirement to those who are directly employed by the Government or to those who are employed upon public works situate upon land owned by the United States. This construction prevented its application to government battle ships and other vessels built in private shipyards and to heavy guns and armor plate contracted for and made at private establishments.

Pending Bill

The proposed act provides that no laborer or mechanic doing any part of the work contemplated by a contract with the United States in the employ of the contractor or any subcontractor shall be required or permitted to work more than eight hours a day in any one calendar day.

It seems to me from the past history that the Government has been committed to a policy of encouraging the limitation of the day's work to eight hours in all works of construction initiated by itself, and it seems to me illogical to maintain a difference between government work done on government soil and government work done in a private establishment, when the work is of such large dimensions and involves the expenditure of much labor for a considerable period, so that the private manufacturer may adjust himself and his establishment to the special terms of employment that he must make with his workmen for this particular job. To require, however, that every small contract of manufacture entered into by the Government should be carried out by the contractor with men working at eight hours would be to impose an intolerable burden upon the Government by limiting its sources of supply and excluding altogether the great majority of those who would otherwise compete for its business.

The proposed act recognizes this in the exceptions which it makes to contracts "for transportation by land or water, for the transmission of intelligence, and for such materials or articles as may usually be bought in the open market whether made to conform to particular specifications or not, or for the purchase of supplies by the Government, whether manufactured to conform to particular specifications or not."

Substitute for Pending Bill

I recommend that instead of enacting the proposed bill, the meaning of which is not clear and definite and might be given a construction embarrassing to the public interest, the present act be enlarged by providing that public works shall be construed to include not only buildings and work upon public ground, but also ships, armor, and large guns when manufactured in private yards or factories.

Provision for Suspension in Emergencies by President

One of the great difficulties in enforcing this eight-hour law is that its application under certain emergencies becomes exceedingly oppressive and there is a great temptation to subordinate officials to evade it. I think that it would be wiser to allow the President, by Executive order, to declare an emergency in special instances in which the limitation might not apply and, in such cases, to permit the payment by the Government of extra compensation for the time worked each day in excess of eight hours. I may add that my suggestions in respect to this legislation have the full concurrence of the Commissioner of Labor.

Workmen's Compensation

In view of the keen, widespread interest now felt in the United States in a system of compensation for industrial accidents to supplant our present thoroughly unsatisfactory system of employers' liability (a subject the importance of which Congress has already recognized by the appointment of a commission), I recommend that the International Congress on Industrial Insurance be invited to hold its meeting in 1913 in Washington, and that an appropriation of $10,000 be made to cover the necessary expenses of organizing and carrying on the meeting.

Bureau of Immigration

Distributing Immigrants

The immigration into this country is increasing each year. A large part of it comes through the immigrant station at Ellis Island in the City of New York. An examination of the station and the methods pursued satisfies me that a difficult task is there performed by the commissioner and his force with common sense, the strictest fairness, and with the most earnest desire to enforce the law equitably and mercifully. It has been proposed to enlarge the accommodations so as to allow more of the immigrants to come by that port. I do not think it wise policy to do this. I have no objection to—on the contrary, I recommend—the construction of additional buildings for the purpose of facilitating a closer and more careful examination of each immigrant as he comes in, but I deprecate the enlargement of the buildings and of the force for the purpose of permitting the examination of more immigrants per day than are now examined. If it is understood that no more immigrants can be taken in at New York than are now taken in, and the steamship companies thus are given a reason and a motive for transferring immigrants to other ports, we can be confident that they will be better distributed through the country and that there will not be that congestion in the City of New York which does not make for the better condition of the immigrant or increase his usefulness as a new member of this community. Everything which tends to send the immigrants west and south into rural life helps the country.

Amendments Recommended

I concur with the Secretary in his recommendations as to the amendments to the immigration law in increasing the fine against the companies for violation of the regulations, and in giving greater power to the commissioner to enforce more care on the part of the steamship companies in accepting immigrants. The recommendation of the Secretary, in which he urges that the law may be amended so as to discourage the separation of families, is, I think, a good one.

Miscellaneous Subjects Not Included in Departments

Bureau of Health

In my message of last year I recommended the creation of a Bureau of Health, in which should be embraced all those Government agencies outside of the War and Navy Departments which are now directed toward the preservation of public health or exercise functions germane to that subject. I renew this recommendation. I greatly regret that the agitation in favor of this bureau has aroused a counteragitation against its creation, on the ground that the establishment of such a bureau is to be in the interest of a particular school of medicine. It seems to me that this assumption is wholly unwarranted, and that those responsible for the Government can be trusted to secure in the personnel of the bureau the appointment of representatives of all recognized schools of medicine, and in the management of the bureau entire freedom from narrow prejudice in this regard.

The Imperial Valley Project

By an act passed by Congress the President was authorized to expend a million dollars to construct the needed work to prevent injury to the lands of the Imperial Valley from the overflow of the Colorado River. I appointed a competent engineer to examine the locality and to report a plan for construction. He has done so. In order to complete the work it is necessary to secure the consent of Mexico, for part of the work must be constructed in Mexican territory. Negotiations looking to the securing of such authority are quite near success. The Southern Pacific Railroad Company proposes to assist us in the work by lending equipment and by the transportation of material at cost price, and it is hoped that the work may be completed before any danger shall arise from the spring floods in the river. The work is being done under the supervision of the Secretary of the Interior and his consulting engineer, General Marshall, late Chief of Engineers, now retired.

This leads me to invite the attention of Congress to the claim made by the Southern Pacific Railroad Company for an amount expended in a similar work of relief called for by a flood and great emergency. This work, as I am informed, was undertaken at the request of my predecessor and under promise to reimburse the railroad company. It seems to me the equity of this claim is manifest, and the only question involved is the reasonable value of the work done. I recommend the payment of the claim in a sum found to be just.

District of Columbia

Character of Government

The government of the District of Columbia is a good government. The police force, while perhaps it might be given, or acquire, more military discipline in bearing and appearance, is nevertheless an efficient body of men, free from graft, and discharges its important duties in this capital of the nation effectively. The parks and the streets of the city and the District are generally kept clean and in excellent condition. The Commissioners of the District have its affairs well in hand, and, while not extravagant, are constantly looking to those municipal improvements that are expensive but that must be made in a modern growing city like Washington. While all this is true, nevertheless the fact that Washington is governed by Congress, and that the citizens are not responsible and have no direct control through popular election in District matters, properly subjects the government to inquiry and criticism by its citizens, manifested through the public press and otherwise; such criticism should command the careful attention of Congress. Washington is the capital of the nation and its maintenance as a great and beautiful city under national control, every lover of his country has much at heart; and it should present in every way a model in respect of economy of expenditure, of sanitation, of tenement reform, of thorough public instruction, of the proper regulation of public utilities, of sensible and extended charities, of the proper care of criminals and of youth needing reform, of healthful playgrounds and opportunity for popular recreation, and of a beautiful system of parks. I am glad to think that progress is being made in all these directions, but I venture to point out certain specific improvements toward these ends which Congress in its wisdom might adopt. Speaking generally, I think there ought to be more concentration of authority in respect to the accomplishment of some of these purposes with more economy of expenditure.

Public Parks

Attention is invited to the peculiar situation existing in regard to the parks of Washington. The park system proper, comprising some 343 different areas, is under the Office of Public Buildings and Grounds, which, however, has nothing to do with the control of Rock Creek Park, the Zoological Park, the grounds of the Department of Agriculture, the Botanic Garden, the grounds of the Capitol, and other public grounds which are regularly open to the public and ought to be part of the park system. Exclusive of the grounds of the Soldiers' Home and of Washington Barracks, the public grounds used as parks in the District of Columbia comprise over 3,100 acres, under ten different controlling officials or bodies. This division of jurisdiction is most unfortunate.

Large sums of money are spent yearly in beautifying and keeping in good condition these parks and the grounds connected with Government buildings and institutions. The work done on all of them is of the same general character—work for which the Office of Public Buildings and Grounds has been provided by Congress with a special organization and equipment, which are lacking for the grounds not under that office. There can be no doubt that if all work of care and improvement upon the grounds belonging to the United States in the District of Columbia were put, as far as possible, under one responsible head, the result would be not only greater efficiency and economy in the work itself, but greater harmony in the development of the public parks and gardens of the city.

Congress at its last session provided for two more parks, called the Meridian Hill and Montrose parks, and the District Commissioners have also included in their estimates a sum to be used for the acquisition of much needed park land adjoining the Zoological Park, known as the Klingle Ford tract. The expense of these three parks, included in the estimates of the Commissioners, aggregates $900,000. I think it would lead to economy if the improvement and care of all these parks and other public grounds above described should be transferred to the Office of Public Buildings and Grounds, which has an equipment well and economically adapted to carrying out the public purpose in respect to improvements of this kind.

To prevent encroachments upon the park area it is recommended that the erection of any permanent structure on any lands in the District of Columbia belonging to the United States be prohibited except by specific authority of Congress.

The District of Columbia in Virginia

I have already in previous communications to Congress referred to the importance of acquiring for the District of Columbia at least a part of the territory on the other side of the Potomac in Virginia which was originally granted for the District by the State of Virginia, and then was retroceded by act of Congress in 1846. It is very evident from conferences that I have had with the Senators and Representatives from Virginia that there is no hope of a regranting by the State of the land thus given back; and I am frank to say that in so far as the tract includes the town of Alexandria and land remote from the Potomac River there would be no particular advantage in bringing that within national control. But the land which lies along the Potomac River above the railroad bridge and across the Potomac, including Arlington Cemetery, Fort Myer, the Government experiment farm, the village of Rosslyn, and the Palisades of the Potomac, reaching to where the old District line intersects the river, is very sparsely settled and could be admirably utilized for increasing the system of the parks of Washington. It has been suggested to me by the same Virginia Senators and Representatives that if the Government were to acquire for a government park the land above described, which is not of very great value, the present law of Virginia would itself work the creation of federal jurisdiction over it, and if that were not complete enough, the legislature of Virginia would in all probability so enlarge the jurisdiction as to enable Congress to include it within the control of the government of the District of Columbia and actually make it a part of Washington. I earnestly recommend that steps be taken to carry out this plan.

Public Utilities

There are a sufficient number of corporations enjoying the use of public utilities in the District of Columbia to justify and require the enactment of a law providing for their supervision and regulation in the public interest consistent with the vested rights secured to them by their charters. A part of these corporations, to wit, the street railways, have been put under the control of the Interstate Commerce Commission, but that Commission recommends that the power be taken from it, and intimates broadly that its other and more important duties make it impossible for it to give the requisite supervision. It seems to me wise to place this general power of supervision and regulation in the District Commissioners. It is said that their present duties are now absorbing and would prevent the proper discharge by them of these new functions, but their present jurisdiction brings them so closely and frequently in contact with these corporations and makes them to know in such detail how the corporations are discharging their duties under the law and how they are serving the public interest that the Commissioners are peculiarly fitted to do this work, and I hope that Congress will impose it upon them by intrusting them with powers in respect to such corporations similar to those of the public utilities commission of New York, New York or similar boards in Massachusetts.

School System

I do not think the present control of the school system of Washington commends itself as the most efficient and economical and thorough instrument for the carrying on of public instruction.

The cost of education in the District of Columbia is excessive as compared with the cost in other cities of similar size, and it is not apparent that the results are in general more satisfactory. The average cost per pupil per day in Washington is about 38 cents, while the average cost in 13 other American cities fairly comparable with Washington in population and standard of education is about 25.5 cents. For each dollar spent in salaries of school teachers and officers in the District about 4.4 days of instruction per pupil are given, while in the 13 cities above referred to each dollar expended for salaries affords on the average 6.8 days of instruction. For the current fiscal year the estimates of the Board of Education amounted to about three-quarters of the entire revenue locally collected for District purposes.

If I may say so, there seems to be a lack of definite plan in the expansion of the school system and the erection of new buildings and of proper economy in the use of these buildings that indicates the necessity for the concentration of control. All plans for improvement and expansion in the school system are with the School Board, while the limitation of expenses is with the District Commissioners. I think it would be much better to put complete control and responsibility in the District Commissioners, and then provide a board of school visitors, to be appointed by the Supreme Court of the District or by the President, from the different school districts of Washington, who, representing local needs, shall meet and make recommendations to the Commissioners and to the Superintendent of Education—an educator of ability and experience who should be an appointee of and responsible to the District Commissioners.

Permanent Improvements

Among other items for permanent improvements appearing in the District estimates for 1912 is one designed to substitute for Willow Tree Alley, notorious in the records of the Police and Health Departments, a playground with a building containing baths, a gymnasium, and other helpful features, and I hope Congress will approve this estimate. Fair as Washington seems with her beautiful streets and shade trees, and free, as the expanse of territory which she occupies would seem to make her, from slums and insanitary congestion of population, there are centers in the interior of squares where the very poor, and the criminal classes as well, huddle together in filth and noisome surroundings, and it is of primary importance that these nuclei of disease and suffering and vice should be removed, and that there should be substituted for them small parks as breathing spaces, and model tenements having sufficient air space and meeting other hygienic requirements. The estimate for the reform of Willow Tree Alley, the worst of these places in the city, is the beginning of a movement that ought to attract the earnest attention and support of Congress, for Congress can not escape its responsibility for the existence of these human pest holes.

The estimates for the District of Columbia for the fiscal year 1912 provide for the repayment to the United States of $616,000, one-fourth of the floating debt that will remain on June 30, 1911. The bonded debt will be reduced in 1912 by about the same amount.

The District of Columbia is now in an excellent financial condition. Its own share of indebtedness will, it is estimated, be less than $6,000,000 on June 30, 1912, as compared with about $9,000,000 on June 30, 1909.

The bonded debt, owed half and half by the United States and the District, will be extinguished by 1924, and the floating debt of the District probably long before that time.

The revenues have doubled in the last ten years, while the population during the same period has increased but 18.78 percent. It is believed that, if due economy be practiced, the District can soon emerge from debt, even while financing its permanent improvements with reasonable rapidity from current revenues.

To this end, I recommend the enactment into law of a bill now before Congress—and known as the Judson Bill—which will insure the gradual extinguishment of the District's debt, while at the same time requiring that the many permanent improvements needed to complete a fitting capital city shall be carried on from year to year and at a proper rate of progress with funds derived from the rapidly increasing revenues.

Freedmen's Bank

I renew my recommendation that the claims of the depositors in the Freedmen's Bank be recognized and paid by the passage of the pending bill on that subject.

Negro Exposition

I also renew my recommendation that steps be taken looking to the holding of a Negro exposition in celebration of the fiftieth anniversary of the issuing by Mr. Lincoln of the Emancipation Proclamation.

Civil Service Commission

The Civil Service Commission has continued its useful duties during the year. The necessity for the maintenance of the provisions of the civil service law was never greater than today. Officers responsible for the policy of the Administration, and their immediate personal assistants or deputies, should not be included within the classified service; but in my judgment, public opinion has advanced to the point where it would support a bill providing a secure tenure during efficiency for all purely administrative officials. I entertain the profound conviction that it would greatly aid the cause of efficient and economical government, and of better politics if Congress could enact a bill providing that the Executive shall have the power to include in the classified service all local offices under the Treasury Department, the Department of Justice, the Post-Office Department, the Interior Department, and the Department of Commerce and Labor, appointments to which now require the confirmation of the Senate, and that upon such classification the advice and consent of the Senate shall cease to be required in such appointments. By their certainty of tenure, dependent on good service, and by their freedom from the necessity for political activity, these local officers would be induced to become more efficient public servants.

The civil service law is an attempt to solve the problem of the proper selection of those who enter the service. A better system under that law for promotions ought to be devised, but, given the selected employee, there remains still the question of promoting his efficiency and his usefulness to the Government, and that can be brought about only by a careful comparison of unit work done by the individual and a pointing out of the necessity for improvement in this regard where improvement is possible.

Inquiry Into Economy and Efficiency

The increase in the activities and in the annual expenditures of the Federal Government has been so rapid and so great that the time has come to check the expansion of government activities in new directions until we have tested the economy and efficiency with which the Government of today is being carried on. The responsibility rests upon the head of the Administration. He is held accountable by the public, and properly so. Despite the unselfish and patriotic efforts of the heads of departments and others charged with responsibility of government, there has grown up in this country a conviction that the expenses of government are too great. The fundamental reason for the existence undetected of waste, duplication, and bad management is the lack of prompt, accurate information. The president of a private corporation doing so vast a business as the Government transacts would, through competent specialists, maintain the closest scrutiny on the comparative efficiency and the comparative costs in each division or department of the business. He would know precisely what the duties and the activities of each bureau or division are in order to prevent overlapping. No adequate machinery at present exists for supplying the President of the United States with such information respecting the business for which he is responsible. For the first time in the history of the Government, Congress in the last session supplied this need and made an appropriation to enable the President to inquire into the economy and efficiency of the executive departments, and I am now assembling an organization for that purpose.

At the outset I find comparison between departments and bureaus impossible for the reason that in no two departments are the estimates and expenditures displayed and classified alike. The first step is to reduce all to a common standard for classification and judgment, and this work is now being done. When it is completed, the foundation will be laid for a businesslike national budget, and for such a just comparison of the economy and efficiency with which the several bureaus and divisions are conducted as will enable the President and the heads of Departments to detect waste, eliminate duplication, encourage the intelligent and effective civil servants whose efforts too often go unnoticed, and secure the public service at the lowest possible cost.

The Committees on Appropriations of Congress have diligently worked to reduce the expenses of government and have found their efforts often blocked by lack of accurate information containing a proper analysis of requirements and of actual and reasonable costs. The result of this inquiry should enable the Executive in his communications to Congress to give information to which Congress is entitled and which will enable it to promote economy.

My experience leads me to believe that while Government methods are much criticised, the bad results—if we do have bad results—are not due to a lack of zeal or willingness on the part of the civil servants. On the contrary, I believe that a fine spirit of willingness to work exists in the personnel, which, if properly encouraged, will produce results equal to those secured in the best managed private enterprises. In handling Government expenditure the aim is not profit—the aim is the maximum of public service at the minimum of cost. We wish to reduce the expenditures of the Government, and we wish to save money to enable the Government to go into some of the beneficial projects which we are debarred from taking up now because we ought not to increase our expenditures.

I have requested the head of each Department to appoint committees on economy and efficiency in order to secure full cooperation in the movement by the employees of the Government themselves.

At a later date I shall send to Congress a special message on this general subject.

I urge the continuance of the appropriation of $100,000 requested for the fiscal year 1912.

Civil Service Retirement

It is impossible to proceed far in such an investigation without perceiving the need of a suitable means of eliminating from the service the superannuated. This can be done in one of two ways, either by straight civil pension or by some form of contributory plan.

Careful study of experiments made by foreign governments shows that three serious objections to the civil pension payable out of the public treasury may be brought against it by the taxpayer, the administrative officer, and the civil employee, respectively. A civil pension is bound to become an enormous, continuous, and increasing tax on the public exchequer; it is demoralizing to the service since it makes difficult the dismissal of incompetent employees after they have partly earned their pension; and it is disadvantageous to the main body of employees themselves since it is always taken into account in fixing salaries and only the few who survive and remain in the service until pensionable age receive the value of their deferred pay. For this reason, after a half century of experience under a most liberal pension system, the civil servants of England succeeded, about a year ago, in having the system so modified as to make it virtually a contributory plan with provision for refund of their theoretical contributions.

The experience of England and other countries shows that neither can a contributory plan be successful, human nature being what it is, which does not make provision for the return of contributions, with interest, in case of death or resignation before pensionable age. Followed to its logical conclusion this means that the simplest and most independent solution of the problem for both employee and the Government is a compulsory savings arrangement, the employee to set aside from his salary a sum sufficient, with the help of a liberal rate of interest from the Government, to purchase an adequate annuity for him on retirement, this accumulation to be inalienably his and claimable if he leaves the service before reaching the retirement age or by his heirs in case of his death. This is the principle upon which the Gillett bill now pending is drawn.

The Gillett bill, however, goes further and provides that the Government shall contribute to the pension fund of those employees who are now so advanced in age that their personal contributions will not be sufficient to create their annuities before reaching the retirement age. In my judgment this provision should be amended so that the annuities of those employees shall be paid out of the salaries appropriated for the positions vacated by retirement, and that the difference between the annuities thus granted and the salaries may be used for the employment of efficient clerks at the lower grades. If the bill can be thus amended I recommend its passage, as it will initiate a valuable system and ultimately result in a great saving in the public expenditures

Interstate Commerce Commission

There has not been time to test the benefit and utility of the amendments to the interstate commerce law contained in the act approved June 18, 1910. The law as enacted did not contain all the features which I recommended. It did not specifically denounce as unlawful the purchase by one of two parallel and competing roads of the stock of the other. Nor did it subject to the restraining influence of the Interstate Commerce Commission the power of corporations engaged in operating interstate railroads to issue new stock and bonds; nor did it authorize the making of temporary agreements between railroads, limited to thirty days, fixing the same rates for traffic between the same places.

I do not press the consideration of any of these objects upon Congress at this session. The object of the first provision is probably generally covered by the antitrust law. The second provision was in the act referred to the consideration of a commission to be appointed by the Executive and to report upon the matter to Congress. That commission has been appointed, and is engaged in the investigation and consideration of the question submitted under the law. It consists of President Arthur T. Hadley, of Yale University, as chairman; Frederick Strauss, Frederick N. Judson, Walter L. Fisher, and Prof. B. H. Meyer, with William E. S. Griswold as secretary.

The third proposal led to so much misconstruction of its object, as being that of weakening the effectiveness of the antitrust law, that I am not disposed to press it for further consideration. It was intended to permit railroad companies to avoid useless rate cutting by a mere temporary acquiescence in the same rates for the same service over competing railroads, with no obligation whatever to maintain those rates for any time.

Safety Appliances and Provisions

The protection of railroad employees from personal injury is a subject of the highest importance and demands continuing attention. There have been two measures pending in Congress, one for the supervision of boilers and the other for the enlargement of dangerous clearances. Certainly some measures ought to be adopted looking to a prevention of accidents from these causes. It seems to me that with respect to boilers a bill might well be drawn requiring and enforcing by penalty a proper system of inspection by the railway companies themselves which would accomplish our purpose. The entire removal of outside clearances would be attended by such enormous expense that some other remedy must be adopted. By act of May 6, 1910, the Interstate Commerce Commission is authorized and directed to investigate accidents, to report their causes and its recommendations. I suggest that the Commission be requested to make a special report as to injuries from outside clearances and the best method of reducing them.

Valuation of Railroads

The Interstate Commerce Commission has recommended appropriations for the purpose of enabling it to enter upon a valuation of all railroads. This has always been within the jurisdiction of the Commission, but the requisite funds have been wanting. Statistics of the value of each railroad would be valuable for many purposes, especially if we ultimately enact any limitations upon the power of the interstate railroads to issue stocks and bonds, as I hope we may. I think, therefore, that in order to permit a correct understanding of the facts, it would be wise to make a reasonable appropriation to enable the Interstate Commerce Commission to proceed with due dispatch to the valuation of all railroads. I have no doubt that railroad companies themselves can and will greatly facilitate this valuation and make it much less costly in time and money than has been supposed.

Fraudulent Bills of Lading

Forged and fraudulent bills of lading purporting to be issued against cotton, some months since, resulted in losses of several millions of dollars to American and foreign banking and cotton interests. Foreign bankers then notified American bankers that, after October 31, 1910, they would not accept bills of exchange drawn against bills of lading for cotton issued by American railroad companies, unless American bankers would guarantee the integrity of the bills of lading. The American bankers rightly maintained that they were not justified in giving such guarantees, and that, if they did so, the United States would be the only country in the world whose bills were so discredited, and whose foreign trade was carried on under such guaranties.

The foreign bankers extended the time at which these guaranties were demanded until December 31, 1910, relying upon us for protection in the meantime, as the money which they furnish to move our cotton crop is of great value to this country.

For the protection of our own people and the preservation of our credit in foreign trade, I urge upon Congress the immediate enactment of a law under which one who, in good faith, advances money or credit upon a bill of lading issued by a common carrier upon an interstate or foreign shipment can hold the carrier liable for the value of the goods described in the bill at the valuation specified in the bill, at least to the extent of the advances made in reliance upon it. Such liability exists under the laws of many of the States. I see no objection to permitting two classes of bills of lading to be issued: (1) Those under which a carrier shall be absolutely liable, as above suggested, and (2) those with respect to which the carrier shall assume no liability except for the goods actually delivered to the agent issuing the bill. The carrier might be permitted to make a small separate specific charge in addition to the rate of transportation for such guaranteed bill, as an insurance premium against loss from the added risk, thus removing the principal objection which I understand is made by the railroad companies to the imposition of the liability suggested, viz., that the ordinary transportation rate would not compensate them for the liability assumed by the absolute guaranty of the accuracy of the bills of lading.

I further recommend that a punishment of fine and imprisonment be imposed upon railroad agents and shippers for fraud or misrepresentation in connection with the issue of bills of lading issued upon interstate and foreign shipments.

General Conclusion as to Interstate Commerce and Antitrust Law

Except as above, I do not recommend any amendment to the interstate-commerce law as it stands. I do not now recommend any amendment to the anti-trust law. In other words, it seems to me that the existing legislation with reference to the regulation of corporations and the restraint of their business has reached a point where we can stop for a while and witness the effect of the vigorous execution of the laws on the statute books in restraining the abuses which certainly did exist and which roused the public to demand reform. If this test develops a need for further legislation, well and good, but until then let us execute what we have. Due to the reform movements of the present decade, there has undoubtedly been a great improvement in business methods and standards. The great body of business men of this country, those who are responsible for its commercial development, now have an earnest desire to obey the law and to square their conduct of business to its requirements and limitations. These will doubtless be made clearer by the decisions of the Supreme Court in cases pending before it. It is in the interest of all the people of the country that for the time being the activities of government, in addition to enforcing earnestly and impartially the existing laws, should be directed to economy of administration, to the enlargement of opportunities for foreign trade, to the conservation and improvement of our agricultural lands and our other natural resources, to the building up of home industries, and to the strengthening of confidence of capital in domestic investment.

First Appendix to Second Annual Message

Address to the National Conservation Congress in St. Paul, Minnesota,
September 5, 1911

[Figures as to land withdrawals, classifications, and valuations are brought down to November 15, 1910.]

Conservation as an economic and political term has come to mean the preservation of our natural resources for economical use, so as to secure the greatest good to the greatest number. In the development of this country, in the hardships of the pioneer, in the energy of the settler, in the anxiety of the investor for quick returns, there was very little time, opportunity, or desire to prevent waste of those resources supplied by nature which could not be quickly transmuted into money; while the investment of capital was so great a desideratum that the people as a community exercised little or no care to prevent the transfer of absolute ownership of many of the valuable natural resources to private individuals, without retaining some kind of control of their use. The impulse of the whole new community was to encourage the coming of population, the increase of settlement, and the opening up of business; and he who demurred in the slightest degree to any step which promised additional development of the idle resources at hand was regarded as a traitor to his neighbors and an obstructor to public progress. But now that the communities have become old, now that the flush of enthusiastic expansion has died away, now that the would-be pioneers have come to realize that all the richest lands in the country have been taken up, we have perceived the necessity for a change of policy in the disposition of our national resources so as to prevent the continuance of the waste which has characterized our phenomenal growth in the past. Today we desire to restrict and retain under public control the acquisition and use by the capitalist of our natural resources.

The danger to the State and to the people at large from the waste and dissipation of our national wealth is not one which quickly impresses itself on the people of the older communities, because its most obvious instances do not occur in their neighborhood, while in the newer part of the country the sympathy with expansion and development is so strong that the danger is scoffed at or ignored. Among scientific men and thoughtful observers, however, the danger has always been present; but it needed some one to bring home the crying need for a remedy of this evil so as to impress itself on the public mind and lead to the formation of public opinion and action by the representatives of the people. Theodore Roosevelt took up this task in the last two years of his second administration, and well did he perform it.

As President of the United States I have, as it were, inherited this policy, and I rejoice in my heritage. I prize my high opportunity to do all that an Executive can do to help a great people realize a great national ambition. For conservation is national. It affects every man of us, every woman, every child. What I can do in the cause I shall do, not as President of a party, but as President of the whole people. Conservation is not a question of politics, or of factions, or of persons. It is a question that affects the vital welfare of all of us—of our children and our children's children. I urge that no good can come from meetings of this sort unless we ascribe to those who take part in them, and who are apparently striving worthily in the cause, all proper motives, and unless we judicially consider every measure or method proposed with a view to its effectiveness in achieving our common purpose, and wholly without regard to who proposes it or who will claim the credit for its adoption. The problems are of very great difficulty and call for the calmest consideration and clearest foresight. Many of the questions presented have phases that are new in this country, and it is possible that in their solution we may have to attempt first one way and then another. What I wish to emphasize, however, is that a satisfactory conclusion can only be reached promptly if we avoid acrimony, imputations of bad faith, and political controversy.

The public domain of the Government of the United States, including all the cessions from those of the thirteen States that made cessions to the United States and including Alaska, amounted in all to about 1,800,000,000 acres. Of this there is left as purely government property outside of Alaska something like 700,000,000 acres. Of this the national forest reserves in the United States proper embrace 144,000,000 acres. The rest is largely mountain or arid country, offering some opportunity for agriculture by dry farming and by reclamation, and containing metals as well as coal, phosphates, oils, and natural gas. Then the Government owns many tracts of land lying along the margins of streams that have water power, the use of which is necessary in the conversion of the power into electricity and its transmission.

I shall divide my discussion under the heads of (1) agricultural lands; (2) mineral lands—that is, lands containing metalliferous minerals; (3) forest lands; (4) coal lands; (5) oil and gas lands; and (6) phosphate lands.

I feel that it will conduce to a better understanding of the problems presented if I take up each class and describe, even at the risk of tedium, first, what has been done by the last administration and the present one in respect to each kind of land; second, what laws at present govern its disposition; third, what was done by the present Congress in this matter; and, fourth, the statutory changes proposed in the interest of conservation.

(1) Agricultural Lands

Our land laws for the entry of agricultural lands are now as follows:

The original homestead law, with the requirements of residence and cultivation for five years, much more strictly enforced now than ever before.

The enlarged homestead act, applying to nonirrigable lands only, requiring five years' residence and continuous cultivation of one-fourth of the area.

The desert-land act, which requires on the part of the purchaser the ownership of a water right and thorough reclamation of the land by irrigation, and the payment of $1.25 per acre.

The donation or Carey Act, under which the State selects the land and provides for its reclamation, and the title vests in the settler who resides upon the land and cultivates it and pays the cost of reclamation.

The national reclamation homestead law, requiring five years' residence and cultivation by the settler on the land irrigated by the Government, and payment by him to the Government of the cost of the reclamation.

There are other acts, but not of sufficient general importance to call for mention unless it is the stone and timber act, under which every individual, once in his lifetime, may acquire 160 acres of land, if it has valuable timber on it or valuable stone, by paying the price of not less than $2.50 per acre, fixed after examination of the stone or timber by a government appraiser. In times past a great deal of fraud has been perpetrated in the acquisition of lands under this act; but it is now being much more strictly enforced, and the entries made are so few in number that it seems to serve no useful purpose and ought to be repealed.

The present Congress passed a bill of great importance, severing the ownership of coal by the Government in the ground from the surface and permitting homestead entries upon the surface of the land, which, when perfected, give the settler the right to farm the surface, while the coal beneath the surface is retained in ownership by the Government and may be disposed of by it under other laws.

There is no crying need for radical reform in the methods of disposing of what are really agricultural lands. The present laws have worked well. The enlarged homestead law has encouraged the successful farming of lands in the semiarid regions. Of course the teachings of the Agricultural Department as to how these subarid lands may be treated and the soil preserved for useful culture are of the very essence of conservation. Then conservation of agricultural lands is shown in the reclamation of arid lands by irrigation and I should devote a few words to what the Government has done and is doing in this regard.

Reclamation

By the reclamation act a fund has been created of the proceeds of the public lands of the United States with which to construct works for storing great bodies of water at proper altitudes from which, by a suitable system of canals and ditches, the water is to be distributed over the arid and subarid lands of the Government to be sold to settlers at a price sufficient to pay for the improvements. Primarily, the projects are and must be for the improvement of public lands. Incidentally, where private land is also within the reach of the water supply, the furnishing at cost or profit of this water to private owners by the Government is held by the Federal Court of Appeals not to be a usurpation of power. But certainly this ought not to be done except from surplus water not needed for government land. About 30 projects have been set on foot distributed through the public-land States in accord with the statute, by which the allotments from the reclamation fund are required to be as near as practicable in proportion to the proceeds from the sale of the public lands in the respective States. The total sum already accumulated in the reclamation fund is about $69,449,058.76, and of that all but $6,241,058.76 has been allotted. It became very clear to Congress at its last session, from the statements made by experts, that these 30 projects could not be promptly completed with the balance remaining on hand or with the funds likely to accrue in the near future. It was found, moreover, that there are many settlers who have been led into taking up lands with the hope and understanding of having water furnished in a short time, who are left in a most distressing situation. I recommended to Congress that authority be given to the Secretary of the Interior to issue bonds in anticipation of the assured earnings by the projects, so that the projects, worthy and feasible, might be promptly completed, and the settlers might be relieved from their present inconvenience and hardship. In authorizing the issue of these bonds, Congress limited the application of their proceeds to those projects which a board of army engineers, to be appointed by the President, should examine and determine to be feasible and worthy of completion. The board has been appointed and soon will make its report.

(2) Mineral Lands

By mineral lands I mean those lands bearing metals, or what are called metalliferous minerals. The rules of ownership and disposition of these lands were first fixed by custom in the West, and then were embodied in the law, and they have worked, on the whole, so fairly and well that I do not think it is wise now to attempt to change or better them. The apex theory of tracing title to a lode has led to much litigation and dispute and ought not to have become the law, but it is so fixed and understood now that the benefit to be gained by a change is altogether outweighed by the inconvenience that would attend the introduction of a new system. So, too, the proposal for the Government to lease such mineral lands and deposits and to impose royalties might have been in the beginning a good thing, but now that most of the mineral land—I do not refer to coal land, or gas land, or phosphate land—has been otherwise disposed of it would be hardly worth while to assume the embarrassment of a radical change.

(3) Forest Lands

Nothing can be more important in the matter of conservation than the treatment of our forest lands. It was probably the ruthless destruction of forests in the older States that first called attention to the necessity for a halt in the waste of our resources. This was recognized by Congress by an act authorizing the Executive to reserve from entry and set aside public timber lands as national forests. Speaking generally, there has been reserved of the existing forests about 70 percent of all the timber lands of the Government. Within these forests (including 26,000,000 acres in two forests in Alaska) are 192,000,000 of acres, of which 166,000,000 of acres are in the United States proper and include within their boundaries something like 22,000,000 of acres that belong to the State or to private individuals. We have, then, excluding Alaska forests, a total of about 144,000,000 acres of forests belonging to the Government which is being treated in accord with the principles of scientific forestry. The law now prohibits the reservation of any more forest lands in Oregon, Washington, Idaho, Montana, Colorado, and Wyoming, except by act of Congress. I am informed by the Department of Agriculture that the Government owns other tracts of timber land in these States which should be included in the forest reserves. I expect to recommend to Congress that the limitation herein imposed shall be repealed. In the present forest reserves there are lands which are not properly forest land and which ought to be subject to homestead entry. This has caused some local irritation. We are carefully eliminating such lands from forest reserves, or, where their elimination is not practicable, listing them for entry under the forest homestead act. Congress ought to trust the Executive to use the power of reservation only with respect to land covered by timber or which will be useful in the plan of reforestation. During the present administration steps have been initiated which will result in the elimination of 6,250,000 acres of land, largely nontimbered, from forest reserves and in the addition of 3,500,000 acres of land principally valuable for forest purposes, making a net reduction in forest reserves amounting to 2,750,000 acres. The Bureau of Forestry since its creation has initiated reforestation on about 15,000 acres. A great deal of the forest land is available for grazing. During the past year the grazing lessees numbered 25,687, and they pastured upon the forest reserves 1,409,873 cattle, 85,552 horses, and 7,558,650 sheep, for which the Government received $986,909—a decrease from the preceding year of $45,276, due to the fact that no money was collected or received for grazing on the nontimbered lands eliminated from the forest reserve. Another source of profit in the forestry is the receipts for timber sold. This year they amounted to $1,043,428, an increase of $307,326 over the receipts of last year. This increase is due to the improvement in transportation to market and to the greater facility with which the timber can be reached.

The government timber in this country amounts to only one-fourth of all the timber, the rest being in private ownership. Only 3 percent of that which is in private ownership is looked after properly and treated according to modern rules of forestry. The usual destructive waste and neglect continues in the remainder of the forests owned by private persons and corporations. It is estimated that fire alone destroys fifty million dollars' worth of timber a year. The management of forests not on public land is beyond the jurisdiction of the Federal Government. If anything can be done by law it must be done by the state legislatures. I believe that it is within their constitutional power and duty to require the enforcement of regulations in the general public interest, as to fire and other causes of waste in the management of forests owned by private individuals and corporations.

Other Land Withdrawals

When President Roosevelt became fully advised of the necessity for the change in our disposition of public lands, especially those containing coal, oil, gas, phosphates, or water-power sites, he began the exercise of the power of withdrawal by executive order, of lands subject by law to homestead and the other methods of entering for agricultural lands. The precedent he set in this matter was followed by the present administration. Doubt had been expressed in some quarters as to the power in the Executive to make such withdrawals. The confusion and injustice likely to arise if the courts were to deny the power led me to appeal to Congress to give the President the express power. Congress has complied. The law as passed does not expressly validate or confirm previous withdrawals, and therefore as soon as the new law was passed, I myself confirmed all the withdrawals which had theretofore been made by both administrations by making them over again. This power of withdrawal is a most useful one, and I do not think that it is likely to be abused.

(4) Coal Lands

The next subject, and one most important for our consideration, is the disposition of the coal lands in the United States and in Alaska. First, as to those in the United States. At the beginning of this administration there were classified coal lands amounting to 5,476,000 acres, and there were withdrawn from entry for purposes of classification 17,867,000 acres. Since that time there have been withdrawn by my order from entry for classification 78,977,745 acres, making a total withdrawal of 96,844,745 acres. Meantime, of the acres thus withdrawn, 10,061,889 have been classified and found not to contain coal, and have been restored to agricultural entry, and 4,726,091 acres have been classified as coal lands, while 79,903,239 acres remain withdrawn from entry and await classification. In addition 337,000 acres have been classified as coal lands without prior withdrawal, thus increasing the classified coal lands to 10,429,372 acres.

Under the laws providing for the disposition of coal lands in the United States, the minimum price at which lands are permitted to be sold is $10 an acre; but the Secretary of the Interior has the power to fix a maximum price and to sell at that price. By the first regulations governing appraisal, approved April 8, 1907, the minimum was $10, as provided by law, and the maximum was $100, and the highest price actually placed upon any land sold was $75. Under the new regulations, adopted April 10, 1909, the maximum price was increased to $300, except in regions where there are large mines, where no maximum limit is fixed and the price is determined by the estimated tons of coal to the acre. The highest price fixed for any land under this regulation has been $608. The appraised value of the lands classified as coal lands and valued under the new and old regulations is shown to be as follows: 3,795,445 acres, valued under the old regulation at $76,804,337, an average of approximately $20.50 an acre; and 6,633,927 acres classified and valued under the new regulation at $430,050,364, or a total of 10,429,372 acres, valued at $506,854,701.

For the year ended June 30, 1909, 213 coal entries were made, embracing an area of 31,045 acres, which sold for $556,502.03. For the year ended June 30, 1910, there were 248 entries, embracing an area of 38,325 acres, which sold for $772,325.41; and from June 30 to November, 1910, there were 38 entries, with an area of 5,164 acres, which sold for $103,082.75, making the disposition of coal lands within the last two years of about 75,000 acres for $1,431,910.

The present Congress, as already said, has separated the surface of coal lands, either classified or withdrawn for classification, from the coal beneath, so as to permit at all times homestead entries upon the surface of lands useful for agriculture and to reserve the ownership in the coal to the Government. The question which remains to be considered is whether the existing law for the sale of the coal in the ground should continue in force or be repealed and a new method of disposition adopted. Under the present law the absolute title in the coal beneath the surface passes to the grantee of the Government. The price fixed is upon an estimated amount of the tons of coal per acre beneath the surface, and the prices are fixed so that the earnings will only be a reasonable profit upon the amount paid and the investment necessary. But, of course, this is more or less guesswork, and the Government parts with the ownership of the coal in the ground absolutely. Authorities of the Geological Survey estimate that in the United States today there is a supply of about 3,000 billions of tons of coal, and that of this 1,000 billions are in the public domain. Of course, the other 2,000 billions are within private ownership and under no more control as to the use or the prices at which the coal may be sold than any other private property. If the Government leases the coal lands and acts as any landlord would, and imposes conditions in its leases like those which are now imposed by the owners in fee of coal mines in the various coal regions of the East, then it would retain over the disposition of the coal deposits a choice as to the assignee of the lease, a power of resuming possession at the end of the term of the lease, or of readjusting terms at fixed periods of the lease, which might easily be framed to enable it to exercise a limited but effective control in the disposition and sale of the coal to the public. It has been urged that the leasing system has never been adopted in this country, and that its adoption would largely interfere with the investment of capital and the proper development and opening up of the coal resources. I venture to differ entirely from this view. My investigations show that many owners of mining property of this country do not mine it themselves, and do not invest their money in the plants necessary for the mining; but they lease their properties for a term of years varying from twenty to forty years, under conditions requiring the erection of a proper plant and the investment of a certain amount of money in the development of the mines, and fixing a rental and a royalty, sometimes an absolute figure and sometimes one proportioned to the market value of the coal. Under this latter method the owner of the mine shares in the prosperity of his lessees when coal is high and the profits good, and also shares to some extent in their disappointment when the price of coal falls.

I have looked with some care into a report made at the instance of President Roosevelt upon the disposition of coal lands in Australia, Tasmania, and New Zealand. These are peculiarly mining countries, and their experience ought to be most valuable. In all these countries the method for the disposition and opening of coal mines originally owned by the Government is by granting leasehold, and not by granting an absolute title. The terms of the leases run all the way from twenty to fifty years, while the amount of land which may be leased to any individual there is from 320 acres to 2,000 acres. It appears that a full examination was made and the opinions of all the leading experts on the subject were solicited and given, and that with one accord they approved in all respects the leasing system. Its success is abundantly shown. It is possible that at first considerable latitude will have to be given to the Executive in drafting these forms of lease, but as soon as experiment shall show which is the most workable and practicable, its use should be provided for specifically by statute.

The question as to how great an area ought to be included in a lease to one individual or corporation is not free from difficulty; but in view of the fact that the Government retains control as owner, I think there might be some liberality in the amount leased, and that 2,500 acres would not be too great a maximum. The leases should only be granted after advertisement and public competition.

By the opportunity to readjust the terms upon which the coal shall be held by the tenant, either at the end of each lease or at periods during the term, the Government may secure the benefit of sharing in the increased price of coal and the additional profit made by the tenant. By imposing conditions in respect to the character of work to be done in the mines, the Government may control the character of the development of the mines and the treatment of employees with reference to safety. By denying the right to transfer the lease except by the written permission of the governmental authorities, it may withhold the needed consent when it is proposed to transfer the leasehold to persons interested in establishing a monopoly of coal production in any State or neighborhood. As one-third of all the coal supply is held by the Government, it seems wise that it should retain such control over the mining and the sale as the relation of lessor to lessee furnishes.

Alaska Coal Lands

The investigations of the Geological Survey show that the coal properties in Alaska cover about 1,200 square miles, and that there are known to be available about 15 billion tons. This is, however, an underestimate of the coal in Alaska, because further developments will probably increase this amount many times; but we can say with considerable certainty that there are two fields on the Pacific slope which can be reached by railways at a reasonable cost from deep water—in one case of about 50 miles and in the other case of about 150 miles—which will afford certainly 6 billion tons of coal, more than half of which is of a very high grade of bituminous and of anthracite. It is estimated to be worth, in the ground, one-half cent a ton, which makes its value per acre from $50 to $500. The coking-coal lands of Pennsylvania are worth from $800 to $2,000 an acre, while other Appalachian fields are worth from $10 to $386 an acre, and the fields in the Central States from $10 to $2,000 an acre, and in the Rocky Mountains from $10 to $500 an acre. The demand for coal on the Pacific coast is for about 4,500,000 tons a year. It would encounter the competition of cheap fuel oil, of which the equivalent of 12,000,000 tons of coal a year is used there. It is estimated that the coal could be laid down at Seattle or San Francisco, a high-grade bituminous, at 4 a ton and anthracite at $5 or $6 a ton. The price of coal on the Pacific slope varies greatly from time to time in the year and from year to year—from $4 to $12 a ton. With a regular coal supply established, the expert of the Geological Survey, Mr. Brooks, who has made a report on the subject, does not think there would be an excessive profit in the Alaska coal mining because the price at which the coal could be sold would be considerably lowered by competition from these fields and by the presence of crude fuel oil. The history of the laws affecting the disposition of Alaska coal lands shows them to need amendment badly. Speaking of them, Mr. Brooks says:

> The first act, passed June 6, 1900, simply extended to Alaska the provisions of the coal-land laws in the United States. The law was ineffective, for it provided that only subdivided lands could be taken up, and there were then no land surveys in Alaska. The matter was rectified by the act of April 28, 1904, which permitted unsurveyed lands to be entered and the surveys to be made at the expense of the entrymen. Unfortunately, the law provided that only tracts of 160 acres could be taken up, and no recognition was given to the fact that it was impracticable to develop an isolated coal field requiring the expenditure of a large amount of money by such small units Many claims were staked, however, and surveys were made for patents. It was recognized by everybody familiar with the conditions that after patent was obtained these claims would be combined in tracts large enough to assure successful mining operations. No one experienced in mining would, of course, consider it feasible to open a coal field on the basis of single 160-acre tracts. The claims for the most part were handled in groups, for which one agent represented the several different owners. Unfortunately, a strict interpretation of the statute raised the question whether even a tacit understanding between claim owners to combine after patents had been obtained was not illegal. Remedial legislation was sought and enacted in the statute of May 28, 1908. This law permitted the consolidation of claims staked previous to November 12, 1906, in tracts of 2,560 acres. One clause of this law invalidated the title if any individual or corporation at any time in the future owned any interest whatsoever, directly or indirectly, in more than one tract. The purpose of this clause was to prevent the monopolization of

coal fields; its immediate effect was to discourage capital. It was felt by many that this clause might lead to forfeiture of title through the accidents of inheritance, or might even be used by the unscrupulous in blackmailing. It would appear that land taken up under this law might at any time be forfeited to the Government through the action of any individual who, innocently or otherwise, obtained interest in more than one coal company. Such a title was felt to be too insecure to warrant the large investments needed for mining developments. The net result of all this is that no titles to coal lands have been passed.

On November 12, 1906, President Roosevelt issued an executive order withdrawing all coal lands from location and entry in Alaska. On May 16, 1907, he modified the order so as to permit valid locations made prior to the withdrawal on November 12, 1906, to proceed to entry and patent. Prior to that date some 900 claims had been filed, most of them said to be illegal because either made fraudulently by dummy entrymen in the interest of one individual or corporation, or because of agreements made prior to location between the applicants to cooperate in developing the lands. There are 33 claims for 160 acres each, known as the "Cunningham claims," which are claimed to be valid on the ground that they were made by an attorney for 33 different and bona fide claimants who, as alleged, paid their money and took the proper steps to locate their entries and protect them. The representatives of the Government, on the other hand, in the hearings before the Land Office have attacked the validity of these Cunningham claims on the ground that prior to their location there was an understanding between the claimants to pool their claims after they had been perfected and unite them in one company. The trend of decision seems to show that such an agreement would invalidate the claims, although under the subsequent law of May 28, 1998, the consolidation of such claims was permitted, after location and entry, in tracts of 2,560 acres. It would be, of course, improper for me to intimate what the result of the issue as to the Cunningham and other Alaska claims is likely to be, but it ought to be distinctly understood that no private claims for Alaska coal lands have as yet been allowed or perfected, and also that whatever the result as to pending claims, the existing coal-land laws of Alaska are most unsatisfactory and should be radically amended. To begin with, the purchase price of the land is a flat rate of $10 per acre with no power to increase it beyond that, although, as we have seen, the estimate of the agent of the Geological Survey would carry up the maximum of value to $500 an acre. In my judgment it is essential to the proper development of Alaska that these coal lands should be opened, and that the Pacific slope should be given the benefit of the comparatively cheap coal of fine quality which can be furnished at a reasonable price from these fields; but the public, through the Government, ought certainly to retain a wise control and interest in these coal deposits, and I think it may do so safely if Congress will authorize the granting of leases, as already suggested, for government coal lands in the United States, with provisions forbidding the transfer of the leases except with the consent of the Government, thus preventing their acquisition by a combination or monopoly and upon limitations as to the area to be included in any one lease to one individual, and at a certain moderate rental, with royalties upon the coal mined proportioned to the market value of the coal laid down either at Seattle or at San Francisco. Of course such leases should contain conditions requiring the erection of proper plants, the proper development by modern mining methods of the properties leased, and the use of every known and practical means and device for saving the life of the miners.

The Government of the United States has much to answer for in not having given proper attention to the government of Alaska and the development of her resources for the benefit of all the people of the country. I would not force development at the expense of a present or future waste of resources; but the problem as to the disposition of the coal lands for present and future use can be wisely and safely settled in one session if Congress gives it careful attention.

(5) Oil and Gas Lands

In the last administration there were withdrawn from agricultural entry 2,820,000 acres of supposed oil land in California; 1,451,520 acres in Louisiana, of which only 6,500 acres were known to be vacant unappropriated land; and 74,849 acres in Oregon, making a total of 4,346,369 acres. In September, 1909, I directed that all public oil lands, whether then withdrawn or not, should be withheld from disposition pending congressional action, for the reason that the existing placer mining law, although made applicable to deposits of this character, is not suitable to such lands, and for the further reason that it seemed desirable to reserve certain fuel-oil deposits for the use of the American navy. Accordingly the form of all existing withdrawals was changed, and new withdrawals aggregating 2,750,000 acres were made in Arizona, California, Colorado, New Mexico, Utah, and Wyoming. Field examinations during the year showed that of the original withdrawals 2,190,424 acres were not valuable for oil, and they were restored for agricultural entry. Meantime other withdrawals of public oil lands in these states were made, so that November 15, 1910, the outstanding withdrawals amounted to 4,654,000 acres.

The needed oil and gas law is essentially a leasing law. In their natural occurrence, oil and gas can not be measured in terms of acres, like coal, and it follows that exclusive title to these products can normally be secured only after they reach the surface. Oil should be disposed of as a commodity in terms of barrels of transportable product rather than in acres of real estate. This is, of course, the reason for the practically universal adoption of the leasing system wherever oil land is in private ownership. The Government thus would not be entering on an experiment, but simply putting into effect a plan successfully operated in private contracts. Why should not the Government as a landowner deal directly with the oil producer rather than through the intervention of a middleman to whom the Government gives title to the land?

The principal underlying feature of such legislation should be the exercise of beneficial control rather than the collection of revenue. As not only the largest owner of oil lands, but as a prospective large consumer of oil by reason of the increasing use of fuel oil by the navy, the Federal Government is directly concerned both in encouraging rational development and at the same time insuring the longest possible life to the oil supply. The royalty rates fixed by the Government should neither exceed nor fall below the current rates. But much more important than revenue is the enforcement of regulations to conserve the public interest so that the covenants of the lessees shall specifically safeguard oil fields against the penalties from careless drillings and of production in excess of transportation facilities or of market requirements.

One of the difficulties presented, especially in the California fields, is that the Southern Pacific Railroad owns every other section of land in the oil fields, and in those fields the oil seems to be in a common reservoir, or series of reservoirs, communicating through the oil sands, so that the excessive draining of oil at one well, or on the railroad territory generally, would exhaust the oil in the government land. Hence it is important that if the Government is to have its share of the oil it should begin the opening and development of wells on its own property.

In view of the joint ownership which the Government and the adjoining landowners like the Southern Pacific Railroad have in the oil reservoirs below the surface, it is a most interesting and intricate question, difficult of solution, but one which ought to address itself at once to the state lawmakers, how far the state legislature might impose appropriate restrictions to secure an equitable enjoyment of the common reservoir and to prevent waste and excessive drainage by the various owners having access to this reservoir.

It has been suggested, and I believe the suggestion to be a sound one, that permits be issued to a prospector for oil giving him the right to prospect for two years over a certain tract of government land for the discovery of oil, the right to be evidenced by a license for which he pays a small sum. When the oil is discovered, then he acquires title to a certain tract, much in the same way as he would acquire title under a mining law. Of course if the system of leasing is adopted, then he would be given the benefit of a lease upon terms like that above suggested. What has been said in respect to oil applies also to government gas lands.

Under the proposed oil legislation, especially where the government oil lands embrace an entire oil field, as in many cases, prospectors, operators, consumers, and the public can be benefited by the adoption of the leasing system. The prospector can be protected in the very expensive work that necessarily antedates discovery; the operator can be protected against impairment of the productiveness of the wells which he has leased by reason of control of drilling and pumping of other wells too closely adjacent, or by the prevention of improper methods as employed by careless, ignorant, or irresponsible operators in the same field which result in the admission of water to the oil sands; while of course the consumer will profit by whatever benefits the prospector or operator receives in reducing the first cost of the oil.

(6) Phosphate Lands

Phosphorus is one of the three essentials to plant growth, the other elements being nitrogen and potash. Of these three, phosphorus is by all odds the scarcest element in nature. It is easily extracted in useful form from the phosphate rock, and the United States contains the greatest known deposits of this rock in the world. They are found in Wyoming, Utah, Idaho, and Florida, as well as in South Carolina, Georgia, and Tennessee. The government phosphate lands are confined to Wyoming, Utah, Idaho, and Florida. Prior to March 4, 1909, there were 4,446,298 acres withdrawn from agricultural entry on the ground that the land covered phosphate rock. Since that time, 2,369,776 acres of the land thus withdrawn were found not to contain phosphate in profitable quantities, while 1,678,000 acres were classified properly as phosphate lands. During this administration there have been withdrawn and classified 437,673 acres, so that today there are classified as phosphate-rock land 2,514,195 acres. This rock is most important in the composition of fertilizers to improve the soil, and as the future is certain to create an enormous demand throughout this country for fertilization, the value to the public of such deposits as these can hardly be exaggerated. Certainly with respect to these deposits a careful policy of conservation should be followed. Half of the phosphate of the rock that is mined in private fields in the United States is now exported. As our farming methods grow better the demand for the phosphate will become greater, and it must be arranged so that the supply shall equal the needs of the country. It is uncertain whether the placer or lode law applies to the government phosphate rock. There is, therefore, necessity for some definite and well-considered legislation on this subject, and in aid of such legislation all of the government lands known to contain valuable phosphate rock are now withdrawn from entry. A law that would provide a leasing system for the phosphate deposits, together with a provision for the separation of the surface and mineral rights, as is already provided for in the case of coal, would seem to meet the need of promoting the development of these deposits and their utilization in the agricultural lands of the West. If it is thought desirable to discourage the exportation of phosphate rock and the saving of it for our own lands, this purpose could be accomplished by conditions in the lease granted by the Government to its lessees. Of course, under the Constitution the Government could not tax and could not prohibit the exportation of phosphate, but as proprietor and owner of the lands in which the phosphate is deposited it could impose conditions upon the kind of sales, whether foreign or domestic, which the lessees might make of the phosphate mined.

The tonnage represented by the phosphate lands in government ownership is very great, but the lesson has been learned in the case of such lands that have passed into private ownership in South Carolina, Florida, and Tennessee that the phosphate deposits there are in no sense inexhaustible. Moreover, it is also well understand that in the process of mining phosphate, as it has been pursued, much of the lower grade of phosphate rock, which will eventually all be needed, has been wasted beyond recovery. Such wasteful methods can easily be prevented, so far as the government land is concerned, by conditions inserted in the leases.

(7) Water-Power Sites

Prior to March 4, 1909, there had been, on the recommendation of the Reclamation Service, withdrawn from agricultural entry, because they were regarded as useful for power sites which ought not to be disposed of as agricultural lands, tracts amounting to about 4,000,000 acres. The withdrawals were hastily made and included a great deal of land that was not useful for power sites. They were intended to include the power sites on 29 rivers in 9 States. Since that time 3,475,442 acres of the original 4,000,000 have been restored to settlement because they do not contain power sites; and meantime there have been newly withdrawn 1,240,310 acres of vacant public land and 211,499 acres of entered public land, or a total of 1,451,809 acres. These withdrawals made from time to time cover all the power sites included in the first withdrawals, and many more, on 149 rivers and in 12 States. The disposition of these power sites involves one of the most difficult questions presented in carrying out practical conservation. The Forest Service, under a power found in the statute, has leased a number of these power sites in forest reserves by revocable leases, but no such power exists with respect to power sites that are not located within forest reserves, and the revocable system of leasing is, of course, not a satisfactory one for the purpose of inviting the capital needed to put in proper plants for the transmutation of power.

The statute of 1891 with its amendments permits the Secretary of the Interior to grant perpetual easements or rights of way from water sources over public lands for the primary purpose of irrigation and such electrical current as may be incidentally developed, but no grant can be made under this statute to concerns whose primary purpose is generating and handling electricity. The statute of 1901 authorizes the Secretary of the Interior to issue revocable permits over the public lands to electrical-power companies, but this statute is woefully inadequate because it does not authorize the collection of a charge or fix a term of years. Capital is slow to invest in an enterprise founded on a permit revocable at will.

The subject is one that calls for new legislation. It has been thought that there was danger of combination to obtain possession of all the power sites and to unite them under one control. Whatever the evidence of this, or lack of it, at present we have had enough experience to know that combination would be profitable, and the control of a great number of power sites would enable the holders or owners to raise the price of power at will within certain sections; and the temptations would promptly attract investors, and the danger of monopoly would not be a remote one.

However this may be, it is the plain duty of the Government to see to it that in the utilization and development of all this immense amount of water power, conditions shall be imposed that will prevent monopoly, and will prevent extortionate charges, which are the accompaniment of monopoly. The difficulty of adjusting the matter is accentuated by the relation of the power sites to the water, the fall and flow of which create the power. In the States where these sites are the riparian owner does not control or own the power in the water which flows past his land. That power is under the control and within the grant of the State, and generally the rule is that the first user is entitled to the enjoyment. Now, the possession of the bank or water-power site over which the water is to be conveyed in order to make the power useful, gives to its owner an advantage and a certain kind of control over the use of the water power, and it is proposed that the Government in dealing with its own lands should use this advantage and lease lands for power sites to those who would develop the power, and impose conditions on the leasehold with reference to the reasonableness of the rates at which the power, when transmuted, is to be furnished to the public, and forbidding the union of the particular power with a combination of others made for the purpose of monopoly by forbidding assignment of the lease save by consent of the Government. Serious difficulties are anticipated by some in such an attempt on the part of the General Government, because of the sovereign control of the State over the water power in its natural condition and the mere proprietorship of the Government in the riparian lands. It is contended that through its mere proprietary right in the site the Central Government has no power to attempt to exercise police jurisdiction with reference to how the water power in a river owned and controlled by the State shall be used, and that it is a violation of the State's rights. I question the validity of this objection. The Government may impose any conditions that it chooses in its lease of its own property, even though it may have the same purpose, and in effect accomplish just what the State would accomplish by the exercise of its sovereignty. There are those (and the Director of the Geological Survey, Mr. Smith, who has given a great deal of attention to this matter, is one of them) who insist that this matter of transmuting water power into electricity, which can be conveyed all over the country and across State lines, is a matter that ought to be retained by the General Government, and that it should avail itself of the ownership of these power sites for the very purpose of coordinating in one general plan the power generated from these government-owned sites.

On the other hand, it is contended that it would relieve a complicated situation if the control of the water-power site and the control of the water were vested in the same sovereignty and ownership, viz., the States, and then were disposed of for development to private lessees under the restrictions needed to preserve the interests of the public from the extortions and abuses of monopoly. Therefore, bills have been introduced in Congress providing that whenever the State authorities deem a water power useful they may apply to the Government of the United States for a grant to the State of the adjacent land for a water-power site, and that this grant from the Federal Government to the State shall contain a condition that the State shall never part with the title to the water-power site or the water power, but shall lease it only for a term of years not exceeding fifty, with provisions in the lease by which the rental and the rates for which the power is furnished to the public shall be readjusted at periods less than the term of the lease, say, every ten years. The argument is urged against this disposition of power sites that legislators and state authorities are more subject to corporate influence and control than would be the Central Government; in reply it is claimed that a readjustment of the terms of leasehold every ten years would secure to the public and the State just and equitable terms. Then it is said that the State authorities are better able to understand the local need and what is a fair adjustment in the particular locality than would be the authorities at Washington. It has been argued that after the Federal Government parts with title to a power site it can not control the action of the State in fulfilling the conditions of the deed, to which it is answered that in the grant from the Government there may be easily inserted a condition specifying the terms upon which the State may part with the temporary control of the water-power sites, and, indeed, the water power, and providing for a forfeiture of the title to the water-power sites in case the condition is not performed; and giving to the President, in case of such violation of conditions, the power to declare forfeiture and to direct proceedings to restore to the Central Government the ownership of the power sites with all the improvements thereon, and that these conditions could be promptly enforced and the land and plants forfeited to the General Government by suit of the United States against the State, which is permissible under the Constitution.

I do not express an opinion upon the controversy thus made or a preference as to the two methods of treating water-power sites. I submit the matter to Congress and urge that one or the other of the two plans be promptly adopted.

At the risk of wearying my audience I have attempted to state as succinctly as may be the questions of conservation as they apply to the public domain of the Government, the conditions to which they apply, and the proposed solution of them. In the outset I alluded to the fact that conservation had been made to include a great deal more than what I have discussed here. Of course, as I have referred only to the public domain of the Federal Government I have left untouched the wide field of conservation with respect to which a heavy responsibility rests upon the States and individuals as well. But I think it of the utmost importance that after the public attention has been roused to the necessity of a change in our general policy to prevent waste and a selfish appropriation to private and corporate purposes of what should be controlled for the public benefit, those who urge conservation shall feel the necessity of making clear how conservation can be practically carried out, and shall propose specific methods and legal provisions and regulations to remedy actual adverse conditions. I am bound to say that the time has come for a halt in general rhapsodies over conservation, making the word mean every known good in the world; for, after the public attention has been roused, such appeals are of doubtful utility and do not direct the public to the specific course that the people should take, or have their legislators take, in order to promote the cause of conservation. The rousing of emotions on a subject like this, which has only dim outlines in the minds of the people affected, after a while ceases to be useful, and the whole movement will, if promoted on these lines, die for want of practical direction and of demonstration to the people that practical reforms are intended.

I have referred to the course of the last administration and of the present one in making withdrawals of government lands from entry under homestead and other laws and of Congress in removing all doubt as to the validity of these withdrawals as a great step in the direction of practical conservation. But it is only one of two necessary steps to effect what should be our purpose. It has produced a status quo and prevented waste and irrevocable disposition of the lands until the method for their proper disposition can be formulated. But it is of the utmost importance that such withdrawals should not be regarded as the final step in the course of conservation, and that the idea should not be allowed to spread that conservation is the tying up of the natural resources of the Government for indefinite withholding from use and the remission to remote generations to decide what ought to be done with these means of promoting present general human comfort and progress. For, if so, it is certain to arouse the greatest opposition to conservation as a cause, and if it were the correct expression of the purpose of conservationists it ought to arouse such opposition. Real conservation involves wise, nonwasteful use in the present generation, with every possible means of preservation for succeeding generations, and though the problem to secure this end may be difficult, the burden is on the present generation promptly to solve it and not to run away from it as cowards, lest in the attempt to meet it we may make some mistake. As I have said elsewhere, the problem is how to save and how to utilize, how to conserve and still develop; for no sane person can contend that it is for the common good that nature's blessings should be stored only for unborn generations.

I beg of you, therefore, in your deliberations and in your informal discussion, when men come forward to suggest evils that the promotion of conservation is to remedy, that you invite them to point out the specific evils and the specific remedies; that you invite them to come down to details in order that their discussions may flow into channels that shall be useful rather than into periods that shall be eloquent and entertaining, without shedding real light on the subject. The people should be shown exactly what is needed in order that they make their representatives in Congress and the state legislature do their intelligent bidding.

Second Appendix to Second Annual Message

The White House, December 21, 1910

To the Senate and House of Representatives:

The constitutional convention recently held in the Territory of New Mexico has submitted for acceptance or rejection the draft of a constitution to be voted upon by the voters of the proposed new State, which contains a clause purporting to fix the boundary line between New Mexico and Texas which may reasonably be construed to be different from the boundary lines heretofore legally run, marked, established, and ratified by the United States and the State of Texas, and under which claims might be set up and litigation instigated of an unnecessary and improper character. A joint resolution has been introduced in the House of Representatives for the purpose of authorizing the President of the United States and the State of Texas to mark the boundary lines between the State of Texas and the Territory or proposed State of New Mexico, or to reestablish and re-mark the boundary line heretofore established and marked; and to enact that any provision of the proposed constitution of New Mexico that in any way tends to annul or change the boundary lines between Texas and New Mexico shall be of no force or effect. I recommend the adoption of such joint resolution.

The act of June 5, 1858 (vol. 11, U. S. Stats., 310), "authorizing the President of the United States in conjunction with the State of Texas, to run and mark the boundary lines between the Territories of the United States and the State of Texas," under which a survey was made in 1859–60 by one John H. Clark, and in the act of Congress approved March 3, 1891 (vol. 26, U. S. Stats., 971), "the boundary line between said public land strip and Texas, and between Texas and New Mexico, established under the act of June fifth, eighteen hundred and fifty-eight, is hereby confirmed," and a joint resolution was passed by the Legislature of Texas and became a law March 25, 1891, "confirming the location of the boundary line established by the United States commission between No Man's Land and Texas, and Texas and New Mexico under the act of Congress of June 5, 1858." (Laws of Texas, 1891, p. 193, Resolutions.)

The Committee on Indian Affairs, in its report of May 2, 1910 (No. 1250, 61st Cong., 2d sess.), recommended a joint resolution in the fourth section of which appears the following:

> *Provided,* That the part of a line run and marked by monument along the thirty-second parallel of north latitude, and that part of the line run and marked along the one hundred and third degree of longitude west of Greenwich, the same being the east and west and north and south lines between Texas and New Mexico, and run by authority of act of Congress approved June fifth, eighteen hundred and fifty-eight, and known as the Clark lines, and that part of the line along the parallel of thirty-six degrees and thirty minutes of north latitude, forming the north boundary line of the Panhandle of Texas, and which said parts of said lines have been confirmed by acts of Congress of March third, eighteen hundred and ninety-one, shall remain the true boundary lines of Texas and Oklahoma and the Territory of New Mexico: *Provided further,* That it shall be the duty of the commissioners appointed under this act to re-mark said old Clark monuments and lines where they can be found and identified.

The lines referred to in the paragraph above are the same as contained in the proposed joint resolution above referred to.

Under the act of Congress approved June 20, 1910, "An act to enable the people of New Mexico to form a constitution and State government and be admitted into the Union," etc. (vol. 36, U. S. Stats., 557), section 4 provides that when a constitution has been duly ratified by the people of New Mexico, a certified copy of the same shall be submitted to the President of the United States, and in section 5 it provides that after certain elections shall have been held and the result certified to the President of the United States, the President shall immediately issue his proclamation, upon which the proposed State of New Mexico shall be deemed admitted by Congress into the Union, by virtue of said act of June 20, 1910. The required acts have not taken place and therefore to all intents and purposes the proposed State of New Mexico is still a Territory and under the control of Congress.

As the boundary line between Texas and New Mexico is established under the act of June 5, 1858, and confirmed by Congress under the act of March 3, 1891, and ratified by the State of Texas, March 25, 1891, and as the Territory of New Mexico has not up to the present time fulfilled all the requirements under the act of June 20, 1910, for admission to the Union, there is no reason why the joint resolution should not be adopted as above provided, and I recommend the adoption of such resolution for the purpose of conferring indisputable authority upon the President in conjunction with the State of Texas to reestablish and re-mark a boundary already established and confirmed by Congress and the State of Texas.

2

Special Message on Canadian Reciprocity

The White House, January 26, 1911

To the Senate and House of Representatives:

In my annual message of December 6, 1910, I stated that the policy of broader and closer trade relations with the Dominion of Canada, which was initiated in the adjustment of the maximum and minimum provisions of the tariff act of August 5, 1909, had proved mutually beneficial and that it justified further efforts for the readjustment of the commercial relations of the two countries. I also informed you that, by my direction, the Secretary of State had dispatched two representatives of the Department of State as special commissioners to Ottawa to confer with representatives of the Dominion Government, that they were authorized to take steps to formulate a reciprocal trade agreement, and that the Ottawa conferences thus begun, had been adjourned to be resumed in Washington.

On the seventh of the present month two cabinet ministers came to Washington as representatives of the Dominion Government, and the conferences were continued between them and the Secretary of State. The result of the negotiations was that on the twenty-first instant a reciprocal trade agreement was reached, the text of which is herewith transmitted with accompanying correspondence and other data.

One by one the controversies resulting from the uncertainties which attended the partition of British territory on the American Continent at the close of the Revolution, and which were inevitable under the then conditions, have been eliminated—some by arbitration and some by direct negotiation. The merits of these disputes, many of them extending through a century, need not now be reviewed. They related to the settlement of boundaries, the definition of rights of navigation, the interpretation of treaties, and many other subjects.

Through the friendly sentiments, the energetic efforts, and the broadly patriotic views of successive administrations, and especially of that of my immediate predecessor, all these questions have been settled. The most acute related to the Atlantic fisheries, and this long-standing controversy, after amicable negotiation, was referred to The Hague Tribunal. The judgment of that august international court has been accepted by the people of both countries and a satisfactory agreement in pursuance of the judgment has ended completely the controversy. An equitable arrangement has recently been reached between our Interstate Commerce Commission and the similar body in Canada in regard to through rates on the transportation lines between the two countries.

The path having been thus opened for the improvement of commercial relations, a reciprocal trade agreement is the logical sequence of all that has been accomplished in disposing of matters of a diplomatic and controversial character. The identity of interest of two peoples linked together by race, language, political institutions, and geographical proximity offers the foundation. The contribution to the industrial advancement of our own country by the migration across the boundary of the thrifty and industrious Canadians of English, Scotch, and French origin is now repaid by the movement of large numbers of our own sturdy farmers to the northwest of Canada, thus giving their labor, their means, and their experience to the development of that section, with its agricultural possibilities.

The guiding motive in seeking adjustment of trade relations between two countries so situated geographically should be to give play to productive forces as far as practicable, regardless of political boundaries. While equivalency should be sought in an arrangement of this character, an exact balance of financial gain is neither imperative nor attainable. No yardstick can measure the benefits to the two peoples of this freer commercial intercourse and no trade agreement should be judged wholly by custom house statistics.

We have reached a stage in our own development that calls for a statesmanlike and broad view of our future economic status and its requirements. We have drawn upon our natural resources in such a way as to invite attention to their necessary limit. This has properly aroused effort to conserve them, to avoid their waste, and to restrict their use to our necessities. We have so increased in population and in our consumption of food products and the other necessities of life, hitherto supplied largely from our own country, that unless we materially increase our production we can see before us a change in our economic position, from that of a country selling to the world food and natural products of the farm and forest, to one consuming and importing them. Excluding cotton, which is exceptional, a radical change is already shown in our exports in the falling off in the amount of our agricultural products sold abroad and a corresponding marked increase in our manufactures exported. A farsighted policy requires that if we can enlarge our supply of natural resources, and especially of food products and the necessities of life, without substantial injury to any of our producing and manufacturing classes, we should take steps to do so now. We have on the north of us a country contiguous to ours for three thousand miles, with natural resources of the same character as ours which have not been drawn upon as ours have been, and in the development of which the conditions as to wages and character of the wage earner and transportation to market differ but little from those prevailing with us. The difference is not greater than it is between different States of our own country or between different Provinces of the Dominion of Canada. Ought we not, then, to arrange a commercial agreement with Canada, if we can, by which we shall have direct access to her great supply of natural products without an obstructing or prohibitory tariff? This is not a violation of the protective principle, as that has been authoritatively announced by those who uphold it, because that principle does not call for a tariff between this country and one whose conditions as to production, population, and wages are so like ours, and when our common boundary line of three thousand miles in itself must make a radical distinction between our commercial treatment of Canada and of any other country.

The Dominion has greatly prospered. It has an active, aggressive, and intelligent people. They are coming to the parting of the ways. They must soon decide whether they are to regard themselves as isolated permanently from our markets by a perpetual wall or whether we are to be commercial friends. If we give them reason to take the former view, can we complain if they adopt methods denying access to certain of their natural resources except upon conditions quite unfavorable to us? A notable instance of such a possibility may be seen in the conditions surrounding the supply of pulp wood and the manufacture of print paper, for which we have made a conditional provision in the agreement, believed to be equitable. Should we not now, therefore, before their policy has become too crystallized and fixed for change, meet them in a spirit of real concession, facilitate commerce between the two countries, and thus greatly increase the natural resources available to our people?

I do not wish to hold out the prospect that the unrestricted interchange of food products will greatly and at once reduce their cost to the people of this country. Moreover, the present small amount of Canadian surplus for export as compared with that of our own production and consumption would make the reduction gradual. Excluding the element of transportation, the price of staple food products, especially of cereals, is much the same the world over, and the recent increase in price has been the result of a world-wide cause. But a source of supply as near as Canada would certainly help to prevent speculative fluctuations, would steady local price movements, and would postpone the effect of a further world increase in the price of leading commodities entering into the cost of living, if that be inevitable.

In the reciprocal trade agreement numerous additions are made to the free list. These include not only food commodities, such as cattle, fish, wheat and other grains, fresh vegetables, fruits, and dairy products, but also rough lumber and raw materials useful to our own industries. Free lumber we ought to have. By giving our people access to Canadian forests we shall reduce the consumption of our own, which, in the hands of comparatively few owners, now have a value that requires the enlargement of our available timber resources.

Natural, and especially food, products being placed on the free list, the logical development of a policy of reciprocity in rates on secondary food products, or foodstuffs partly manufactured, is, where they cannot also be entirely exempted from duty, to lower the duties in accord with the exemption of the raw material from duty. This has been followed in the trade agreement which has been negotiated. As an example, wheat is made free and the rate on flour is equalized on a lower basis. In the same way, live animals being made free, the duties on fresh meats and on secondary meat products and on canned meats are substantially lowered. Fresh fruits and vegetables being placed on the free list, the duties on canned goods of these classes are reduced.

Both countries in their industrial development have to meet the competition of lower priced labor in other parts of the world. Both follow the policy of encouraging the development of home industries by protective duties within reasonable limits. This has made it difficult to extend the principle of reciprocal rates to many manufactured commodities, but after much negotiation and effort we have succeeded in doing so in various and important instances.

The benefit to our widespread agricultural implement industry from the reduction of Canadian duties in the agreement is clear. Similarly the new, widely distributed and expanding motor vehicle industry of the United States is given access to the Dominion market on advantageous terms.

My purpose in making a reciprocal trade agreement with Canada has been not only to obtain one which would be mutually advantageous to both countries, but one which also would be truly national in its scope as applied to our own country and would be of benefit to all sections. The currents of business and the transportation facilities that will be established forward and back across the border cannot but inure to the benefit of the boundary States. Some readjustments may be needed, but in a very short period the advantage of the free commercial exchange between communities separated only by short distances will strikingly manifest itself. That the broadening of the sources of food supplies, that the opening of the timber resources of the Dominion to our needs, that the addition to the supply of raw materials, will be limited to no particular section does not require demonstration. The same observation applies to the markets which the Dominion offers us in exchange. As an illustration, it has been found possible to obtain free entry into Canada for fresh fruits and vegetables—a matter of special value to the South and to the Pacific coast in disposing of their products in their season. It also has been practicable to obtain free entry for the cottonseed oil of the South—a most important product with a rapidly expanding consumption in the Dominion.

The entire foreign trade of Canada in the last fiscal year, 1910, was $655,000,000. The imports were $376,000,000, and of this amount the United States contributed more than $223,000,000. The reduction in the duties imposed by Canada will largely increase this amount and give us even a larger share of her market than we now enjoy, great as that is.

The data accompanying the text of the trade agreement exhibit in detail the facts which are here set forth briefly and in outline only. They furnish full information on which the legislation recommended may be based. Action on the agreement submitted will not interfere with such revision of our own tariff on imports from all countries as Congress may decide to adopt.

Reciprocity with Canada must necessarily be chiefly confined in its effect on the cost of living to food and forest products. The question of the cost of clothing as affected by duty on textiles and their raw materials, so much mooted, is not within the scope of an agreement with Canada, because she raises comparatively few wool sheep, and her textile manufactures are unimportant.

This trade agreement, if entered into, will cement the friendly relations with the Dominion which have resulted from the satisfactory settlement of the controversies that have lasted for a century, and further promote good feeling between kindred peoples. It will extend the market for numerous products of the United States among the inhabitants of a prosperous neighboring country with an increasing population and an increasing purchasing power. It will deepen and widen the sources of food supply in contiguous territory, and will facilitate the movement and distribution of these foodstuffs.

The geographical proximity, the closer relation of blood, common sympathies, and identical moral and social ideas furnish very real and striking reasons why this agreement ought to be viewed from a high plane.

Since becoming a nation, Canada has been our good neighbor, immediately contiguous across a wide continent without artificial or natural barrier except navigable waters used in common.

She has cost us nothing in the way of preparations for defense against her possible assault, and she never will. She has sought to agree with us quickly when differences have disturbed our relations. She shares with us common traditions and aspirations. I feel I have correctly interpreted the wish of the American people by expressing, in the arrangement now submitted to Congress for its approval, their desire for a more intimate and cordial relationship with Canada. I therefore earnestly hope that the measure will be promptly enacted into law.

3

Special Message

[Recommending approval by Congress of
constitution of New Mexico]
The White House, February 24, 1911

To the Senate and House of Representatives:

The act to enable the people of New Mexico to form a constitution and State government and be admitted into the Union on an equal footing with the original States, etc., passed June 20, 1910, provides that when the constitution, for the adoption of which provision is made in the act, shall have been duly ratified by the people of New Mexico in the manner provided in the statute, a certified copy of the same will be submitted to the President of the United States and to Congress for approval, and that if Congress and the President approve of such constitution, or if the President approve the same and Congress fails to disapprove the same during the next regular session thereof, then that the President shall certify said facts to the governor of New Mexico, who shall proceed to issue his proclamation for the election of State and county officers, etc.

The constitution prepared in accordance with the act of Congress has been duly ratified by the people of New Mexico, and a certified copy of the same has been submitted to me and also to the Congress for approval, in conformity with the provisions of the act. Inasmuch as the enabling act requires affirmative action by the President, I transmit herewith a copy of the constitution, which, I am advised, has also been separately submitted to Congress, according to the provisions of the act, by the authorities of New Mexico, and to which I have given my formal approval.

I recommend the approval of the same by the Congress.

4

Proclamation of March 4, 1911

[Convening extra session of Congress on April 4, 1911, to consider
the Canadian-American reciprocal tariff agreement]

Whereas, by the special message dated January 26, 1911, there was transmitted to the Senate, and the House of Representatives an agreement between the Department of State and the Canadian Government in regard to reciprocal tariff legislation, together with an earnest recommendation that the necessary legislation be promptly adopted; and *Whereas,* a bill to carry into effect said agreement has passed the House of Representatives, but has failed to reach a vote in the Senate; and

Whereas, the agreement stipulates not only that "the President of the United States will communicate to Congress the conclusions now reached and recommend the adoption of such legislation as maybe necessary on the part of the United States to give effect to the proposed arrangement," but also that "the Governments of the two countries will use their utmost efforts to bring about such changes by concurrent legislation at Washington and at Ottawa":

Now, Therefore, I, William Howard Taft, President of the United States of America, by virtue of the power vested in me by the Constitution, do hereby proclaim and declare that an extraordinary occasion requires the convening of both Houses of the Congress of the United States at their respective chambers in the city of Washington on the fourth day of April, 1911, at 12 o'clock noon, to the end that they may consider and determine whether the Congress shall, by the necessary legislation, make operative the agreement.

All persons entitled to act as Members of the Sixty-second Congress are required to take notice of this proclamation.

Given under my hand and the seal of the United States at Washington the fourth day of March, A.D. 1911, and of the independence of the United States the one hundred and thirty-fifth.

[Seal]

William H. Taft

By the President:

P. C. Knox, Secretary of State

5

Special Message

[Directing attention of Congress to the reciprocal tariff agreement
between the Dominion of Canada and the United States]
The White House, April 5, 1911

To the Senate and House of Representatives:

I transmitted to the Sixty-first Congress on January twenty-sixth last
the text of the reciprocal trade agreement which had been negotiated,
under my direction, by the Secretary of State with the representatives of
the Dominion of Canada. This agreement was the consummation of earnest efforts, extending over a period of nearly a year, on the part of both
governments to effect a trade arrangement which, supplementing as it did
the amicable settlement of various questions of a diplomatic and political
character that had been reached, would mutually promote commerce and
would strengthen the friendly relations now existing.

The agreement in its intent and in its terms was purely economic and
commercial. While the general subject was under discussion by the commissioners, I felt assured that the sentiment of the people of the United
States was such that they would welcome a measure which would result in
the increase of trade on both sides of the boundary line, would open up
the reserve productive resources of Canada to the great mass of our own
consumers on advantageous conditions, and at the same time offer a

broader outlet for the excess products of our farms and many of our industries. Details regarding a negotiation of this kind necessarily could not be
made public while the conferences were pending. When, however, the full
text of the agreement, with the accompanying correspondence and data
explaining both its purpose and its scope, became known to the people
through the message transmitted to Congress, it was immediately apparent
that the ripened fruits of the careful labors of the commissioners met with
widespread approval. This approval has been strengthened by further consideration of the terms of the agreement in all their particulars. The volume
of support which has developed shows that its broadly national scope is
fully appreciated and is responsive to the popular will.

The House of Representatives of the Sixty-first Congress, after the full
text of the arrangement with all the details in regard to the different provisions had been before it, as they were before the American people, passed
a bill confirming the agreement as negotiated and as transmitted to Congress. This measure failed of action in the Senate.

In my transmitting message of the twenty-sixth of January I fully set
forth the character of the agreement and emphasized its appropriateness
and necessity as a response to the mutual needs of the people of the two
countries as well as its common advantages. I now lay that message, and
the reciprocal trade agreement as integrally part of the present message,
before the Sixty-second Congress and again invite earnest attention to the
considerations therein expressed.

I am constrained, in deference to popular sentiment and with a realizing sense of my duty to the great masses of our people whose welfare is
involved, to urge upon your consideration early action on this agreement.
In concluding the negotiations, the representatives of the two countries
bound themselves to use their utmost efforts to bring about the tariff
changes provided for in the agreement by concurrent legislation at Washington and Ottawa. I have felt it my duty, therefore, not to acquiesce in
relegation of action until the opening of the Congress in December, but
to use my constitutional prerogative and convoke the Sixty-second Congress in extra session in order that there shall be no break of continuity in
considering and acting upon this most important subject.

6

Speech of President Taft on the Reciprocal Tariff Agreement with Canada

Delivered in New York on April 27, 1911

The treaty provides for free trade in all agricultural products, and in rough lumber down to the point of planing. It reduces the duties on secondary food products by a very substantial percentage, and it makes such reductions on a number of manufactured articles that those engaged in making them have assured us that the reductions will substantially increase the already large Canadian demand for them.

We tendered to the Canadian commissioners absolutely free trade in all products of either country, manufactured or natural, but the Canadian commissioners did not feel justified in going so far. It is only reasonable to infer, therefore, that with respect to those articles upon which they refused free trade to us they felt that the profitable price at which they could be sold by our manufacturers in Canada was less than the price at which their manufacturers could afford to sell the same either to their own people or to us. Hence it follows that their refusal to agree to free trade in these articles, as we proposed, is the strongest kind of evidence that if we should take off the existing duty from such articles coming into the United States it would not affect in the slightest degree the price at which those articles could be furnished to the public here. In other words, the proposition to put on the free list for entrance into the United States all articles that Canada has declined to make free in both countries would not lower the price to the consumer here. Thus the reason why meats were not put on the free list in this Canadian agreement was because Canada felt that the competition of our packers would injuriously affect the products of their packing houses. If that be true, how would it help our consumer or lower the price of meat in our markets if we let their meat in free while they retained a duty on our meat?

The same thing is true of flour. They would not consent to free trade in flour, because they knew that our flour mills could under sell their millers. If that were so, then how much competition and lowering of the price of flour could we expect from putting Canadian flour on the free list?

And yet gentlemen insist that the farmer has been unjustly treated because we have not put Canadian flour and meat on the free list. And it is proposed to satisfy the supposed grievance of the farmers by now doing so, without any compensating concession from Canada. This proposal would be legislation passed for political-platform uses, without accomplishing any real good.

In another aspect, however, the effect of the proposal might be serious. Of course a mere reduction of our tariff, or the putting of any article on our free list, without insisting on a corresponding change in the Canadian tariff, will not interfere with the contract as made with Canada. Canada cannot object to our giving her greater tariff concessions than we have agreed to give her under the contract. But if we do make such concessions, without any consideration on the part of Canada, without any *quid pro quo,* so to speak, after the contract has been tentatively agreed upon by those authorized to make contracts for ratification in both governments, then we are in danger of creating an obligation against us in favor of all other foreign countries with whom we have existing treaties containing what is called the "favored-nation" clause. By this clause we agree to give the same commercial privileges to the country with whom we have made the treaty as we give to any other nation. This clause has been construed by our statesmen not to involve us in an obligation to extend a privilege to all nations which we confer upon one nation in consideration of an equally valuable privilege received from that one nation. In other words, it has been held not to include special bargains or contracts where there is a consideration moving to each side for the obligation of the other.

But the serious question that would arise is whether if, now that the contract has been tentatively agreed upon and is about to be confirmed by Canada, we should grant to Canada more than the contract requires, we could claim that this extra concession was not a pure gratuity and one which was necessarily extended to all other nations under the "favored-nation" clause. There are two objections, therefore, to inserting in the bill confirming this Canadian contract additions to our free list from Canada. The first is that they are a concession that is of no value to those whom it is proposed to propitiate by adopting it, and the second is that it may involve us indirectly in a doubtful obligation in respect to trade with other countries. If we desire to put meat and flour and other commodities on the free list for the entire world, that is one thing; we can do it with our eyes open and with a knowledge of what it entails after an investigation, but to put such a provision in a Canadian treaty and then have it operate as a free list for the entire world is legislation necessarily ill considered.

More than this, those proposed gratuitous concessions are in the nature of an admission that in some way or other we have done an injury to a particular class by this Canadian reciprocity agreement. I deny it. It is said that it injures the farmers. I deny it. It is strictly in accordance with the protective principle that we should only have a protective tariff between us and countries in which the conditions are so dissimilar as to make a difference in the cost of production. Now, it is known of all men that the general conditions that prevail in Canada are the same as those which obtain in the United States in the matter of agricultural products. Indeed, if there is any advantage, the advantage is largely on the side of the United States, because we have much greater variety of products, in view of the varieties of our climate, than they can have in Canada.

We raise cotton as no other country does. Of course they raise none in Canada.

We raise corn, and hogs and cattle fed on corn, and with the exception of a very small part of the acreage of Canada, in Ontario, it is not possible to raise corn at all in the Dominion.

With respect to wheat and barley and oats, conditions differ in different parts of Canada and in different parts of the United States. Classing them together, and on the whole, the conditions are substantially the same. In prices of farm land the differences are no greater between Canada and the United States than between the different states in the United States. In the matter of farm wages, they differ in different parts of Canada as they do in the United States; but, on the whole, they are about the same— higher in Canada at some places than in the United States and less at others. But there is no pauper class of labor in either country, and the only difference between the two countries is that Canada is farther north than the United States, a difference which, as already said, gives the advantage agriculturally to our side of the border.

It is said that this is an agreement that affects agricultural products more than manufactures. That is true; but if we are to have an interchange of products between the two countries of any substantial amount the chief part of it must necessarily be in agricultural products. As it is we export to Canada more agricultural products than we receive from her, and so it will be afterwards. The effect is not going to lower, in my judgment, the specific prices of agricultural products in our country. It is going to steady them; it is going to reduce the rapid fluctuations, and it is going to produce an interchange of products at a profit which will be beneficial to both countries.

If objection can be made to the treaty on the ground that a particular class derive less benefit from it than other classes, then it is the manufacturer of the country who ought to object, because the treaty, in its nature, will not enlarge his market as much as it will that of the farmer.

I am quite aware that, from one motive or another, a great deal of effort and money have been spent in sending circulars to farmers to convince them that this Canadian treaty, if adopted, will do them injury. I do not know that it is possible to allay such fears by argument, pending the consideration of the treaty by the Senate. It usually takes a considerable time by argument to clarify erroneous economic views of this kind having no foundation in fact, but only in fear, stimulated by misrepresentation and exaggeration. But there is one way—and that a conclusive way—of demonstrating the fallacy and unfounded character of their fears to the farmers, or any other class that believes itself to be unjustly affected by this treaty, and that is to try it on. There is no obligation on either nation to continue the reciprocity arrangement any longer than it desires, and if it be found by actual practice that there is an injury, and a permanent injury, to the farmers of this country, everybody knows that they can sufficiently control legislation to bring about a change and a return to the old conditions. Those of us who are responsible for the Canadian treaty are willing and anxious to subject it to that kind of a test, and we have no doubt that when it is put in operation the ghosts which have been exhibited to frighten the agricultural classes will be laid forever.

Another and a very conclusive reason for closing the contract is the opportunity which it gives us to increase the supply of our natural resources which, with the wastefulness of children, we have wantonly exhausted. The timber resources of Canada, which will open themselves to us inevitably under the operation of this agreement, are now apparently inexhaustible. I say "apparently inexhaustible," for if the same procedure were to be adopted in respect to them that we have followed in respect to our own forests I presume that they, too, might be exhausted. But fortunately for Canada and for us we and they have learned much more than we realized two decades ago with respect to the necessity for proper methods of forestry and of lumber cutting. Hence, we may be safe in saying that under proper modern methods the timber resources open to us in Canada may be made inexhaustible and we may derive ample supplies of timber from Canadian sources, to the profit of Canada and for our own benefit.

There are other natural resources, which I need not stop to enumerate, that will become available to us as if our own if we adopt and maintain commercial union with Canada; and this is one of the chief reasons that ought to commend the Canadian agreement to the farseeing statesmanship of leaders of American public opinion.

But there are other, even broader, grounds than this that should lead to the adoption of the agreement. Canada's superficial area is greater than that of the United States between the oceans. Of course it has a good deal of waste land in the far north, but it has enormous tracts of unoccupied land, or land settled so sparsely as to be substantially unoccupied, which in the next two or three decades will rapidly acquire a substantial and valuable population. The Government is one entirely controlled by the people, and the bond uniting the Dominion with the mother country is light and almost imperceptible. There are no restrictions upon the trade or economic development of Canada which will interfere in the slightest with her carving out her independent future. The attitude of the people is that of affection toward the mother country, and of a sentimental loyalty toward her royal head. But for practical purposes the control exercised from England by Executive or Parliament is imponderable.

Canada has now between seven and eight millions of people. They are a hardy, temperate, persistent race, brave, intelligent, and enterprising, sharing or inheriting the good qualities of all their ancestors, and with a national pride in their Dominion that grows with the wonderful success and prosperity that have attended them in the last three decades. They are good neighbors; we could not have better neighbors. It is more than a hundred years since a hostile shot was fired across the border, and they are like us because our conditions are similar and because our traditions are similar.

They are more restrictive in their immigration laws than we, and perhaps they grow less rapidly; but they have before them a wonderful expansion in population, in agriculture, and in business, and they offer to any nation with whom they have sympathetic relations, and with whom it is profitable for them to deal, a constantly increasing market and an ever-expanding trade.

The question which we now have to answer is whether we propose to maintain an artificial wall across the country of 3,700 miles in length and of indefinite height to prevent the natural trade that would flow between two great nations of people of the same language, of similar character, tradition, business habits, and moral aspirations, when the removal of that wall would furnish to each country the economic advantage of its corresponding enlargement of prosperous population and territory without the added responsibility of government and political control.

The theory that trade is not profitable to one party unless it is done at a loss to the other party is at the bottom of a great deal of the economic fallacies of the past and the present. Trade is mutually beneficial. It is profitable to both parties, for if it is not it cannot and ought not continue. As between Canada and the United States, the trade and the mutual benefit from the trade will increase.

It is amusing—and I am not sure that it has not some elements of consolation in it—to find that all the buncombe and all of the exaggeration and misrepresentation in politics and all of the political ghosts are not confined to our own country, and that there has entered into the discussion in Canada, as a reason for defeating the adoption of this contract by the Canadian Parliament, a fear that we desire to annex the Dominion; and the dreams of Americans with irresponsible imaginations, who like to talk of the starry flag's floating from Panama to the Pole, are exhibited by the opponents of the Canadian treaty in Canada as the declaration of a real policy by this country and as an announcement of our purpose to push political control over our neighbor of the North.

I am not an anti-imperialist, but I have had considerable experience in the countries over which we have assumed temporary control. I do not know when that control will end, but I do know that in respect to those countries we have taken over heavy duties and obligations, the weight of which ought to destroy any temptation to further acquisition of territory.

It would be invidious to institute a comparison between the Government of Canada and this country, but there is one part of our jurisdiction and that of Canada that come together sufficiently close to enable the Canadians and ourselves to realize that the sample of government that we exhibit is not alluring. I refer to the control of Alaska as compared with the control by Canada of her northwest territory. The talk of annexation is bosh. Everyone who knows anything about it realizes that it is bosh. Canada is a great, strong youth, anxious to test his muscles, rejoicing in the race he is ready to run. The United States has all it can attend to with the territory it is now governing, and to make the possibility of the annexation of Canada to the United States a basis for objection to any steps toward their greater economic and commercial union should be treated as one of the jokes of the platform, and should not enter into the consideration of serious men engaged in solving a serious problem.

Why should we not have a closer union with Canada? Think of the absurdity of separating Manitoba and Minneapolis by as great a distance as Manitoba and Liverpool when certainly Providence intended that their separation, socially and commercially, should only be that of their geographical distance. Canadians have furnished us a large number of our best citizens. We are giving them a large number of the pick of our young farmers. Let us open the gateways between us. Let us give to both countries the profit of the trade that God intended between us. Let the political governments remain as they are. Let us abolish arbitrary and artificial obstructions to our association with our friends upon the North and derive the mutual profit that it will certainly bring.

The Canadian contract has passed the House substantially as adopted and in such form that, if adopted in the same way by the Senate, it will go into effect as soon as the bill now pending in the Canadian Parliament shall be passed by that Parliament.

I desire to express my high appreciation of the manner in which the present House of Representatives have treated the reciprocity agreement. It has not "played politics." It has taken the statesmanlike course in respect to it.

I am very hopeful that the Senate will treat the agreement in the same way and that no amendments will there be added to the bill. For the reasons given, I think they are dangerous. It is not for me to question the good faith of those who propose to introduce and adopt them, but it is appropriate to say that the use of amendments is a very common method of defeating legislation when the responsibility for its defeat is one that the movers of such amendments do not desire openly to assume.

It may be that the Canadian contract does not go far enough. In making it we were limited by the reluctance of Canada to go as far as we would wish to have her go, but the fact that it does not go far enough is the poorest reason for not going as far as we can. We were making a contract, we were balancing considerations; we were not making a general tariff law or a general tariff revision. It was no part of our duty to reduce the tariff generally in this contract with other countries. If that is to be done, and if there is a sincere desire to have it done, then it ought to be done by separate legislation, and the passage of the present agreement, which I regard as epoch making in the commercial relations between the two countries, should not be endangered by making its passage conditioned on the passage of tariff revision or other legislation having no real relevancy to the contract.

I appeal to this company, representing as it does the press of the United States, to see to it that it is made clear to the public that this contract ought to stand or fall by its own terms, and that its passage or defeat ought not to be affected in any regard by other amendments to the tariff law. Such a method is a recurrence to the old way of making a tariff bill, which has been properly criticized and condemned, by which its passage is secured not on the merits of particular schedules, but by the support that may be secured in the House or Senate through giving a tariff on particular products of particular localities.

I think there is a general sentiment now in favor of revising the tariff, schedule by schedule, and of making this revision dependent on exact information as to each schedule, gathered by impartial investigators. To amend this Canadian contract and to make its passage dependent on other tariff legislation is to continue the old method of tariff revision characterized, not without reason, as a local issue.

I have said that this was a critical time in the solution of the question of reciprocity. It is critical, because, unless it is now decided favorably to reciprocity, it is exceedingly probable that no such opportunity will ever again come to the United States. The forces which are at work in England and in Canada to separate her by a Chinese wall from the United States and to make her part of an imperial commercial band, reaching from England around the world to England again, by a system of preferential tariffs, will derive an impetus from the rejection of this treaty, and if we would have reciprocity with all the advantages that I have described, and that I earnestly and sincerely believe will follow its adoption, we must take it now or give it up forever.

7

Special Message

[Explaining the Administration's reasons for eliminating from
the Chugach National Forest of Alaska 12,800 acres of land
fronting on Controller Bay]
The White House, July 26, 1911

To the Senate of the United States:

On June twenty-seventh last, your honorable body adopted the following resolution:

Resolved, That the President of the United States be, and he is hereby, requested to transmit to the Senate of the United States copies of all letters, maps, executive or departmental orders or instructions, surveys, also applications to enter land, or for rights of way for railroads or otherwise, and all other official reports, recommendations, documents, or records in the Departments of War, Interior, and Agriculture, or by any of the officials or bureaus of these departments, not included in the report of the Secretary of the Interior of April 26, 1911, printed as Senate Document No. 12, Sixty-second Congress, first session, relating in any way to the elimination from the Chugach National Forest, in Alaska, of land fronting upon Controller Bay, approximating 12,800 acres; especially referring to such papers, documents, etc., as relate to the applications of the Controller Railroad & Navigation Co. for rights of way or confirmation of its maps of rights of way or harbor rights or privileges in or near to the said Controller Bay, or upon the Chugach National Forest, or upon lands eliminated therefrom, or upon the tide lands or shore lands of the said Controller Bay, with such information, if any, as is in the possession of the War Department, relating to the character of Controller Bay as a harbor, its soundings, and a designation of those portions of the harbor which are available for the use of deep-water vessels.

Also, to include in the report hereby requested the names of the soldiers whose claims are to be used as bases for the applications for the land referred to, the mesne and subsequent assignments, and other data relating thereto, with a statement of the present status of all said applications to enter said lands or for rights of way thereon.

I herewith submit copies of all the documents above requested. The records in the Department of Commerce and Labor are not asked for in the resolution, but the Secretary of the Interior has secured from the Secretary of Commerce and Labor certain documents relating to the subject matter on file or of record in the Bureau of Coast and Geodetic Survey, and those are transmitted as part of the documents furnished me by the Secretary of the Interior. I also submit such documents as are on the Executive Office files relating to the Executive order of October 28, last.

I deem it wise and proper to accompany the submission of these documents with a statement in narrative form of the action of the administration with the reasons therefor.

The Executive Order of October 28, 1910, referred to in the resolution, was in the terms following:

The White House, October 28, 1910
Under authority of the act of Congress of June 4, 1897 (30 Stat., 11, at 34 and 36), and on the recommendation of the Secretary of Agriculture, it is hereby ordered that the proclamation of February 23, 1909, enlarging the Chugach National Forest, be modified to reduce the area of such national forest by eliminating therefrom the following-described tract, containing approximately 12,800 acres of land, which has been found, upon examination, to be not chiefly valuable for national forest purposes:

Beginning at a point where the meridian of longitude 144 degrees 5' west crosses the coast line of Controller Bay, thence north along said meridian line to the parallel of latitude at 60 degrees and 10' north; thence west along said parallel to a point where the same crosses the coast line at or near the mouth of Behring River, and thence along the coast to the place of beginning.

The tract above described is hereby restored to the public domain.

Controller Bay is upward of twenty miles in total length and five or six miles in width and is land-locked by a number of islands. It was supposed for some time to be so shallow as to make its use for navigation impossible, but in 1907 a channel was discovered, which passed from the ocean to the southeast of the island of Kanaka and curving into the bay extended southeasterly some seven miles. Mr. McCabe, solicitor of the Agricultural Department, states in the memorandum prepared by him for submission to the secretary and to me, that investigation had shown that for a distance of six miles the frontage of Controller Bay was on deep water, to be reached by trestles of ordinary length.

A more exact description of the channel is as follows: For four miles it is about three quarters of a mile wide and for three miles about 2,000 feet wide, gradually approaching nearer to the shore of the mainland. The channel is eleven fathoms where it enters the bay, and continues for more than five miles to have a 30-foot depth, and then gradually shallows until it is from twelve to fifteen feet at mean low water. The mean high tide would increase its depth nine feet. The bottom of the channel is glacial silt and very easily dredgible, so that it would be entirely practicable to widen the channel and deepen it the full length of seven miles. The tract eliminated by the Executive order has a right-angled triangular form, with the shore line or high-water mark as the hypotenuse, between six and seven miles long and roughly about the same length as the channel I have described. The north shore opposite the entrance of the channel to the bay is between two and three miles from low-water mark, and is separated therefrom by tidal mud flats that are covered at high water. The 30-foot contour line is about a mile farther from the shore line.

All the territory surrounding Controller Bay was included in the Chugach Forest Reservation in 1909 by a proclamation of President Roosevelt. The importance of Controller Bay is that it lies about twenty-five miles from very valuable coal deposits, known as the Bering coal fields. Katalla Bay is to the west of Controller Bay and almost immediately adjoins it. It is an open roadstead upon the shore of which an attempt was made by the

Morgan-Guggenheim syndicate to establish a railway terminal, and thence to build a road to the Bering coal fields, already mentioned. The attempt failed for the reason that the breakwater protecting the terminals was destroyed by storms and the terminals became impracticable. Some fifty miles or more farther west of Katalla Bay is the mouth of the Copper River, where there is an excellent harbor, on which is the town of Cordova. There the Copper River Railroad, owned by the Morgan-Guggenheim interests, has its terminals, and the line runs to the northeast along the Copper River and has nearly reached certain rich copper mines in the interior. A branch from this main line is projected to the Bering coal fields and is feasible.

When the channel in the Controller Bay was discovered, Mr. Tittmann, superintendent of the Coast Survey, as shown by his letter in the record, was of opinion that it was of great value and ought to be maintained as a naval reservation because of its proximity to the coal fields. His letter was submitted by the Secretary of Commerce and Labor to the Secretary of the Interior, who invited the comment of the Director of the Geological Survey. That officer replied that the harbor was a poor one, and that it would not be as good for a naval reservation as one already selected, but that he thought that private capital ought to be encouraged to construct a railway from the channel over the mud flats to the shore and thence to the coal fields. Captain Pillsbury of the Army Engineers, in a report in the record made in 1908, mentions three possible objections to Controller Bay: First, that the surrounding islands may prove to be so low as not fully to protect the channel; second, that the flats extend two or three miles from the shore; and, third, that ice formed in the rivers entering the bay and affected by tidal currents may destroy structures put upon the flats and especially a long trestle built over them.

In December, 1909, Mr. Richard S. Ryan, representing the Controller Railway & Navigation Company, applied to Mr. Pinchot, the then Forester, for an elimination from the Chugach Forest Reservation of a tract of land to enable his company to secure railroad terminals, bunkers, railroad shops, etc., on the northeast shore of Controller Bay. This application was referred by the Associate Forester to the District Forester at Portland, Ore., and by him to the Forester in Alaska. The result of these references and the application was that early in 1910 Mr. Graves, who had in the meantime become Forester, reported that there was no objection from the standpoint of forestry interests to the elimination of the tract indicated, or, indeed, of 18,000 acres on the northeast shore of Controller Bay.

The attention of the Navy Department was invited by the Forestry Bureau to the proposal to open the shore of Controller Bay to entry and occupation, and inquiry was made whether the Navy Department desired to use Controller Bay as a reservation and whether it objected to its being opened up. The answer was in the negative.

The matter was considered by the Forestry Bureau, by the Secretary of Agriculture, by the Secretary of the Interior, and by the General Land Office, and the result was a recommendation to me in May, 1910, that an elimination be made of 320 acres with a frontage of 160 rods on the northeast shore of Controller Bay. I entertained some question about the matter and stated my objections at a cabinet meeting. Thereafter, some time in June, I had an interview with Mr. Richard S. Ryan, the promoter of the Controller Railway & Navigation Company, to whom the Secretary of the Interior had stated my objections, which led to Ryan's sending a communication to the Secretary of the Interior under date of July 13, 1910. This letter was, in the secretary's absence, sent by the department to me at once. I considered the whole case in August, 1910, and directed that the 320 acres, recommended by both departments, be eliminated as recommended. Nothing was done, however, in the matter until I returned to Washington in October, 1910, when a formal order, which had been drawn in the Interior Department and was subsequently specifically approved by the Secretary of Agriculture and returned to the Interior Department, was submitted to me by the Acting Secretary of the Interior, with the approval of that department. The order was as follows:

> Under authority of the act of Congress of June 4, 1897 (30 Stat., 11, at 34 and 36), and on the recommendation of the Secretary of Agriculture, it is hereby ordered that the proclamation of February 23, 1909, enlarging the Chugach National Forest, be modified to reduce the area of such national forest by eliminating therefrom the following described tract, containing approximately 320 acres of land, which has been found, upon examination, to be not chiefly valuable for national forest purposes and which is necessary for terminal purposes and desired by the Controller Railway & Navigation Co. for such purposes:
>
> Beginning at a point on Controller Bay which bears south 17° 22'

west, 1,196.7 feet from U. S. Location Monument No. 842; thence north 5,720.5 feet; thence east 2,202.1 feet; thence south 7,044.2 feet to a point on Controller Bay; thence following the meanders of the bay north 52° 30' west 1,460 feet; thence north 79° 26' west 800 feet; thence north 42° 34' west 380 feet, to the point of beginning, containing 320 acres, approximately, the same being in approximate longitude 144° 11' west from Greenwich, latitude 60° 8' north.

The tract above described is hereby restored to the public domain.

The question finally came before the Cabinet late in October. After a full discussion of the matter, and after a consideration of the law, I expressed dissatisfaction with the order because it purported on its face to make the elimination for the benefit of a railroad company of a tract of land which the company could not secure under the statute, for it was a tract 320 acres in one body when only 160 acres could be thus acquired. In the second place, I preferred to make a much larger elimination of a tract facing the entire channel, and with sufficient room for a terminal railway town. I was willing to do this because I found the restrictions in the law sufficient to prevent the possibility of any monopoly of either the upland or the harbor or channel by the Controller Railway & Navigation Company, or any other persons, or company. For lack of time sufficient to draft a memorandum myself, I requested the Secretary of the Interior, who, with the Secretary of Agriculture, after full discussion, had agreed in my conclusion, to prepare a letter setting forth the reasons for making the larger elimination, so that it might become part of the record. The letter is of even date with the order. It does not set forth the reasons for the larger order as fully as I did in discussing it.

It had been originally suggested by the Forestry Bureau that 18,000 acres might safely be eliminated so far as forestry purposes were concerned, but fear had been expressed by one of the District Foresters that such a large elimination would offer an opportunity to the company to use land scrip and acquire title to extensive town sites, and the result of the joint consideration of both departments had been the reduction to 320 acres.

I wish to be as specific as possible upon this point and to say that I alone am responsible for the enlargement of the proposed elimination from 320 acres to 12,800 acres, and that I proposed the change and stated my reasons therefor, and while both secretaries cordially concurred in it, the suggestion was mine.

The statement of Mr. Ryan, who had been properly vouched to the Forester by two gentlemen whom I know, Mr. Chester Lyman and Mr. Fred Jennings, and who had produced a letter from a reputable financial firm, Probst, Wetzler & Company, was that the railway company which he represented had expended more than $75,000 in making preparations for the construction of a railway from Controller Bay to the coal fields, twenty-five miles away, but that they were obstructed in so doing by the order reserving the Chugach Forest Reservation, which covered all of the Controller Bay shore. He, as well as Probst, Wetzler & Company, gave every assurance that the Copper River Railway Company, owned by Messrs. Morgan and Guggenheim, had no connection with them, and that they were engaged in an independent enterprise in good faith to build an independent railroad. No evidence to the contrary has been brought to my attention since.

Of course it was possible that the owners of the Copper River Railway Company might attempt to buy this railroad when, and if, it was built. It was possible that Mr. Ryan was acting in the interests of the Copper River Railroad, although I did not believe it; but, whether this was true or not, it was clear that the order of elimination by reason of the restrictions of the act of Congress hereafter explained, would not permit the owners of either railroad to shut out any other capitalists who might desire to construct a railroad from the channel of Controller Bay to the coal fields; and if by this order we could secure the construction of a railroad from Controller Bay to the coal fields, it would be a distinct step in the useful development of Alaska. The rates of freight for coal to be charged, of course, would always be subject to congressional control, and if Government ownership seemed a wise policy under the peculiar circumstances, ample land for right of way, harbor frontage, and terminals must always remain available under the law for Government use, or if it is preferred to take over to the Government a railway built by private enterprise, condemnation is easy.

The thing which Alaska needs is development, and where rights and franchises can be properly granted to encourage investment and construction of railroads without conferring exclusive privileges, I believe it to be in accordance with good policy to grant them.

Full authority is given in the Federal statutes for the location of rail-roads and the acquisition of a right of way over public lands by such location and construction of the road in Alaska (30 Stat. L., 409), and this is permitted even in the forest reservations. (30 Stat. L., 1233.) Pains are taken in the statute to prevent one railroad from excluding another by the appropriation of the only possible pass or canyon or defile through which a road can be built between two points. The difficulty presented by a forest reservation in a case like this is that there is no opportunity to secure town sites or proper terminals for a coal road and shipping point in such a reservation. When, on the recommendation of Forester Pinchot, the Chugach National Forest was created by proclamation of President Roosevelt in July, 1907, there were excepted from the forest the several areas contained within boundaries formed by circles described with a radius of a mile each from the centers of ten small towns or settlements. Among these were Eyak, on Orca Bay, and Valdez, on Valdez Arm. A little later (September 18, 1907), there was eliminated from the reservation approximately 33,000 acres of the waterfront on Valdez Arm, the tract thus eliminated being a mile wide, abutting on the shore, and following the contour of the arm or bay for a distance of more than thirty miles. At this time, Valdez was deemed important as a future port. Both Orca Bay and Valdez Arm are excellent harbors and have deep water near the shore.

While it does not appear that the creation of railway terminals and harbor facilities was one of the reasons for the exclusion from the national forest of the lands around the town of Eyak, or for the elimination of 33,000 acres at Valdez Arm, it certainly was not regarded as necessary to include or to retain these lands within the national forest for fear they would be entered by a railroad, because on April 24, 1907, Mr. Ballinger, then Commissioner of the General Land Office, had called the attention of Secretary Garfield to the fact that a number of transportation companies were seeking to obtain rights of way through the lands included in the general area proposed to be reserved. Doubtless the rights of the public were thought to be sufficiently safeguarded against monopoly of harbor facilities under the limitations of the statute hereafter mentioned, which were the same then as now. As a matter of fact, the Copper River Railway Company, owned by the Morgan-Guggenheim Syndicate, having applied for terminal and station grounds at what was then called Eyak shortly before the Chugach Forest Reservation was proclaimed, has established its terminals there and thus has been developed in the immediate neighborhood the well-known terminal town of Cordova. Whenever the Bering coal fields are opened this company can readily reach them by a branch line, the construction of which has already been considered and is entirely practicable. Indeed, its promoters have insisted to the Secretary of the Interior that this is the proper method of developing these coal fields, and that they would not be interested in building a direct line to Controller Bay, where it would be necessary for them to duplicate terminal facilities they already have at Cordova on a better harbor, and where coal is not the only commodity seeking transportation. If this position is correct, and it seems to have sound economic reasons behind it, the only effect of preventing railroad construction at Controller Bay would be to leave the field entirely to the Copper River Railroad.

If a railroad was to be constructed from Controller Bay to the Bering coal fields, it was perfectly evident that there must be a terminal town on the shore of Controller Bay, and I was therefore glad and anxious to throw it open to entry and settlement as one important step in encouraging railroad enterprise. I was certain that Congress had provided, in the statutes affecting the entry and settlement of land in Alaska, limitations which would prevent the possibility of the exclusive appropriation of the harbor and channel of Controller Bay or its shores or upland to any one railroad. This, I propose now to show.

The only practicable method for securing title from the Government in such a tract as this after its elimination is by the use of what is called "soldiers' additional homestead right," evidences by scrip. The statutory limitations upon this method of acquiring title are threefold:

1. No more than 160 acres can be entered in any single body by such scrip. (30 Stat. L., 409; 32 Stat. L., 1028.)
2. No location of scrip along any navigable waters can be made within the distance of eighty rods of any lands already located along such waters. No entry can be allowed extending more than 160 rods along the shore of any navigable water, and along such shore a space of at least eighty rods must be reserved from entry between all such

claims. (30 Stat. L., 409; 32 Stat. L., 1028.) Moreover, the statute expressly provides that a roadway sixty feet in width, parallel to the shore line as near as may be practicable, shall be reserved for the use of the public as a highway. (30 Stat. L., 413.)

3. Nothing in the act contained is to be construed to authorize entries to be made or title to be acquired to the shore of any navigable waters within said district. (30 Stat. L., 409; 32 Stat. L., 1029.)

Under the first limitation the navigation company and every other person is prevented from locating more than 160 acres in one body. By the construction of the land department, as shown in the record, this requires a separation between any two entries by the same person or in the same interest of a tract of forty acres. This would prevent the possibility of any one person or any one interest acquiring an entire tract like that of 12,800 acres.

The second limitation is important in that it prevents the entry of claims at any point on the shore having a greater frontage than half a mile, and requires that between that and the next claim taken up there shall be a frontage reserved to the public and kept in public control of a quarter of a mile. The consequence is that in the seven miles of the frontage of this eliminated tract there must be reserved for Government control and use, and such disposition as Congress may see fit to make, and free from private appropriation, a frontage aggregating about 2³/₄ miles, and so distributed along the shore in frontages of eighty rods as to make certain of a public frontage of this width having all the advantage that any private frontage can have. In other words, if a tract with a half-mile frontage is located at a particularly advantageous place with reference to the harbor, then on each side of that frontage must be reserved to the public a frontage of a quarter of a mile, or a half mile in all, for public uses. These public frontages are to be connected by a sixty-foot street reserved parallel to the shore.

These two restrictions necessarily prevent a monopoly of land abutting on the shore, and as they necessarily prevent a monopoly by any one locator, or in the interest of any company for whom locators are acting, they take away the motive for the acquisition of land and frontage merely for the purpose of excluding other companies and possible competitors and tend to confine locators to the acquisition of land to be profitable in its use.

Since the executive order was issued, October 28, 1910, there have been four locations under soldiers' scrip—three of them of 160 rods each along the bay, separated by two divisions of eighty rods, dated November 1, November 10, and November 11, 1910, respectively. I shall assume that all of them are in the interest of the Controller Railway & Navigation Company. None of them has been approved or passed to patent, but I shall assume they can be passed to valid patent. Where the fourth one, dated March 11, 1911, is, does not appear on the map opposite page 2, but it is understood to front 160 rods on the bay shore on the east side of the Campbell River. In addition, upon one of the 80-rod intervals, there is filed what is called a terminal railroad claim of forty acres, covering the entire frontage of eighty rods. This was filed December 14, 1910, after the location of the two scrip entries which it connects. It is plainly invalid because placed on the interval of eighty rods especially reserved by statute for the public. We thus have four frontages of 160 rods now located.

Of the shore frontage unlocated which may be appropriated by scrip, there remain six frontages of 160 rods each on the shore of the tract opened by the Executive order facing the bay and channel, and in addition about 2³/₄ miles of frontage distributed in eleven 80-rod strips, subject to public use and the disposition of Congress. There is thus ample room for many other railroads to reach high-water mark on Controller Bay, and there to acquire tracts for terminals. Of the 12,800 acres, the entries in area have covered not more than 800 acres, and all the rest is available for scrip location or is reserved for the public under the limitations of the act.

But it is said that the three or four locations are the best ones on the bay with reference to the channel and harbor, and are opposite the deepest part. If this is true, it is equally true of the 80-rod reservations between and on each side of these locations. More than that, the channel extends 2¹/₂ miles beyond these locations, and while it narrows some and shallows some, it still has a depth of from fifteen to thirty feet at low water and, if necessary, is easily capable of being dredged to greater depth and greater width because of the character of the bottom.

But there is a third reason why the opening of this tract to settlement and limited private appropriations cannot lead to a monopoly in the Controller Railway & Navigation Company or anyone else. The distance from the dry land—i. e., the shore land—the line of high-water mark—to the line of low-water mark is between two and three miles, and the distance to deeper water is about a mile farther, making it necessary, if a harbor is to be reached and used, to construct a viaduct or trestle three or four miles long from the shore to the channel. This tidal flat is owned by the United States, and the acquisition under the public-land laws of tracts on the shore abutting these tidal flats gives no right or title to those flats. This would be the law if the statute was silent on the subject; but not only the statute of 1898 (30 Stat. L., 409), but also the amending statute of 1903 (32 Stat. L., 1028) expressly imposes the restriction that no title or right can be obtained under the act in the shore of a navigable body of water.

The theory upon which it has been contended that the Controller Bay Railway & Navigation Company has practically acquired an exclusive appropriation of the harbor is that its anticipated ownership of the lands located by it and abutting on the shore will give it the right to build viaducts from these lands to the side of the deep channel, $3^{1}/_{2}$ miles away, and there establish wharves on the channel equal in frontage to that of the locations made on the shore, and that even if it does not itself build such wharves, it can prevent anyone else from enjoying access to the channel for the whole length of its frontage, say two miles. I have shown that even if this were the law, the public reservations and the unlocated frontage would prevent monopoly of the channel. But it is not the law.

The shore runs from high-water mark down to low-water mark. The owners of the upland, by virtue of the title they have acquired from the Government, do not acquire a vested right of access to the deep water and have no right or easement to build viaducts or trestles across the flats or wharves along the deep channel which Congress may not regulate or defeat.

The principle of law is settled by the decision of the Supreme Court of the United States in the case of Shively *v.* Bowlby (152 U. S., 1). In that case it was decided that "grants by Congress of portions of the public lands within a territory to settlers thereon, though bordering on or bounded by navigable waters, convey of their own force no title or right below high-water mark" and do not impair the right either of the United States or of the future State, when created, to deal with the tidal land between high and low water mark at pleasure. It was there held that in the State of Oregon a person who took title to land acquired under an act of Congress while Oregon was a Territory, abutting on the tidal water of the Columbia River, could not object to a subsequent grant to another by the State of Oregon of the tidal lands upon which the land of the grantee under the act of Congress abutted.

It follows that no matter what the ownership of the upland abutting on the tidal flats, Congress has complete power to regulate the trestles and wharves which shall be built from the shore to the channel and along it, and to determine their character and the distance along the channel they may occupy, and in the absence of congressional action, the abutting lot owners can possibly acquire at best only a revocable license or permit from the War Department to put in such structures as that department will certify do not interfere with navigation.

Is congressional action wanting or has Congress given abutting lot owners any permission or easement of this kind? In only two instances has Congress conferred any such authority.

There is a provision of the act of May 14, 1898 (30 Stat. L., 409), providing a right of way for located railways in Alaska that reads as follows:

And when such railway shall connect with any navigable stream or tide water, such company shall have power to construct and maintain necessary piers and wharves for connection with water transportation, subject to the supervision of the Secretary of the Treasury.

But this is not a right incident to, or commensurate with, ownership of abutting land, but it is incident only to the location of a right of way of a railway. It secures to the railway only such trestles or viaducts to the wharves along the deep channel as the Secretary of the Treasury may deem necessary.

In the second place, there is a provision in the same act by which the Secretary of the Interior may permit the extension of piers and the construction of wharves from the 80-rod frontages reserved to the public, to the navigable channel, but such piers and wharves must be open to public use for reasonable tolls to be fixed by the secretary (30 Stat. L., 413).

There is no provision or intimation in the statute that abutting landowners as such shall have an easement of this kind. The consequence is that even if the Controller Railway & Navigation Company were to obtain control of the entire frontage on the north shore—which, of course, it cannot do because of the 80-rod reservations—it still could not appropriate the channel or exclude anyone from its occupancy.

The whole contention that the executive order and the opening to settlement of the shore of Controller Bay grants a monopoly to the railway company rests on the claim that it has given an opportunity to persons using scrip to appropriate the control of the only available and practicable parts of the channel by the location of the scrip opposite to those parts. If now the location of the scrip opposite to the harbor gives no right to reach the harbor except as Congress may expressly give it, clearly the Controller Railway & Navigation Company has not the slightest opportunity for exclusive appropriation of the harbor facilities unless Congress shall by future act deliberately and voluntarily confer it.

I should be lacking in candor if I allowed it to be inferred that this third reason for saying that there is not the slightest danger of this order giving a monopoly of the channel to the Controller Railway & Navigation Company was present in my mind when I made the order. I was, of course, satisfied because of the other restrictions mentioned that no monopoly of the channel could follow, but I did not examine the law as to this point at that time. But the law is as I have stated it, and the consequences are inevitable.

The owners of the Controller Railway & Navigation Company realized the difficulty there might be in asserting a right as abutting owners to construct trestles and wharves on the tidal flats to the channel, and without even relying on the express privilege conferred on railway companies to apply to the Secretary of the Treasury for such permission, already quoted, went direct to Congress and secured from Congress an act which gives to the company expressly a right of way 200 feet wide across the tidal flats to the deep water; but this grant of an exclusive easement is carefully drawn and is accompanied and surrounded with every safeguard. Express power to repeal it is reserved to Congress, and the character and extent of the structures on the channels are placed in the control of the War Department upon recommendation of the Chief of Engineers. This easement was granted in an act passed March fourth of this year (36 Stat. at Large, 1360), and only after full examination by the Interstate Commerce Committee of the House, after recommendations by the War Department and the Interior Department and a clarifying discussion in the House of Representatives.

In the records of the War Department will be found one permit to construct a trestle from the Controller Bay shore to the channel, which, by extension, is still in force and will remain so until January 1, 1912. This was given to the Controller Bay & Bering Coal Railway Company, a different company from the Controller Railway & Navigation Company. It does not appear upon what authority such permit could be given by the War Department. Under the statute, the Secretary of the Treasury is charged with supervision over such a case, and before a lawful license can be granted his consent must be obtained (30 Stat. L., 409).

It follows from what has been said that the question of how the channel of Controller Bay shall be used is wholly in the control of Congress and nothing that has been done by the executive order or otherwise imperils that control. With the opportunity that any projected railway has to secure access to the harbor by locating its right of way to the line of the shore under supervision of the Secretary of the Treasury, or by application to Congress, the mere private ownership of land abutting on the shore is relatively unimportant. If a railway company thus secures access by trestle and wharf to the deepwater channel, it may conveniently establish its terminal yards, stations, warehouses, and elevators wherever in the eliminated tract it can secure title, and extended frontage on the tidal flats is of no particular advantage. As 12,000 acres in the tract eliminated still remain open to entry, the prospect of a monopoly in one railroad company is most remote. I submit to all fair-minded men who may have been disturbed over the charges made in respect to the executive order of October 28, 1910, that it has been demonstrated by the foregoing that no public interest has suffered from its issue; that great good may come from it; and that no dishonest or improper motive is needed to explain it. I might, therefore, stop here; but rather for the purpose of the moral to be drawn from them than to vindicate the order, I propose to consider the attacks upon the order that misinformation, hysteria, or rancor has prompted.

The order has been criticized because it was not in form a proclamation instead of an order. This was determined by Mr. Graves, the Forester, who, in letter of March 24, 1910, speaking of the proposed elimination, says to his assistant: "Action in this instance will be taken by executive order rather than by proclamation accompanied by diagram," and he gives the reasons in a note dated July 6, 1911:

When a comparatively small area is to be eliminated from a national forest the executive order is very commonly used instead of the proclamation, especially when other changes in boundaries may be made in a short time. The preparation of the diagrams which accompany a proclamation is necessarily expensive and laborious, and the issuance of repeated proclamations with their diagrams is avoided when an executive order will serve the purpose. In the present case reports were pending, recommending other changes in boundaries of the Chugach Forest, and since the proposed eliminations would be described without the use of a diagram, the executive order form of elimination was chosen.

The fact is that in law there is in effect no difference between a proclamation and an executive order. (Wood *v.* Beach, 156 U. S., 548–50.) In practice the same publicity is given to each. Both are sent to the State Department for record. The custom of the State Department is to advertise neither a proclamation nor an executive order. Each is merely handed to the representatives of the press after being executed, and is sent to the large mailing list of the State Department. That course was here pursued in respect to the executive order of October 28, 1910. In accordance with custom, copies were sent to the Interior Department and the Agricultural Department, because they were especially concerned.

The charge has been made that this was a secret order, and that though it was made in October, 1910, no one knew of it until April, 1911. This is utterly unfounded. The statement of Mr. Vernon, the correspondent of the *Post-Intelligencer,* of Seattle, a newspaper of wide circulation among a people most interested in Alaska, shows that ten days before the order was made, news of the details of Ryan's application and the probability of its being granted was given wide publicity. It further appears from the records of the Interior Department that the evening the order was signed, October 28, 1910, a full notice of the issue of the order and its details was furnished by the department to all correspondents in the form of a news bulletin. Finally, the agent of the Associated Press certifies that at 7.23 p.m., October 28, 1910, there was sent out by that association to all its newspaper clients a telegram taken from a typewritten statement issued by the Interior Department, as follows:

Washington, *October 28.*—Approximately 12,800 acres of land in the Chugach National Forest, Alaska, have been restored by the President for disposition under appropriate land laws, according to information made public today by the Interior Department. These lands are situated on the coast line of Controller Bay in Southern Alaska near the Cunningham claims, and have been found upon examination to be of little value for forestry purposes.

It would be difficult to prepare an advertisement more informing to the public or more likely to attract the attention of all likely to desire acquisition of land on Controller Bay. On the twenty-ninth, the Chief Forester sent a telegram making a similar announcement to his district forester at Portland, Ore.

The order has been attacked on the ground that it did not contain a provision delaying its taking effect for thirty days after its local publication as orders restoring land to settlement by homesteaders frequently do. An examination of the record furnishes an explanation of this feature of the order as made. When in October the two departments had agreed, with my acquiescence, that the order should be an elimination of only 320 acres, an order describing the 320 acres directing its restoration to settlement and containing the usual provision postponing its taking effect thirty days was prepared in the Forestry Bureau and forwarded to the Interior Department. There it was deemed wiser to spread on the face of the order a specific declaration that it was made to afford terminals for the Controller Railway & Navigation Company, and as no one else was expected to intervene and take up any part of the eliminated tract, the restoration was made immediate.

The form thus amended was submitted to the Secretary of Agriculture, who expressed his preference for the immediate restoration order through his solicitor's memorandum on the face of the order, as follows:

Mr. Clements [Assistant Attorney in the Interior Department],
We think this O. K. The Secretary says it is the direct way, and appeals to him.
Geo. P. McCabe

The idea of the Secretary doubtless was that the short form of order was preferable because on its face it was directly indicative of the purpose to secure an opportunity to the railway company by proper entry to settle on the land eliminated, and as no one else was expected to intervene no postponement was needed. Accordingly when the case came for decision in the Cabinet, the order was without any postponement clause. This was the form sent me for my signature by the Acting Secretary of the Interior Department.

When I directed the striking out of the reference to the railway company and the enlargement of the area from 320 acres to 12,800 acres, the form of the order in its provision for immediate restoration was not changed. I have no doubt that this was the reason why the order issued took the form it did. Had the postponement clause been suggested, I would, doubtless, have directed it to be embodied in the order. But the event has proven that it was really not important in this case, for in now nearly nine months only the Controller Railway & Navigation Company has made any scrip entries on the eliminated tract and this, although 12,000 acres and about two and one half miles of waterfront still remain open to entry, and there are several different railway companies in addition to the Controller Railway & Navigation Company that had filed locations for rights of way in the vicinity in the last two years who have had in the last nine months the fullest notice of their opportunity if they wished to enter on this land.

Before closing, I desire to allude to a circumstance which the terms of this resolution make apt and relevant. It is a widely published statement attributed to a newspaper correspondent that in an examination of the files of the Interior Department a few weeks ago a postscript was found attached to a letter of July 13, 1910, addressed by Mr. Richard S. Ryan to Secretary Ballinger—and in the present record—urging the elimination of land enough for terminals for the Controller Railway & Navigation Company. The postscript was said to read as follows:

Dear Dick:

I went to see the President the other day. He asked me who it was I represented. I told him, according to our agreement, that I represented myself. But this didn't seem to satisfy him. So I sent for Charlie Taft and asked him to tell his brother, the President, who it was I really represented. The President made no further objection to my claim.

Yours,

Dick

The postscript is not now on the files of the department. If it were, it would be my duty to transmit it under this resolution. Who is really responsible for its wicked fabrication if it ever existed, or for the viciously false statement made as to its authenticity, is immaterial for the purposes of this communication. The purport of the alleged postscript is, and the intention of the fabricator was, to make Mr. Richard S. Ryan testify through its words to the public that although I was at first opposed in the public interest to granting the elimination which he requested, nevertheless through the undue influence of my brother, Mr. Charles P. Taft, and the disclosure of the real persons in interest, I was induced improperly and for the promotion of their private gain, to make the order.

The statement in so far as my brother is concerned—and that is the chief feature of the postscript—is utterly unfounded. He never wrote to me or spoke to me in reference to Richard S. Ryan or on the subject of Controller Bay or the granting of any privileges or the making of any orders in respect to Alaska. He has no interest in Alaska, never had, and knows nothing of the circumstances connected with this transaction. He does not remember that he ever met Richard S. Ryan. He never heard of the Controller Railway & Navigation Company until my cablegram of inquiry reached him, which, with his answer, is in the record.

Mr. Ballinger says in a telegram in answer to my inquiry, both of which are in the record, that he never received such a postscript and that he was in Seattle on the date of July thirteenth, when it was said to have been written.

Mr. Richard S. Ryan, in a letter which he has sent me without solicitation, and which is in the record, says that he never met my brother, Mr. Charles P. Taft, and that so far as he knows, Mr. Charles P. Taft never had the slightest interest in Controller Bay, in the Controller Railway & Navigation Company, or in any Alaskan company, that he utterly denies writing or signing the alleged postscript. The utter improbability of his writing such a postscript to Mr. Ballinger at Washington, when the latter was away for his vacation for two months, must impress everyone.

The fact is that Mr. Ballinger never saw the letter of July 13, 1910, to which this postscript is said to have been attached. It was sent to me by Mr. Carr, Secretary Ballinger's private secretary, at Beverly, on July fourteenth—the next day. I read the letter at Beverly in August with other papers and sent them to the White House. It was placed upon the White House files and remained there until April 22, 1911, when it was, by request of Secretary Fisher, for use in connection with his answer to a Senate inquiry, returned to the Interior Department, and it was after this that the correspondent is said to have seen the letter with the postscript attached. Mr. Carr saw no such postscript when he sent the letter to me. I did not see it when I read it. No one saw it in the Executive Office, but it remained to appear as a postscript when it is said that the correspondent saw the letter in April or May on the files of the Interior Department. All others were denied the sight.

The person upon whose statement the existence of what has been properly characterized as an amazing postscript is based, is a writer for newspapers and magazines, who was given permission by Secretary Fisher, after consultation with me, to examine all the files in respect to the Controller Bay matter—and this under the supervision of Mr. Brown, then private secretary to the Secretary of the Interior. After the examination, at which it is alleged this postscript was received from the hand of Mr. Brown, the correspondent prepared an elaborate article on the subject of this order and Controller Bay, which was submitted to Mr. Fisher, and which was discussed with Mr. Fisher at length, but never in the conversation between them or in the article submitted did the correspondent mention the existence of the postscript. Mr. Brown states that there was no such postscript in the papers when he showed them to the correspondent and that he never saw such a postscript. Similar evidence is given by Mr. Carr and other custodians of the records in the Interior Department.

Stronger evidence of the falsity and maliciously slanderous character of the alleged postscript could not be had. Its only significance is the light it throws on the bitterness and venom of some of those who take active part in every discussion of Alaskan issues. The intensity of their desire to besmirch all who invest in that district, and all who are officially connected with its administration, operates upon the minds of weak human instruments and prompts the fabrication of such false testimony as this postscript. I dislike to dwell upon this feature of the case, but it is so full of a lesson that ought to be taken to heart of every patriotic citizen that I cannot pass it over in silence.

When I made this order, I was aware that the condition of public opinion in reference to investments in Alaska, fanned by charges of fraud—some well founded and others of an hysterical and unjust or false character—would lead to an attack upon it and to the questioning of my motives in signing it. I remarked this when I made the order, and I was not mistaken. But a public officer, when he conceives it his duty to take affirmative action in the public interest, has no more right to allow fear of unjust criticism and attack to hinder him from taking that action than he would to allow personal and dishonest motives to affect him. It is easy in cases like this to take the course which timidity prompts, and to do nothing, but such a course does not inure to the public weal.

I am in full sympathy with the concern of reasonable and patriotic men that the valuable resources of Alaska should not be turned over to be exploited for the profit of greedy, absorbing, and monopolistic corporations or syndicates. Whatever the attempts which have been made, no one, as a matter of fact, has secured in Alaska any undue privilege or franchise not completely under the control of Congress. I am in full agreement with the view that every care, both in administration and in legislation, must be observed to prevent the corrupt or unfair acquisition of undue privilege, franchise, or right from the Government in that district. But everyone must know that the resources of Alaska can never become available either to the people of Alaska or to the public of the United States unless reasonable opportunity is granted to those who would invest their money to secure a return proportionate to the risk run in the investment and reasonable under all the circumstances.

On the other hand, the acrimony of spirit and the intense malice that have been engendered in respect of the administration of the government in Alaska and in the consideration of measures proposed for her relief and the wanton recklessness and eagerness with which attempts have been made to besmirch the characters of high officials having to do with the Alaskan government, and even of persons not in public life, present a condition that calls for condemnation and requires that the public be warned of the demoralization that has been produced by the hysterical suspicions of good people and the unscrupulous and corrupt misrepresentations of the wicked. The helpless state to which the credulity of some and the malevolent scandal-mongering of others have brought the people of Alaska in their struggle for its development ought to give the public pause, for until a juster and fairer view be taken, investment in Alaska, which is necessary to its development, will be impossible, and honest administrators and legislators will be embarrassed in the advocacy and putting into operation of those policies in regard to the Territory which are necessary to its progress and prosperity.

Special Messages

[Transmitting authenticated copies of the treaties between the
United States and Great Britain and France, negotiated August 3,
1911]

The White House, August 4, 1911

I

To the Senate:

With a view to receiving the advice and consent of the Senate to the
ratification of the treaty, I transmit herewith an authenticated copy of a
treaty signed by the plenipotentiaries of the United States and Great Britain on August 3, 1911, extending the scope and obligation of the policy of
arbitration adopted in the present arbitration treaty of April 4, 1908, between the two countries, so as to exclude certain exceptions contained in
that treaty and to provide means for the peaceful solution of all questions
of difference which it shall be found impossible in future to settle by diplomacy.

2

To the Senate:

With a view to receiving the advice and consent of the Senate to the
ratification of the treaty, I transmit herewith an authenticated copy.

8

Veto Message

[Returning without approval a joint resolution for the
admission of the Territories of New Mexico and Arizona
into the Union as States]
The White House, August 22, 1911

To the House of Representatives:

I return herewith, without my approval, House joint resolution No.
14, "To admit the Territories of New Mexico and Arizona as States into
the Union on an equal footing with the original States."

Congress, by an enabling act approved June 20, 1910, provided for
the calling of a constitutional convention in each of these Territories, the
submission of the constitution proposed by the convention to the electors
of the Territory, the approval of the constitution by the President and Congress, the proclamation of the fact by the President, and the election of
State officers. Both in Arizona and New Mexico conventions have been
held, constitutions adopted and ratified by the people and submitted to
the President and Congress. I have approved the constitution of New Mexico, and so did the House of Representatives of the Sixty-first Congress.
The Senate, however, failed to take action upon it. I have not approved
the Arizona constitution, nor have the two Houses of Congress, except as
they have done so by the joint resolution under consideration. The resolution admits both Territories to statehood with their constitutions, on condition that at the time of the election of State officers New Mexico shall

submit to its electors an amendment to its new constitution altering and modifying its provision for future amendments, and on the further condition that Arizona shall submit to its electors, at the time of the election of its State officers, a proposed amendment to its constitution by which judicial officers shall be excepted from the section permitting a recall of all elective officers.

If I sign this joint resolution, I do not see how I can escape responsibility for the judicial recall of the Arizona constitution. The joint resolution admits Arizona with the judicial recall, but requires the submission of the question of its wisdom to the voters. In other words, the resolution approves the admission of Arizona with the judicial recall, unless the voters themselves repudiate it. Under the Arizona constitution all elective officers, and this includes county and State judges, six months after their election are subject to the recall. It is initiated by a petition signed by electors equal to 25 percent of the total number of votes cast for all the candidates for the office at the previous general election. Within five days after the petition is filed the officer may resign. Whether he does or not, an election ensues in which his name, if he does not resign, is placed on the ballot with that of all other candidates. The petitioners may print on the official ballot 200 words showing their reasons for recalling the officer, and he is permitted to make defense in the same place in 200 words. If the incumbent receives the highest number of the votes, he continues in his office; if not, he is removed from office and is succeeded by the candidate who does receive the highest number.

This provision of the Arizona constitution, in its application to county and State judges, seems to me so pernicious in its effect, so destructive of independence in the judiciary, so likely to subject the rights of the individual to the possible tyranny of a popular majority, and, therefore, to be so injurious to the cause of free government, that I must disapprove a constitution containing it. I am not now engaged in performing the office given me in the enabling act already referred to, approved June 20, 1910, which was that of approving the constitutions ratified by the peoples of the Territories. It may be argued from the text of that act that in giving or withholding the approval under the act my only duty is to examine the proposed constitution, and if I find nothing in it inconsistent with the Federal Constitution, the principles of the Declaration of Independence, or the enabling act, to register my approval. But now I am discharging my constitutional function in respect to the enactment of laws, and my discretion is equal to that of the Houses of Congress. I must therefore withhold my approval from this resolution if in fact I do not approve it as a matter of governmental policy. Of course, a mere difference of opinion as to the wisdom of details in a State constitution ought not to lead me to set up my opinion against that of the people of the Territory. It is to be their government, and while the power of Congress to withhold or grant statehood is absolute, the people about to constitute a State should generally know better the kind of government and constitution suited to their needs than Congress or the Executive. But when such a constitution contains something so destructive of free government as the judicial recall, it should be disapproved.

A government is for the benefit of all the people. We believe that this benefit is best accomplished by popular government, because in the long run each class of individuals is apt to secure better provision for themselves through their own voice in government than through the altruistic interest of others, however intelligent or philanthropic. The wisdom of ages has taught that no government can exist except in accordance with laws and unless the people under it either obey the laws voluntarily or are made to obey them. In a popular government the laws are made by the people—not by all the people—but by those supposed and declared to be competent for the purpose, as males over 21 years of age, and not by all of these—but by a majority of them only. Now, as the government is for all the people, and is not solely for a majority of them, the majority in exercising control either directly or through its agents is bound to exercise the power for the benefit of the minority as well as the majority. But all have recognized that the majority of a people, unrestrained by law, when aroused and without the sobering effect of deliberation and discussion, may do injustice to the minority or to the individual when the selfish interest of the majority prompts. Hence arises the necessity for a constitution by which the will of the majority shall be permitted to guide the course of the government only under controlling checks that experience has shown to be necessary to secure for the minority its share of the benefit to the whole people that a popular government is established to bestow. A popular government is not a government of a majority, by a majority, for a majority of the people. It is a government of the whole people, by a majority of the whole people under such rules and checks as will secure a wise, just, and beneficent government for all the people. It is said you can always trust the people to do justice. If that means all the people and they all agree, you can. But ordinarily they do not all agree, and the maxim is interpreted to mean that you can always trust a majority of the people. This is not invariably true; and every limitation imposed by the people upon the power of the majority in their constitutions is an admission that it is not always true. No honest, clear-headed man, however great a lover of popular government, can deny that the unbridled expression of the majority of a community converted hastily into law or action would sometimes make a government tyrannical and cruel. Constitutions are checks upon the hasty action of the majority. They are the self-imposed restraints of a whole people upon a majority of them to secure sober action and a respect for the rights of the minority, and of the individual in his relation to other individuals, and in his relation to the whole people in their character as a state or government.

The Constitution distributes the functions of government into three branches—the legislative, to make the laws; the executive, to execute them; and the judicial, to decide in cases arising before it the rights of the individual as between him and others and as between him and the Government. This division of government into three separate branches has always been regarded as a great security for the maintenance of free institutions, and the security is only firm and assured when the judicial branch is independent and impartial. The executive and legislative branches are representative of the majority of the people which elected them in guiding the course of the Government within the limits of the Constitution. They must act for the whole people, of course; but they may properly follow, and usually ought to follow, the views of the majority which elected them in respect to the governmental policy best adapted to secure the welfare of the whole people. But the judicial branch of the Government is not representative of a majority of the people in any such sense, even if the mode of selecting the judges is by popular election. In a proper sense, judges are servants of the people; that is, they are doing work which must be done for the Government and in the interest of all the people, but it is not work in the doing of which they are to follow the will of the majority except as that is embodied in statutes lawfully enacted according to constitutional limitations. They are not popular representatives. On the contrary, to fill their office properly, they must be independent. They must decide every question which comes before them according to law and justice. If this question is between individuals, they will follow the statute, or the unwritten law if no statute applies, and they take the unwritten law growing out of tradition and custom from previous judicial decisions. If a statute or ordinance affecting a cause before them is not lawfully enacted, because it violates the constitution adopted by the people, then they must ignore the statute and decide the question as if the statute had never been passed. This power is a judicial power imposed by the people on the judges by the written constitution. In early days some argued that the obligations of the Constitution operated directly on the conscience of the legislature, and only in that manner, and that it was to be conclusively presumed that whatever was done by the legislature was constitutional. But such a view did not obtain with our hard-headed, courageous, and far-sighted statesmen and judges, and it was soon settled that it was the duty of judges in cases properly arising before them to apply the law and so to declare what was the law, and that if what purported to be statutory law was at variance with the fundamental law, i. e., the Constitution, the seeming statute was not law at all, was not binding on the courts, the individuals, or any branch of the Government, and that it was the duty of the judges so to decide. This power conferred on the judiciary in our form of government is unique in the history of governments, and its operation has attracted and deserved the admiration and commendation of the world. It gives to our judiciary a position higher, stronger, and more responsible than that of the judiciary of any other country, and more effectively secures adherence to the fundamental will of the people.

What I have said has been to little purpose if it has not shown that judges to fulfill their functions properly in our popular Government must be more independent than in any other form of government, and that need of independence is greater where the individual is one litigant and the State, guided by the successful and governing majority, is the other. In order to maintain the rights of the minority and the individual and to preserve our constitutional balance we must have judges with courage to decide against the majority when justice and law require.

By the recall in the Arizona constitution it is proposed to give to the majority power to remove arbitrarily, and without delay, any judge who may have the courage to render an unpopular decision. By the recall it is proposed to enable a minority of 25 percent of the voters of the district or

State, for no prescribed cause, after the judge has been in office six months, to submit the question of his retention in office to the electorate. The petitioning minority must say on the ballot what they can against him in 200 words, and he must defend as best he can in the same space. Other candidates are permitted to present themselves and have their names printed on the ballot, so that the recall is not based solely on the record or the acts of the judge, but also on the question whether some other and more popular candidate has been found to unseat him. Could there be a system more ingeniously devised to subject judges to momentary gusts of popular passion than this? We can not be blind to the fact that often an intelligent and respectable electorate may be so roused upon an issue that it will visit with condemnation the decision of a just judge, though exactly in accord with the law governing the case, merely because it affects unfavorably their contest. Controversies over elections, labor troubles, racial or religious issues, issues as to the construction or constitutionality of liquor laws, criminal trials of popular or unpopular defendants, the removal of county seats, suits by individuals to maintain their constitutional rights in obstruction of some popular improvement—these and many other cases could be cited in which a majority of a district electorate would be tempted by hasty anger to recall a conscientious judge if the opportunity were open all the time. No period of delay is interposed for the abatement of popular feeling. The recall is devised to encourage quick action, and to lead the people to strike while the iron is hot. The judge is treated as the instrument and servant of a majority of the people and subject to their momentary will, not after a long term in which his qualities as a judge and his character as a man have been subjected to a test of all the varieties of judicial work and duty so as to furnish a proper means of measuring his fitness for continuance in another term. On the instant of an unpopular ruling, while the spirit of protest has not had time to cool and even while an appeal may be pending from his ruling in which he may be sustained, he is to be haled before the electorate as a tribunal, with no judicial hearing, evidence, or defense, and thrown out of office, and disgraced for life because he has failed, in a single decision, it may be, to satisfy the popular demand. Think of the opportunity such a system would give to unscrupulous political bosses in control, as they have been in control not only of conventions but elections! Think of the enormous power for evil given to the sensational, muckraking portion of the press in rousing prejudice against a just judge by false charges and insinuations, the effect of which in the short period of an election by recall it would be impossible for him to meet and offset! Supporters of such a system seem to think that it will work only in the interest of the poor, the humble, the weak and the oppressed; that it will strike down only the judge who is supposed to favor corporations and be affected by the corrupting influence of the rich. Nothing could be further from the ultimate result. The motive it would offer to unscrupulous combinations to seek to control politics in order to control judges is clear. Those would profit by the recall who have the best opportunity of rousing the majority of the people to action on a sudden impulse. Are they likely to be the wisest or the best people in a community? Do they not include those who have money enough to employ the firebrands and slanderers in a community and the stirrers-up of social hate? Would not self-respecting men well hesitate to accept judicial office with such a sword of Damocles hanging over them? What kind of judgments might those on the unpopular side expect from courts whose judges must make their decisions under such legalized terrorism? The character of the judges would deteriorate to that of trimmers and time-servers, and independent judicial action would be a thing of the past. As the possibilities of such a system pass in review, is it too much to characterize it as one which will destroy the judiciary, its standing, and its usefulness?

The argument has been made to justify the judicial recall that it is only carrying out the principle of the election of the judges by the people. The appointment by the executive is by the representative of the majority, and so far as future bias is concerned there is no great difference between the appointment and the election of judges. The independence of the judiciary is secured rather by a fixed term and fixed and irreducible salary. It is true that when the term of judges is for a limited number of years and reelection is necessary, it has been thought and charged sometimes that shortly before election in cases in which popular interest is excited, judges have leaned in their decisions toward the popular side.

As already pointed out, however, in the election of judges for a long and fixed term of years, the fear of popular prejudice as a motive for unjust decisions is minimized by the tenure on the one hand, while the opportunity which the people have calmly to consider the work of a judge for a full term of years in deciding as to his reelection generally insures from them a fair and reasonable consideration of his qualities as a judge. While, therefore, there have been elected judges who have bowed before unjust popular prejudice, or who have yielded to the power of political bosses in their decisions, I am convinced that these are exceptional, and that, on the whole, elected judges have made a great American judiciary. But the success of an elective judiciary certainly furnishes no reason for so changing the system as to take away the very safeguards which have made it successful.

Attempt is made to defend the principle of judicial recall by reference to States in which judges are said to have shown themselves to be under corrupt corporate influence and in which it is claimed that nothing but a desperate remedy will suffice. If the political control in such States is sufficiently wrested from corrupting corporations to permit the enactment of a radical constitutional amendment like that of judicial recall, it would seem possible to make provision in its stead for an effective remedy by impeachment in which the cumbrous features of the present remedy might be avoided, but the opportunity for judicial hearing and defense before an impartial tribunal might be retained. Real reforms are not to be effected by patent short cuts or by abolishing those requirements which the experience of ages has shown to be essential in dealing justly with everyone. Such innovations are certain in the long run to plague the inventor or first user and will come readily to the hand of the enemies and corrupters of society after the passing of the just popular indignation that prompted their adoption.

Again judicial recall is advocated on the ground that it will bring the judges more into sympathy with the popular will and the progress of ideas among the people. It is said that now judges are out of touch with the movement toward a wider democracy and a greater control of governmental agencies in the interest and for the benefit of the people. The righteous and just course for a judge to pursue is ordinarily fixed by statute or clear principles of law, and the cases in which his judgment may be affected by his political, economic, or social views are infrequent. But even in such cases, judges are not removed from the people's influence. Surround the judiciary with all the safeguards possible, create judges by appointment, make their tenure for life, forbid diminution of salary during their term, and still it is impossible to prevent the influence of popular opinion from coloring judgments in the long run. Judges are men, intelligent, sympathetic men, patriotic men, and in those fields of the law in which the personal equation unavoidably plays a part, there will be found a response to sober popular opinion as it changes to meet the exigency of social, political, and economic changes. Indeed this should be so. Individual instances of a hidebound and retrograde conservatism on the part of courts in decisions which turn on the individual economic or sociological views of the judges may be pointed out; but they are not many, and do not call for radical action. In treating of courts we are dealing with a human machine, liable like all the inventions of man to err, but we are dealing with a human institution that likens itself to a divine institution because it seeks and preserves justice. It has been the corner stone of our gloriously free government in which the rights of the individual and of the minority have been preserved, while governmental action of the majority has lost nothing of beneficent progress, efficacy, and directness. This balance was planned in the Constitution by its framers and has been maintained by our independent judiciary.

Precedents are cited from State constitutions said to be equivalent to a popular recall. In some, judges are removable by a vote of both houses of the legislature. This is a mere adoption of the English address of Parliament to the Crown for the removal of judges. It is similar to impeachment in that a form of hearing is always granted. Such a provision forms no precedent for a popular recall without adequate hearing and defense, and with new candidates to contest the election.

It is said the recall will be rarely used. If so, it will be rarely needed. Then why adopt a system so full of danger? But it is a mistake to suppose that such a powerful lever for influencing judicial decisions and such an opportunity for vengeance because of adverse ones will be allowed to remain unused.

But it is said that the people of Arizona are to become an independent State when created, and even if we strike out judicial recall now, they can reincorporate it in their constitution after statehood.

To this I would answer that in dealing with the courts, which are the corner stone of good government, and in which not only the voters, but the nonvoters and nonresidents, have a deep interest as a security for their rights of life, liberty, and property, no matter what the future action of the State may be, it is necessary for the authority which is primarily responsible for its creation to assert in no doubtful tones the necessity for an independent and untrammeled judiciary.

9

Annual Message

Part I
[On the Anti-Trust Statute]
The White House, December 5, 1911

To the Senate and House of Representatives:

This message is the first of several which I shall send to Congress during the interval between the opening of its regular session and its adjournment for the Christmas holidays. The amount of information to be communicated as to the operations of the Government, the number of important subjects calling for comment by the Executive, and the transmission to Congress of exhaustive reports of special commissions, make it impossible to include in one message of a reasonable length a discussion of the topics that ought to be brought to the attention of the National Legislature at its first regular session.

The Anti-Trust Law—To Supreme Court Decisions

In May last the Supreme Court handed down decisions in the suits in equity brought by the United States to enjoin the further maintenance of the Standard Oil Trust and of the American Tobacco Trust, and to secure their dissolution. The decisions are epoch-making and serve to advise the business world authoritatively of the scope and operation of the Anti-Trust Act of 1890. The decisions do not depart in any substantial way from the previous decisions of the court in construing and applying this important statute, but they clarify those decisions by further defining the already admitted exceptions to the literal construction of the act. By the decrees, they furnish a useful precedent as to the proper method of dealing with the capital and property of illegal trusts. These decisions suggest the need and wisdom of additional or supplemental legislation to make it easier for the entire business community to square with the rule of action and legality thus finally established and to preserve the benefit, freedom, and spur of reasonable competition without loss of real efficiency or progress.

No Change in the Rule of Decision—Merely in Its Form of Expression

The statute in its first section declares to be illegal "every contract, combination in the form of trust or otherwise, or conspiracy, in restraint of trade or commerce among the several States or with foreign nations," and in the second, declares guilty of a misdemeanor "every person who shall monopolize or attempt to monopolize or combine or conspire with any other person to monopolize any part of the trade or commerce of the several States or with foreign nations."

In two early cases, where the statute was invoked to enjoin a transportation rate agreement between interstate railroad companies, it was held that it was no defense to show that the agreement as to rates complained of was reasonable at common law, because it was said that the statute was directed against all contracts and combinations in restraint of trade whether reasonable at common law or not. It was plain from the record, however, that the contracts complained of in those cases would not have been deemed reasonable at common law. In subsequent cases the court said that the statute should be given a reasonable construction and refused to include within its inhibition, certain contractual restraints of trade which it denominated as incidental or as indirect.

These cases of restraint of trade that the court excepted from the operation of the statute were instances which, at common law, would have been called reasonable. In the Standard Oil and Tobacco cases, therefore, the court merely adopted the tests of the common law, and in defining exceptions to the literal application of the statute, only substituted for the test of being incidental or indirect, that of being reasonable, and this, without varying in the slightest the actual scope and effect of the statute. In other words, all the cases under the statute which have now been decided would have been decided the same way if the court had originally accepted in its construction the rule at common law.

It has been said that the court, by introducing into the construction of the statute common-law distinctions, has emasculated it. This is obviously untrue. By its judgment every contract and combination in restraint of interstate trade made with the purpose or necessary effect of controlling prices by stifling competition, or of establishing in whole or in part a monopoly of such trade, is condemned by the statute. The most extreme critics can not instance a case that ought to be condemned under the statute which is not brought within its terms as thus construed.

The suggestion is also made that the Supreme Court by its decision in the last two cases has committed to the court the undefined and unlimited discretion to determine whether a case of restraint of trade is within the terms of the statute. This is wholly untrue. A reasonable restraint of trade at common law is well understood and is clearly defined. It does not rest in the discretion of the court. It must be limited to accomplish the purpose of a lawful main contract to which, in order that it shall be enforceable at all, it must be incidental. If it exceed the needs of that contract, it is void.

The test of reasonableness was never applied by the court at common law to contracts or combinations or conspiracies in restraint of trade whose purpose was or whose necessary effect would be to stifle competition, to control prices, or establish monopolies. The courts never assumed power to say that such contracts or combinations or conspiracies might be lawful if the parties to them were only moderate in the use of the power thus secured and did not exact from the public too great and exorbitant prices. It is true that many theorists, and others engaged in business violating the statute, have hoped that some such line could be drawn by courts; but no court of authority has ever attempted it. Certainly there is nothing in the decisions of the latest two cases from which such a dangerous theory of judicial discretion in enforcing this statute can derive the slightest sanction.

Force and Effectiveness of Statute a Matter of Growth

We have been twenty-one years making this statute effective for the purposes for which it was enacted. The Knight case was discouraging and seemed to remit to the States the whole available power to attack and suppress the evils of the trusts. Slowly, however, the error of that judgment was corrected, and only in the last three or four years has the heavy hand of the law been laid upon the great illegal combinations that have exercised such an absolute dominion over many of our industries. Criminal prosecutions have been brought and a number are pending, but juries have felt averse to convicting for jail sentences, and judges have been most reluctant to impose such sentences on men of respectable standing in society whose offense has been regarded as merely statutory. Still, as the offense becomes better understood and the committing of it partakes more of studied and deliberate defiance of the law, we can be confident that juries will convict individuals and that jail sentences will be imposed.

The Remedy in Equity by Dissolution

In the Standard Oil case the Supreme and Circuit Courts found the combination to be a monopoly of the interstate business of refining, transporting, and marketing petroleum and its products, effected and maintained through thirty-seven different corporations, the stock of which was held by a New Jersey company. It in effect commanded the dissolution of this combination, directed the transfer and *pro rata* distribution by the New Jersey company of the stock held by it in the thirty-seven corporations to and among its stockholders; and the corporations and individual defendants were enjoined from conspiring or combining to restore such monopoly; and all agreements between the subsidiary corporations tending to produce or bring about further violations of the act were enjoined.

In the Tobacco case, the court found that the individual defendants, twenty-nine in number, had been engaged in a successful effort to acquire complete dominion over the manufacture, sale, and distribution of tobacco in this country and abroad, and that this had been done by combinations made with a purpose and effect to stifle competition, control prices, and establish a monopoly, not only in the manufacture of tobacco, but also of tin-foil and licorice used in its manufacture and of its products of cigars, cigarettes, and snuffs. The tobacco suit presented a far more complicated and difficult case than the Standard Oil suit for a decree which would effectuate the will of the court and end the violation of the statute. There was here no single holding company as in the case of the Standard Oil Trust. The main company was the American Tobacco Company, a manufacturing, selling, and holding company. The plan adopted to destroy the combination and restore competition involved the redivision of the capital and plants of the whole trust between some of the companies constituting the trust and new companies organized for the purposes of the decree and made parties to it, and numbering, new and old, fourteen.

Situation After Readjustment

The American Tobacco Company (old), readjusted capital, $92,000,000; the Liggett & Meyers Tobacco Company (new), capital, $67,000,000; the P. Lorillard Company (new), capital, $47,000,000; and the R. J. Reynolds Tobacco Company (old), capital, $7,525,000, are chiefly engaged in the manufacture and sale of chewing and smoking tobacco and cigars. The former one tin-foil company is divided into two, one of $825,000 capital and the other of $400,000. The one snuff company is divided into three companies, one with a capital of $15,000,000, another with a capital of $8,000,000, and a third with a capital of $8,000,000. The licorice companies are two, one with a capital of $5,758,300 and another with a capital of $2,000,000. There is, also, the British-American Tobacco Company, a British corporation, doing business abroad with a capital of $26,000,000, the Puerto Rican Tobacco Company, with a capital of $1,800,000, and the corporation of United Cigar Stores, with a capital of $9,000,000.

Under this arrangement, each of the different kinds of business will be distributed between two or more companies with a division of the prominent brands in the same tobacco products, so as to make competition not only possible but necessary. Thus the smoking-tobacco business of the country is divided so that the present independent companies have 21.39 percent, while the American Tobacco Company will have 33.08 percent, the Liggett & Meyers 20.05 percent, the Lorillard Company 22.82 percent, and the Reynolds Company 2.66 percent. The stock of the other thirteen companies, both preferred and common, has been taken from the defendant American Tobacco Company and has been distributed among its stockholders. All covenants restricting competition have been declared null and further performance of them has been enjoined. The preferred stock of the different companies has now been given voting power which was denied it under the old organization. The ratio of the preferred stock to the common was as 78 to 40. This constitutes a very decided change in the character of the ownership and control of each company.

In the original suit there were twenty-nine defendants who were charged with being the conspirators through whom the illegal combination acquired and exercised its unlawful dominion. Under the decree these defendants will hold amounts of stock in the various distributee companies ranging from 41 percent as a maximum to 28½ percent as a minimum, except in the case of one small company, the Puerto Rican Tobacco Company, in which they will hold 45 percent. The twenty-nine individual defendants are enjoined for three years from buying any stock except from each other, and the group is thus prevented from extending its control during that period. All parties to the suit, and the new companies who are made parties, are enjoined perpetually from in any way effecting any combination between any of the companies in violation of the statute by way of resumption of the old trust. Each of the fourteen companies is enjoined from acquiring stock in any of the others. All these companies are enjoined from having common directors or officers, or common buying or selling agents, or common offices, or lending money to each other.

Size of New Companies

Objection was made by certain independent tobacco companies that this settlement was unjust because it left companies with very large capital in active business, and that the settlement that would be effective to put all on an equality would be a division of the capital and plant of the trust into small fractions in amount more nearly equal to that of each of the independent companies. This contention results from a misunderstanding of the anti-trust law and its purpose. It is not intended thereby to prevent the accumulation of large capital in business enterprises in which such a combination can secure reduced cost of production, sale, and distribution. It is directed against such an aggregation of capital only when its purpose is that of stifling competition, enhancing or controlling prices, and establishing a monopoly. If we shall have by the decree defeated these purposes and restored competition between the large units into which the capital and plant have been divided, we shall have accomplished the useful purpose of the statute.

Confiscation Not the Purpose of the Statute

It is not the purpose of the statute to confiscate the property and capital of the offending trusts. Methods of punishment by fine or imprisonment of the individual offenders, by fine of the corporation or by forfeiture of its goods in transportation, are provided, but the proceeding in equity is a specific remedy to stop the operation of the trust by injunction and prevent the future use of the plant and capital in violation of the statute.

Effectiveness of Decree

I venture to say that not in the history of American law has a decree more effective for such a purpose been entered by a court than that against the Tobacco Trust. As Circuit Judge Noyes said in his judgment approving the decree:

> The extent to which it has been necessary to tear apart this combination and force it into new forms with the attendant burdens ought to demonstrate that the Federal anti-trust statute is a drastic statute which accomplishes effective results; which so long as it stands on the statute books must be obeyed, and which can not be disobeyed without incurring far-reaching penalties. And, on the other hand, the successful reconstruction of this organization should teach that the effect of enforcing this statute is not to destroy, but to reconstruct; not to demolish, but to re-create in accordance with the conditions which the Congress has declared shall exist among the people of the United States.

Common Stock Ownership

It has been assumed that the present *pro rata* and common ownership in all these companies by former stockholders of the trust would insure a continuance of the same old single control of all the companies into which the trust has by decree been disintegrated. This is erroneous and is based upon the assumed inefficacy and innocuousness of judicial injunctions. The companies are enjoined from cooperation or combination; they have different managers, directors, purchasing and sales agents. If all or many of the numerous stockholders, reaching into the thousands, attempt to secure concerted action of the companies with a view to the control of the market, their number is so large that such an attempt could not well be concealed, and its prime movers and all its participants would be at once subject to contempt proceedings and imprisonment of a summary character. The immediate result of the present situation will necessarily be activity by all the companies under different managers, and then competition must follow, or there will be activity by one company and stagnation by another. Only a short time will inevitably lead to a change in ownership of the stock, as all opportunity for continued cooperation must disappear. Those critics who speak of this disintegration in the trust as a mere change of garments have not given consideration to the inevitable working of the decree and understand little the personal danger of attempting to evade or set at naught the solemn injunction of a court whose object is made plain by the decree and whose inhibitions are set forth with a detail and comprehensiveness unexampled in the history of equity jurisprudence.

Voluntary Reorganizations of Other Trusts at Hand

The effect of these two decisions has led to decrees dissolving the combination of manufacturers of electric lamps, a southern wholesale grocers' association, an interlocutory decree against the Powder Trust with directions by the circuit court compelling dissolution, and other combinations of a similar history are now negotiating with the Department of Justice looking to a disintegration by decree and reorganization in accordance with law. It seems possible to bring about these reorganizations without general business disturbance.

Movement for Repeal of the Anti-Trust Law

But now that the anti-trust act is seen to be effective for the accomplishment of the purpose of its enactment, we are met by a cry from many different quarters for its repeal. It is said to be obstructive of business progress, to be an attempt to restore old-fashioned methods of destructive competition between small units, and to make impossible those useful combinations of capital and the reduction of the cost of production that are essential to continued prosperity and normal growth.

In the recent decisions the Supreme Court makes clear that there is nothing in the statute which condemns combinations of capital or mere bigness of plant organized to secure economy in production and a reduction of its cost. It is only when the purpose or necessary effect of the organization and maintenance of the combination or the aggregation of immense size are the stifling of competition, actual and potential, and the enhancing of prices and establishing a monopoly, that the statute is violated. Mere size is no sin against the law. The merging of two or more business plants necessarily eliminates competition between the units thus combined, but this elimination is in contravention of the statute only when the combination is made for purpose of ending this particular competition in order to secure control of, and enhance, prices and create a monopoly.

Lack of Definiteness in the Statute

The complaint is made of the statute that it is not sufficiently definite in its description of that which is forbidden, to enable business men to avoid its violation. The suggestion is, that we may have a combination of two corporations, which may run on for years, and that subsequently the Attorney General may conclude that it was a violation of the statute, and that which was supposed by the combiners to be innocent then turns out to be a combination in violation of the statute. The answer to this hypothetical case is that when men attempt to amass such stupendous capital as will enable them to suppress competition, control prices and establish a monopoly, they know the purpose of their acts. Men do not do such a thing without having it clearly in mind. If what they do is merely for the purpose of reducing the cost of production, without the thought of suppressing competition by use of the bigness of the plant they are creating, then they can not be convicted at the time the union is made, nor can they be convicted later, unless it happen that later on they conclude to suppress competition and take the usual methods for doing so, and thus establish for themselves a monopoly. They can, in such a case, hardly complain if the motive which subsequently is disclosed is attributed by the court to the original combination.

New Remedies Suggested

Much is said of the repeal of this statute and of constructive legislation intended to accomplish the purpose and blaze a clear path for honest merchants and business men to follow. It may be that such a plan will be evolved, but I submit that the discussions which have been brought out in recent days by the fear of the continued execution of the anti-trust law have produced nothing but glittering generalities and have offered no line of distinction or rule of action as definite and as clear as that which the Supreme Court itself lays down in enforcing the statute.

Supplemental Legislation Needed—Not Repeal or Amendment

I see no objection—and indeed I can see decided advantages—in the enactment of a law which shall describe and denounce methods of competition which are unfair and are badges of the unlawful purpose denounced in the anti-trust law. The attempt and purpose to suppress a competitor by underselling him at a price so unprofitable as to drive him out of business, or the making of exclusive contracts with customers under which they are required to give up association with other manufacturers, and numerous kindred methods for stifling competition and effecting monopoly, should be described with sufficient accuracy in a criminal statute on the one hand to enable the Government to shorten its task by prosecuting single misdemeanors instead of an entire conspiracy, and, on the other hand, to serve the purpose of pointing out more in detail to the business community what must be avoided.

Federal Incorporation Recommended

In a special message to Congress on January 7, 1910, I ventured to point out the disturbance to business that would probably attend the dissolution of these offending trusts. I said:

> But such an investigation and possible prosecution of corporations whose prosperity or destruction affects the comfort not only of stockholders but of millions of wage earners, employees, and associated tradesmen must necessarily tend to disturb the confidence of the business community, to dry up the now flowing sources of capital from its places of hoarding, and produce a halt in our present prosperity that will cause suffering and strained circumstances among the innocent many for the faults of the guilty few. The question which I wish in this message to bring clearly to the consideration and discussion of Congress is whether, in order to avoid such a possible business danger, something can not be done by which these business combinations may be offered a means,

without great financial disturbance, of changing the character, organization, and extent of their business into one within the lines of the law under Federal control and supervision, securing compliance with the anti-trust statute.

Generally, in the industrial combinations called 'trusts,' the principal business is the sale of goods in many States and in foreign markets; in other words, the interstate and foreign business far exceeds the business done in any one State. This fact will justify the Federal Government in granting a Federal charter to such a combination to make and sell in interstate and foreign commerce the products of useful manufacture under such limitations as will secure a compliance with the anti-trust law. It is possible so to frame a statute that while it offers protection to a Federal company against harmful, vexatious, and unnecessary invasion by the States, it shall subject it to reasonable taxation and control by the States with respect to its purely local business.

Corporations organized under this act should be prohibited from acquiring and holding stock in other corporations (except for special reasons, upon approval by the proper Federal authority), thus avoiding the creation under national auspices of the holding company with subordinate corporations in different States, which has been such an effective agency in the creation of the great trusts and monopolies.

If the prohibition of the anti-trust act against combinations in restraint of trade is to be effectively enforced, it is essential that the National Government shall provide for the creation of national corporations to carry on a legitimate business throughout the United States. The conflicting laws of the different States of the Union with respect to foreign corporations make it difficult, if not impossible, for one corporation to comply with their requirements so as to carry on business in a number of different States.

I renew the recommendation of the enactment of a general law providing for the voluntary formation of corporations to engage in trade and commerce among the States and with foreign nations. Every argument which was then advanced for such a law, and every explanation which was at that time offered to possible objections, have been confirmed by our experience since the enforcement of the antitrust statute has resulted in the actual dissolution of active commercial organizations.

It is even more manifest now than it was then that the denunciation of conspiracies in restraint of trade should not and does not mean the denial of organizations large enough to be intrusted with our interstate and foreign trade. It has been made more clear now than it was then that a purely negative statute like the anti-trust law may well be supplemented by specific provisions for the building up and regulation of legitimate national and foreign commerce.

Government Administrative Experts Needed to Aid Courts in Trust Dissolutions

The drafting of the decrees in the dissolution of the present trusts, with a view to their reorganization into legitimate corporations, has made it especially apparent that the courts are not provided with the administrative machinery to make the necessary inquiries preparatory to reorganization, or to pursue such inquiries, and they should be empowered to invoke the aid of the Bureau of Corporations in determining the suitable reorganization of the disintegrated parts. The circuit court and the Attorney General were greatly aided in framing the decree in the Tobacco Trust dissolution by an expert from the Bureau of Corporations.

Federal Corporation Commission Proposed

I do not set forth in detail the terms and sections of a statute which might supply the constructive legislation permitting and aiding the formation of combinations of capital into Federal corporations. They should be subject to rigid rules as to their organization and procedure, including effective publicity, and to the closest supervision as to the issue of stock and bonds by an executive bureau or commission in the Department of Commerce and Labor, to which in times of doubt they might well submit their proposed plans for future business. It must be distinctly understood that incorporation under Federal law could not exempt the company thus formed and its incorporators and managers from prosecution under the anti-trust law for subsequent illegal conduct, but the publicity of its procedure and the opportunity for frequent consultation with the bureau or commission in charge of the incorporation as to the legitimate purpose of its transactions would offer it as great security against successful prosecutions for violations of the law as would be practical or wise.

Such a bureau or commission might well be invested also with the duty already referred to, of aiding courts in the dissolution and recreation of trusts within the law. It should be an executive tribunal of the dignity and power of the Comptroller of the Currency or the Interstate Commerce Commission, which now exercise supervisory power over important classes of corporations under Federal regulation.

The drafting of such a Federal incorporation law would offer ample opportunity to prevent many manifest evils in corporate management today, including irresponsibility of control in the hands of the few who are not the real owners.

Incorporation Voluntary

I recommend that the Federal charters thus to be granted shall be voluntary, at least until experience justifies mandatory provisions. The benefit to be derived from the operation of great businesses under the protection of such a charter would attract all who are anxious to keep within the lines of the law. Other large combinations that fail to take advantage of the Federal incorporation will not have a right to complain if their failure is ascribed to unwillingness to submit their transactions to the careful official scrutiny, competent supervision, and publicity attendant upon the enjoyment of such a charter.

Only Supplemental Legislation Needed

The opportunity thus suggested for Federal incorporation, it seems to me, is suitable constructive legislation needed to facilitate the squaring of great industrial enterprises to the rule of action laid down by the anti-trust law. This statute as construed by the Supreme Court must continue to be the line of distinction for legitimate business. It must be enforced, unless we are to banish individualism from all business and reduce it to one common system of regulation or control of prices like that which now prevails with respect to public utilities, and which when applied to all business would be a long step toward State socialism.

Importance of the Anti-Trust Act

The anti-trust act is the expression of the effort of a freedom-loving people to preserve equality of opportunity. It is the result of the confident determination of such a people to maintain their future growth by preserving uncontrolled and unrestricted the enterprise of the individual, his industry, his ingenuity, his intelligence, and his independent courage.

For twenty years or more this statute has been upon the statute book. All knew its general purpose and approved. Many of its violators were cynical over its assumed impotence. It seemed impossible of enforcement. Slowly the mills of the courts ground, and only gradually did the majesty of the law assert itself. Many of its statesmen-authors died before it became a living force, and they and others saw the evil grow which they had hoped to destroy. Now its efficacy is seen; now its power is heavy; now its object is near achievement. Now we hear the call for its repeal on the plea that it interferes with business prosperity, and we are advised in most general terms, how by some other statute and in some other way the evil we are just stamping out can be cured, if we only abandon this work of twenty years and try another experiment for another term of years.

It is said that the act has not done good. Can this be said in the face of the effect of the Northern Securities decree? That decree was in no way so drastic or inhibitive in detail as either the Standard Oil decree or the Tobacco decree; but did it not stop for all time the then powerful movement toward the control of all the railroads of the country in a single hand? Such a one-man power could not have been a healthful influence in the Republic, even though exercised under the general supervision of an interstate commission.

Do we desire to make such ruthless combinations and monopolies lawful? When all energies are directed, not toward the reduction of the cost of production for the public benefit by a healthful competition, but toward new ways and means for making permanent in a few hands the absolute control of the conditions and prices prevailing in the whole field of industry, then individual enterprise and effort will be paralyzed and the spirit of commercial freedom will be dead.

Part II
[On foreign relations]
The White House, December 7, 1911

To the Senate and House of Representatives:
  The relations of the United States with other countries have continued during the past twelve months upon a basis of the usual good will and friendly intercourse.

Arbitration

The year just passed marks an important general movement on the part of the Powers for broader arbitration. In the recognition of the manifold benefits to mankind in the extension of the policy of the settlement of international disputes by arbitration rather than by war, and in response to a widespread demand for an advance in that direction on the part of the people of the United States and of Great Britain and of France, new arbitration treaties were negotiated last spring with Great Britain and France, the terms of which were designed, as expressed in the preamble of these treaties, to extend the scope and obligations of the policy of arbitration adopted in our present treaties with those Governments. To pave the way for this treaty with the United States, Great Britain negotiated an important modification in its alliance with Japan, and the French Government also expedited the negotiations with signal good will. The new treaties have been submitted to the Senate and are awaiting its advice and consent to their ratification. All the essentials of these important treaties have long been known, and it is my earnest hope that they will receive prompt and favorable action.

Claim of Alsop & Co. Settled

I am glad to report that on July 5 last the American claim of Alsop & Co. against the Government of Chile was finally disposed of by the decision of His Britannic Majesty George V, to whom, as *amiable compositeur,* the matter had been referred for determination. His Majesty made an award of nearly $1,000,000 to the claimants, which was promptly paid by Chile. The settlement of this controversy has happily eliminated from the relations between the Republic of Chile and the United States the only question which for two decades had given the two foreign offices any serious concern and makes possible the unobstructed development of the relations of friendship which it has been the aim of this Government in every possible way to further and cultivate.

Arbitrations—Panama and Costa Rica—Colombia and Haiti

In further illustration of the practical and beneficent application of the principle of arbitration and the underlying broad spirit of conciliation, I am happy to advert to the part of the United States in facilitating amicable settlement of disputes which menaced the peace between Panama and Costa Rica and between Haiti and the Dominican Republic.

Since the date of their independence, Colombia and Costa Rica had been seeking a solution of a boundary dispute, which came as an heritage from Colombia to the new Republic of Panama, upon its beginning life as an independent nation. Although the disputants had submitted this question for decision to the President of France under the terms of an arbitration treaty, the exact interpretation of the provisions of the award rendered had been a matter of serious disagreement between the two countries, both contending for widely different lines even under the terms of the decision. Subsequently and since 1903 this boundary question had been the subject of fruitless diplomatic negotiations between the parties. In January, 1910, at the request of both Governments the agents representing them met in conference at the Department of State and subsequently concluded a protocol submitting this long-pending controversy to the arbitral judgment of the Chief Justice of the United States, who consented to act in this capacity. A boundary commission, according to the international agreement, has now been appointed, and it is expected that the arguments will shortly proceed and that this long-standing dispute will be honorably and satisfactorily terminated.

Again, a few months ago it appeared that the Dominican Republic and Haiti were about to enter upon hostilities because of complications growing out of an acrimonious boundary dispute which the efforts of many years had failed to solve. The Government of the United States, by a friendly interposition of good offices, succeeded in prevailing upon the parties to place their reliance upon some form of pacific settlement. Accordingly, on the friendly suggestion of this Government, the two Governments empowered commissioners to meet at Washington in conference at the State Department in order to arrange the terms of submission to arbitration of the boundary controversy.

Chamizal Arbitration Not Satisfactory

Our arbitration of the Chamizal boundary question with Mexico was unfortunately abortive, but with the earnest efforts on the part of both Governments which its importance commands, it is felt that an early practical adjustment should prove possible.

Latin America

Venezuela

During the past year the Republic of Venezuela celebrated the one hundredth anniversary of its independence. The United States sent, in honor of this event, a special embassy to Caracas, where the cordial reception and generous hospitality shown it were most gratifying as a further proof of the good relations and friendship existing between that country and the United States.

Mexico

The recent political events in Mexico received attention from this Government because of the exceedingly delicate and difficult situation created along our southern border and the necessity for taking measures properly to safeguard American interests. The Government of the United States, in its desire to secure a proper observance and enforcement of the so-called neutrality statutes of the Federal Government, issued directions to the appropriate officers to exercise a diligent and vigilant regard for the requirements of such rules and laws. Although a condition of actual armed conflict existed, there was no official recognition of belligerency involving the technical neutrality obligations of international law.

On the sixth of March last, in the absence of the Secretary of State, I had a personal interview with Mr. Wilson, the ambassador of the United States to Mexico, in which he reported to me that the conditions in Mexico were much more critical than the press dispatches disclosed; that President Diaz was on a volcano of popular uprising; that the small outbreaks which had occurred were only symptomatic of the whole condition; that a very large percent of the people were in sympathy with the insurrection; that a general explosion was probable at any time, in which case he feared that the 40,000 or more American residents in Mexico might be assailed, and that the very large American investments might be injured or destroyed.

After a conference with the Secretary of War and the Secretary of the Navy, I thought it wise to assemble an Army division of full strength at San Antonio, Tex., a brigade of three regiments at Galveston, a brigade of Infantry in the Los Angeles district of southern California, together with a squadron of battleships and cruisers and transports at Galveston, and a small squadron of ships at San Diego. At the same time, through our representative at the City of Mexico, I expressed to President Diaz the hope that no apprehensions might result from unfounded conjectures as to these military maneuvers, and assured him that they had no significance which should cause concern to his Government.

The mobilization was effected with great promptness, and on the fifteenth of March, through the Secretary of War and the Secretary of the Navy, in a letter addressed to the Chief of Staff, I issued the following instructions:

It seems my duty as Commander in Chief to place troops in sufficient number where, if Congress shall direct that they enter Mexico to save American lives and property, an effective movement may be promptly made. Meantime, the movement of the troops to Texas and elsewhere near the boundary, accompanied with sincere assurances of the utmost goodwill toward the present Mexican Government and with larger and more frequent patrols along the border to prevent insurrectionary expeditions from American soil, will hold up the hands of the existing Government and will have a healthy moral effect to prevent attacks upon Americans and their property in any subsequent general internecine strife. Again, the sudden mobilization of a division of troops has been a great test of our Army and full of useful instruction, while the maneuvers that are thus made possible can occupy the troops and their officers to great advantage.

The assumption by the press that I contemplate intervention on Mexican soil to protect American lives or property is of course gratuitous, because I seriously doubt whether I have such authority under any circumstances, and if I had I would not exercise it without express congressional approval. Indeed, as you know, I have already declined, without Mexican consent, to order a troop of Cavalry to protect the breakwater we are constructing just across the border in Mexico at the mouth of the Colorado River to save the Imperial Valley, although the *insurrectos* had scattered the Mexican troops and were taking our horses and supplies and frightening our workmen away. My determined purpose, however, is to be in a position so that when danger to American lives and property in Mexico threatens and the existing Government is rendered helpless by the insurrection, I can promptly execute congressional orders to protect them, with effect.

Meantime, I send you this letter, through the Secretary, to call your attention to some things in connection with the presence of the division in the Southwest which have doubtless occurred to you, but which I wish to emphasize.

In the first place, I want to make the mobilization a first-class training for the Army, and I wish you would give your time and that of the War College to advising and carrying out maneuvers of a useful character, and plan to continue to do this during the next three months. By that time we may expect that either Ambassador Wilson's fears will have been realized and chaos and its consequences have ensued, or that the present Government of Mexico will have so readjusted matters as to secure tranquility—a result devoutly to be wished. The troops can then be returned to their posts. I understood from you in Washington that Gen. Aleshire said that you could probably meet all the additional expense of this whole movement out of the present appropriations if the troops continue in Texas for three months. I sincerely hope this is so. I observe from the newspapers that you have no blank cartridges, but I presume that this is an error, or that it will be easy to procure those for use as soon as your maneuvers begin.

Second. Texas is a State ordinarily peaceful, but you can not put 20,000 troops into it without running some risk of a collision between the people of that State, and especially the Mexicans who live in Texas near the border and who sympathize with the *insurrectos,* and the Federal soldiers. For that reason I beg you to be as careful as you can to prevent friction of any kind. We were able in Cuba, with the army of pacification there of something more than 5,000 troops, to maintain them for a year without any trouble, and I hope you can do the same thing in Texas. Please give your attention to this, and advise all the officers in command of the necessity for very great circumspection in this regard.

Third. One of the great troubles in the concentration of troops is the danger of disease, and I suppose that you have adopted the most modern methods for preventing and, if necessary, for stamping out epidemics. That is so much a part of a campaign that it hardly seems necessary for me to call attention to it.

Finally, I wish you to examine the question of the patrol of the border and put as many troops on that work as is practicable, and more than are now engaged in it, in order to prevent the use of our borderland for the carrying out of the insurrection. I have given assurances to the Mexican ambassador on this point.

I sincerely hope that this experience will always be remembered by the Army and Navy as a useful means of education, and I should be greatly disappointed if it resulted in any injury or disaster to our forces from any cause. I have taken a good deal of responsibility in ordering this mobilization, but I am ready to answer for it if only you and those under you use the utmost care to avoid the difficulties which I have pointed out.

You may have a copy of this letter made and left with Gen. Carter and such other generals in command as you may think wise and necessary to guide them in their course, but to be regarded as confidential.

I am more than happy to here record the fact that all apprehensions as to the effect of the presence of so large a military force in Texas proved groundless; no disturbances occurred; the conduct of the troops was exemplary and the public reception and treatment of them was all that could have been desired, and this notwithstanding the presence of a large number of Mexican refugees in the border territory.

From time to time communications were received from Ambassador Wilson, who had returned to Mexico, confirming the view that the massing of American troops in the neighborhood had had good effect. By dispatch of April 3, 1911, the ambassador said:

> The continuing gravity of the situation here and the chaos that would ensue should the constitutional authorities be eventually overthrown, thus greatly increasing the danger to which American lives and property are already subject, confirm the wisdom of the President in taking those military precautions which, making every allowance for the dignity and the sovereignty of a friendly state, are due to our nationals abroad.
>
> Charged as I am with the responsibility of safeguarding these lives and property, I am bound to say to the department that our military dispositions on the frontier have produced an effective impression on the Mexican mind and may, at any moment, prove to be the only guaranties for the safety of our nationals and their property. If it should eventuate that conditions here require more active measures by the President and Congress, sporadic attacks might be made upon the lives and property of our nationals, but the ultimate result would be order and adequate protection.

The insurrection continued and resulted in engagements between the regular Mexican troops and the insurgents, and this along the border, so that in several instances bullets from the contending forces struck American citizens engaged in their lawful occupations on American soil.

Proper protests were made against these invasions of American rights to the Mexican authorities. On April 17, 1911, I received the following telegram from the governor of Arizona:

> As a result of today's fighting across the international line, but within gunshot range of the heart of Douglas, five Americans wounded on this

side of the line. Everything points to repetition of these casualties on tomorrow, and while the Federals seem disposed to keep their agreement not to fire into Douglas, the position of the insurrectionists is such that when fighting occurs on the east and southeast of the intrenchments people living in Douglas are put in danger of their lives. In my judgment radical measures are needed to protect our innocent people, and if anything can be done to stop the fighting at Agua Prieta the situation calls for such action. It is impossible to safeguard the people of Douglas unless the town be vacated. Can anything be done to relieve situation, now acute?

After a conference with the Secretary of State, the following telegram was sent to Governor Sloan, on April 18, 1911, and made public:

Your dispatch, received. Have made urgent demand upon Mexican Government to issue instructions to prevent firing across border by Mexican federal troops, and am waiting reply. Meantime I have sent direct warning to the Mexican and insurgent forces near Douglas. I infer from your dispatch that both parties attempt to heed the warning, but that in the strain and exigency of the contest wild bullets still find their way into Douglas. The situation might justify me in ordering our troops to cross the border and attempt to stop the fighting, or to fire upon both combatants from the American side. But if I take this step, I must face the possibility of resistance and greater bloodshed, and also the danger of having our motives misconstrued and misrepresented, and of thus inflaming Mexican popular indignation against many thousand Americans now in Mexico and jeopardizing their lives and property. The pressure for general intervention under such conditions it might not be practicable to resist. It is impossible to foresee or reckon the consequences of such a course, and we must use the greatest self-restraint to avoid it. Pending my urgent representation to the Mexican Government, I can not therefore order the troops at Douglas to cross the border, but I must ask you and the local authorities, in case the same danger recurs, to direct the people of Douglas to place themselves where bullets can not reach them and thus avoid casualty. I am loath to endanger Americans in Mexico, where they are necessarily exposed, by taking a radical step to prevent injury to Americans on our side of the border who can avoid it by a temporary inconvenience.

I am glad to say that no further invasion of American rights of any substantial character occurred.

The presence of a large military and naval force available for prompt action, near the Mexican border, proved to be most fortunate under the somewhat trying conditions presented by this invasion of American rights. Had no movement theretofore taken place, and because of these events it had been necessary then to bring about the mobilization, it must have had sinister significance. On the other hand, the presence of the troops before and at the time of the unfortunate killing and wounding of American citizens at Douglas, made clear that the restraint exercised by our Government in regard to this occurrence was not due to lack of force or power to deal with it promptly and aggressively, but was due to a real desire to use every means possible to avoid direct intervention in the affairs of our neighbor, whose friendship we valued and were most anxious to retain.

The policy and action of this Government were based upon an earnest friendliness for the Mexican people as a whole, and it is a matter of gratification to note that this attitude of strict impartiality as to all factions in Mexico and of sincere friendship for the neighboring nation, without regard for party allegiance, has been generally recognized and has resulted in an even closer and more sympathetic understanding between the two Republics and a warmer regard one for the other. Action to suppress violence and restore tranquility throughout the Mexican Republic was of peculiar interest to this Government, in that it concerned the safeguarding of American life and property in that country. The Government of the United States had occasion to accord permission for the passage of a body of Mexican rurales through Douglas, Arizona, to Tia Juana, Mexico, for the suppression of general lawlessness which had for some time existed in the region of northern Lower California. On May 25, 1911, President Diaz resigned, Señor de la Barra was chosen provisional President. Elections for President and Vice President were thereafter held throughout the Republic, and Señor Francisco I. Madero was formally declared elected on October 15 to the chief magistracy. On November 6 President Madero entered upon the duties of his office.

Since the inauguration of President Madero a plot has been unearthed against the present Government, to begin a new insurrection. Pursuing the same consistent policy which this administration has adopted from the beginning, it directed an investigation into the conspiracy charged, and this investigation has resulted in the indictment of Gen. Bernardo Reyes and others and the seizure of a number of officers and men and horses and accoutrements assembled upon the soil of Texas for the purpose of invading Mexico. Similar proceedings had been taken during the insurrection against the Diaz Government resulting in the indictments and prosecution of persons found to be engaged in violating the neutrality laws of the United States in aid of that uprising.

The record of this Government in respect of the recognition of constituted authority in Mexico therefore is clear.

Central America

Honduras and Nicaragua Treaties Proposed

As to the situation in Central America, I have taken occasion in the past to emphasize most strongly the importance that should be attributed to the consummation of the conventions between the Republics of Nicaragua and of Honduras and this country, and I again earnestly recommend that the necessary advice and consent of the Senate be accorded to these treaties, which will make it possible for these Central American Republics to enter upon an era of genuine economic national development. The Government of Nicaragua which has already taken favorable action on the convention, has found it necessary, pending the exchange of final ratifications, to enter into negotiations with American bankers for the purpose of securing a temporary loan to relieve the present financial tension. In connection with this temporary loan and in the hope of consummating, through the ultimate operation of the convention, a complete and lasting economic regeneration, the Government of Nicaragua has also decided to engage an American citizen as collector general of customs. The claims commission on which the services of two American citizens have been sought, and the work of the American financial adviser should accomplish a lasting good of inestimable benefit to the prosperity, commerce, and peace of the Republic. In considering the ratification of the conventions with Nicaragua and Honduras, there rests with the United States the heavy responsibility of the fact that their rejection here might destroy the progress made and consign the Republics concerned to still deeper submergence in bankruptcy, revolution, and national jeopardy.

Panama

Our relations with the Republic of Panama, peculiarly important, due to mutual obligations and the vast interests created by the canal, have continued in the usual friendly manner, and we have been glad to make appropriate expression of our attitude of sympathetic interest in the endeavors of our neighbor in undertaking the development of the rich resources of the country. With reference to the internal political affairs of the Republic, our obvious concern is in the maintenance of public peace and constitutional order, and the fostering of the general interests created by the actual relations of the two countries, without the manifestation of any preference for the success of either of the political parties.

The Pan American Union

The Pan American Union, formerly known as the Bureau of American Republics, maintained by the joint contributions of all the American nations, has during the past year enlarged its practical work as an international organization, and continues to prove its usefulness as an agency for the mutual development of commerce, better acquaintance, and closer intercourse between the United States and her sister American republics.

The Far East

The Chinese Loans

The past year has been marked in our relations with China by the conclusion of two important international loans, one for the construction of the Hukuang railways, the other for carrying out of the currency reform to which China was pledged by treaties with the United States, Great Britain, and Japan, of which mention was made in my last annual message.

It will be remembered that early in 1909 an agreement was consummated among British, French, and German financial groups whereby they proposed to lend the Chinese Government funds for the construction of railways in the Provinces of Hunan and Hupch, reserving for their nationals the privilege of engineering the construction of the lines and of furnishing the materials required for the work. After negotiations with the Governments and groups concerned an agreement was reached whereby

American, British, French, and German nationals should participate upon equal terms in this important and useful undertaking. Thereupon the financial groups, supported by their respective Governments, began negotiations with the Chinese Government which terminated in a loan to China of $30,000,000, with the privilege of increasing the amount to $50,000,000. The cooperative construction of these trunk lines should be of immense advantage, materially and otherwise, to China and should greatly facilitate the development of the bountiful resources of the Empire. On the other hand, a large portion of these funds is to be expended for materials, American products having equal preference with those of the other three lending nations, and as the contract provides for branches and extensions subsequently to be built on the same terms the opportunities for American materials will reach considerable proportions.

Knowing the interest of the United States in the reform of Chinese currency, the Chinese Government, in the autumn of 1910, sought the assistance of the American Government to procure funds with which to accomplish that all-important reform. In the course of the subsequent negotiations there was combined with the proposed currency loan one for certain industrial developments in Manchuria, the two loans aggregating the sum of $50,000,000. While this was originally to be solely an American enterprise, the American Government, consistently with its desire to secure a sympathetic and practical cooperation of the great powers toward maintaining the principle of equality of opportunity and the administrative integrity of China, urged the Chinese Government to admit to participation in the currency loan the associates of the American group in the Hukuang loan. While of immense importance in itself, the reform contemplated in making this loan is but preliminary to other and more comprehensive fiscal reforms which will be of incalculable benefit to China and foreign interests alike, since they will strengthen the Chinese Empire and promote the rapid development of international trade.

Neutral Financial Adviser

When these negotiations were begun, it was understood that a financial adviser was to be employed by China in connection with the reform, and in order that absolute equality in all respects among the lending nations might be scrupulously observed, the American Government proposed the nomination of a neutral adviser, which was agreed to by China and the other Governments concerned. On September 28, 1911, Dr. Vissering, president of the Dutch Java Bank and a financier of wide experience in the Orient, was recommended to the Chinese Government for the post of monetary adviser.

Especially important at the present, when the ancient Chinese Empire is shaken by civil war incidental to its awakening to the many influences and activities of modernization, are the cooperative policy of good understanding which has been fostered by the international projects referred to above and the general sympathy of view among all the Powers interested in the Far East. While safeguarding the interests of our nationals, this Government is using its best efforts in continuance of its traditional policy of sympathy and friendship toward the Chinese Empire and its people, with the confident hope for their economic and administrative development, and with the constant disposition to contribute to their welfare in all proper ways consistent with an attitude of strict impartiality as between contending factions.

For the first time in the history of the two countries, a Chinese cruiser, the *Haichi,* under the command of Admiral Ching, recently visited New York, where the officers and men were given a cordial welcome.

New Japanese Treaty

The treaty of commerce and navigation between the United States and Japan, signed in 1894, would by a strict interpretation of its provisions have terminated on July 17, 1912. Japan's general treaties with the other powers, however, terminated in 1911, and the Japanese Government expressed an earnest desire to conduct the negotiations for a new treaty with the United States simultaneously with its negotiations with the other powers. There were a number of important questions involved in the treaty, including the immigration of laborers, revision of the customs tariff, and the right of Americans to hold real estate in Japan. The United States consented to waive all technicalities and to enter at once upon negotiations for a new treaty on the understanding that there should be a continuance throughout the life of the treaty of the same effective measures for the restriction of immigration of laborers to American territory which had been in operation with entire satisfaction to both Governments since 1908. The Japanese

Government accepted this basis of negotiation, and a new treaty was quickly concluded, resulting in a highly satisfactory settlement of the other questions referred to.

A satisfactory adjustment has also been effected of the questions growing out of the annexation of Korea by Japan.

The recent visit of Admiral Count Togo to the United States as the Nation's guest afforded a welcome opportunity to demonstrate the friendly feeling so happily existing between the two countries.

Siam

There has been a change of sovereigns in Siam and the American minister at Bangkok was accredited in a special capacity to represent the United States at the coronation ceremony of the new King.

Europe and the Near East

In Europe and the Near East, during the past twelve-month, there has been at times considerable political unrest. The Moroccan question, which for some months was the cause of great anxiety, happily appears to have reached a stage at which it need no longer be regarded with concern. The Ottoman Empire was occupied for a period by strife in Albania and is now at war with Italy. In Greece and the Balkan countries the disquieting potentialities of this situation have been more or less felt. Persia has been the scene of a long internal struggle. These conditions have been the cause of uneasiness in European diplomacy, but thus far without direct political concern to the United States.

In the war which unhappily exists between Italy and Turkey this Government has no direct political interest, and I took occasion at the suitable time to issue a proclamation of neutrality in that conflict. At the same time all necessary steps have been taken to safeguard the personal interests of American citizens and organizations in so far as affected by the war.

Commerce with the Near East

In spite of the attendant economic uncertainties and detriments to commerce, the United States has gained markedly in its commercial standing with certain of the nations of the Near East. Turkey, especially, is beginning to come into closer relations with the United States through the new interest of American manufacturers and exporters in the possibilities of those regions, and it is hoped that foundations are being laid for a large and mutually beneficial exchange of commodities between the two countries. This new interest of Turkey in American goods is indicated by the fact that a party of prominent merchants from a large city in Turkey recently visited the United States to study conditions of manufacture and export here, and to get into personal touch with American merchants, with a view to cooperating more intelligently in opening up the markets of Turkey and the adjacent countries to our manufactures. Another indication of this new interest of America in the commerce of the Near East is the recent visit of a large party of American merchants and manufacturers to central and eastern Europe, where they were entertained by prominent officials and organizations of the large cities, and new bonds of friendship and understanding were established which can not but lead to closer and greater commercial interchange.

Coronation of King George V

The 22d of June of the present year marked the coronation of His Britannic Majesty King George V. In honor of this auspicious occasion I sent a special embassy to London. The courteous and cordial welcome extended to this Government's representatives by His Majesty and the people of Great Britain has further emphasized the strong bonds of friendship happily existing between the two nations.

Settlement of Long-Standing Differences with Great Britain

As the result of a determined effort on the part of both Great Britain and the United States to settle all of their outstanding differences a number of treaties have been entered into between the two countries in recent years, by which nearly all of the unsettled questions between them of any importance have either been adjusted by agreement or arrangements made for their settlement by arbitration. A number of the unsettled questions referred to consist of pecuniary claims presented by each country against the other, and in order that as many of these claims as possible should be settled by arbitration a special agreement for that purpose was entered into between the two Governments on the eighteenth day of August, 1910, in accordance with Article II of the general arbitration treaty with Great Britain of April 4, 1908. Pursuant to the provisions of this special agreement a schedule of claims has already been agreed upon, and the special agreement, together with this schedule, received the approval of the Senate when submitted to it for that purpose at the last session of Congress. Negotiations between the two Governments for the preparation of an additional schedule of claims are already well advanced, and it is my intention to submit such schedule as soon as it is agreed upon to the Senate for its approval, in order that the arbitration proceedings may be undertaken at an early date. In this connection the attention of Congress is particularly called to the necessity for an appropriation to cover the expense incurred in submitting these claims to arbitration.

Presentation to Germany of Replica of Von Steuben Statue

In pursuance of the act of Congress, approved June 23, 1910, the Secretary of State and the Joint Committee on the Library entered into a contract with the sculptor, Albert Jaegers, for the execution of a bronze replica of the statue of Gen. von Steuben erected in Washington, for presentation to His Majesty the German Emperor and the German nation in recognition of the gift of the statue of Frederick the Great made by the Emperor to the people of the United States.

The presentation was made on September 2 last by representatives whom I commissioned as the special mission of this Government for the purpose.

The German Emperor has conveyed to me by telegraph, on his own behalf and that of the German people, an expression of appreciative thanks for this action of Congress.

Russia

By direction of the State Department, our ambassador to Russia has recently been having a series of conferences with the minister of foreign affairs of Russia, with a view to securing a clearer understanding and construction of the treaty of 1832 between Russia and the United States and the modification of any existing Russian regulations which may be found to interfere in any way with the full recognition of the rights of

American citizens under this treaty. I believe that the Government of Russia is addressing itself seriously to the need of changing the present practice under the treaty and that sufficient progress has been made to warrant the continuance of these conferences in the hope that there may soon be removed any justification of the complaints of treaty violation now prevalent in this country.

I expect that immediately after the Christmas recess I shall be able to make a further communication to Congress on this subject.

Liberia

Negotiations for the amelioration of conditions found to exist in Liberia by the American commission, undertaken through the Department of State, have been concluded and it is only necessary for certain formalities to be arranged in securing the loan which it is hoped will place that republic on a practical financial and economic footing.

Recognition of Portuguese Republic

The National Constituent Assembly, regularly elected by the vote of the Portuguese people, having on June 19 last unanimously proclaimed a republican form of government, the official recognition of the Government of the United States was given to the new Republic in the afternoon of the same day.

Spitzbergen Islands

Negotiations for the betterment of conditions existing in the Spitzbergen Islands and the adjustment of conflicting claims of American citizens and Norwegian subjects to lands in that archipelago are still in progress.

International Conventions and Conferences

International Prize Court

The supplementary protocol to The Hague convention for the establishment of an international prize court, mentioned in my last annual message, embodying stipulations providing for an alternative procedure which would remove the constitutional objection to that part of The Hague convention which provides that there may be an appeal to the proposed court from the decisions of national courts, has received the signature of the governments parties to the original convention and has been ratified by the Government of the United States, together with the prize court convention.

The deposit of the ratifications with the Government of the Netherlands awaits action by the powers on the declaration, signed at London on February 26, 1909, of the rules of international law to be recognized within the meaning of article 7 of The Hague convention for the establishment of an International Prize Court.

Fur-Seal Treaty

The fur-seal controversy, which for nearly twenty-five years has been the source of serious friction between the United States and the powers bordering upon the north Pacific Ocean, whose subjects have been permitted to engage in pelagic sealing against the fur-seal herds having their breeding grounds within the jurisdiction of the United States, has at last been satisfactorily adjusted by the conclusion of the north Pacific sealing convention entered into between the United States, Great Britain, Japan, and Russia on the seventh of July last. This convention is a conservation measure of very great importance, and if it is carried out in the spirit of reciprocal concession and advantage upon which it is based, there is every reason to believe that not only will it result in preserving the fur-seal herds of the north Pacific Ocean and restoring them to their former value for the purposes of commerce, but also that it will afford a permanently satisfactory settlement of a question the only other solution of which seemed to be the total destruction of the fur seals. In another aspect, also, this convention is of importance in that it furnishes an illustration of the feasibility of securing a general international game law for the protection of other mammals of the sea, the preservation of which is of importance to all the nations of the world.

Legislation Necessary

The attention of Congress is especially called to the necessity for legislation on the part of the United States for the purpose of fulfilling the obligations assumed under this convention, to which the Senate gave its advice and consent on the twenty-fourth day of July last.

Protection of Industrial Property Union

The conference of the International Union for the Protection of Industrial Property, which, under the authority of Congress, convened at Washington on May 16, 1911, closed its labors on June 2, 1911, by the signature of three acts, as follows:

(1) A convention revising the Paris convention of March 20, 1883, for the protection of industrial property, as modified by the additional act signed at Brussels on December 14, 1900;

(2) An arrangement to replace the arrangement signed at Madrid on April 14, 1891, for the international registration of trademarks, and the additional act with regard thereto signed at Brussels on December 14, 1900; and

(3) An arrangement to replace the arrangement signed at Madrid on April 14, 1891, relating to the repression of false indication of production of merchandise.

The United States is a signatory of the first convention only, and this will be promptly submitted to the Senate.

International Opium Commission

In a special message transmitted to the Congress on the eleventh of January, 1911, in which I concurred in the recommendations made by the Secretary of State in regard to certain needful legislation for the control of our interstate and foreign traffic in opium and other menacing drugs, I quoted from my annual message of December 7, 1909, in which I announced that the results of the International Opium Commission held at Shanghai in February, 1909, at the invitation of the United States, had been laid before this Government; that the report of that commission showed that China was making remarkable progress and admirable efforts toward the eradication of the opium evil; that the interested governments had not permitted their commercial interests to prevent their cooperation in this reform; and, as a result of collateral investigations of the opium question in this country, I recommended that the manufacture, sale, and use of opium in the United States should be more rigorously controlled by legislation.

Prior to that time and in continuation of the policy of this Government to secure the cooperation of the interested nations, the United States proposed an international opium conference with full powers for the purpose of clothing with the force of international law the resolutions adopted by the above-mentioned commission, together with their essential corollaries. The other powers concerned cordially responded to the proposal of this Government, and, I am glad to be able to announce, representatives of all the powers assembled in conference at The Hague on the first of this month.

Since the passage of the opium-exclusion act, more than twenty States have been animated to modify their pharmacy laws and bring them in accord with the spirit of that act, thus stamping out, to a measure, the intrastate traffic in opium and other habit-forming drugs. But, although I have urged on the Congress the passage of certain measures for Federal control of the interstate and foreign traffic in these drugs, no action has yet been taken. In view of the fact that there is now sitting at The Hague so important a conference, which has under review the municipal laws of the different nations for the mitigation of their opium and other allied evils, a conference which will certainly deal with the international aspects of these evils, it seems to me most essential that the Congress should take immediate action on the anti-narcotic legislation to which I have already called attention by a special message.

Buenos Aires Conventions

The four important conventions signed at the Fourth Pan American Conference at Buenos Aires, providing for the regulation of trademarks, patents, and copyrights, and for the arbitration of pecuniary claims, have, with the advice and consent of the Senate, been ratified on the part of the United States and the ratifications have been deposited with the Government of the Argentine Republic in accordance with the requirements of the conventions. I am not advised that similar action has been taken by any other of the signatory governments.

International Arrangement to Suppress Obscene Publications

One of the notable advances in international morality accomplished in recent years was an arrangement entered into on April thirteenth of the present year between the United States and other powers for the repression of the circulation of obscene publications.

Foreign Trade Relations of the United States

In my last annual message I referred to the tariff negotiations of the Department of State with foreign countries in connection with the application, by a series of proclamations, of the minimum tariff of the United States to importations from the several countries, and I stated that, in its general operation, section 2 of the new tariff law had proved a guaranty of continued commercial peace, although there were, unfortunately, instances where foreign governments dealt arbitrarily with American interests within their jurisdiction in a manner injurious and inequitable. During the past year some instances of discriminatory treatment have been removed, but I regret to say that there remain a few cases of differential treatment adverse to the commerce of the United States. While none of these instances now appears to amount to undue discrimination in the sense of section 2 of the tariff law of August 5, 1909, they are all exceptions to that complete degree of equality of tariff treatment that the Department of State has consistently sought to obtain for American commerce abroad. While the double tariff feature of the tariff law of 1909 has been amply justified by the results achieved in removing former and preventing new, undue discriminations against American commerce, it is believed that the time has come for the amendment of this feature of the law in such way as to provide a graduated means of meeting varying degrees of discriminatory treatment of American commerce in foreign countries as well as to protect the financial interests abroad of American citizens against arbitrary and injurious treatment on the part of foreign governments through either legislative or administrative measures. It would seem desirable that the maximum tariff of the United States should embrace within its purview the free list, which is not the case at the present time, in order that it might have reasonable significance to the governments of those countries from which the importations into the United States are confined virtually to articles on the free list.

Record of Highest Amount of Foreign Trade

The fiscal year ended June 30, 1911, shows great progress in the development of American trade. It was noteworthy as marking the highest record of exports of American products to foreign countries, the valuation being in excess of $2,000,000,000. These exports showed a gain over the preceding year of more than $300,000,000.

Facilities for Foreign Trade Furnished by Joint Action of Department of State and of Commerce and Labor

There is widespread appreciation expressed by the business interests of the country as regards the practical value of the facilities now offered by the Department of State and the Department of Commerce and Labor for the furtherance of American commerce. Conferences with their officers at Washington who have an expert knowledge of trade conditions in foreign countries and with consular officers and commercial agents of the Department of Commerce and Labor who, while on leave of absence, visit the principal industrial centers of the United States, have been found of great value. These trade conferences are regarded as a particularly promising method of governmental aid in foreign trade promotion. The Department of Commerce and Labor has arranged to give publicity to the expected arrival and the itinerary of consular officers and commercial agents while on leave in the United States, in order that trade organizations may arrange for conferences with them.

As I have indicated, it is increasingly clear that to obtain and maintain that equity and substantial equality of treatment essential to the flourishing foreign trade, which becomes year by year more important to the industrial and commercial welfare of the United States, we should have a flexibility of tariff sufficient for the give and take of negotiation by the Department of State on behalf of our commerce and industry.

Crying Need for American Merchant Marine

I need hardly reiterate the conviction that there should speedily be built up an American merchant marine. This is necessary to assure favorable transportation facilities to our great ocean-borne commerce as well as to supplement the Navy with an adequate reserve of ships and men. It would have the economic advantage of keeping at home part of the vast sums now paid foreign shipping for carrying American goods. All the great commercial nations pay heavy subsidies to their merchant marine, so that it is obvious that without some wise aid from the Congress the United States must lag behind in the matter of merchant marine in its present anomalous position.

Extension of American Banking to Foreign Countries

Legislation to facilitate the extension of American banks to foreign countries is another matter in which our foreign trade needs assistance.

Chambers of Foreign Commerce Suggested

The interests of our foreign commerce are nonpartisan, and as a factor in prosperity are as broad as the land. In the dissemination of useful information and in the coordination of effort certain unofficial associations have done good work toward the promotion of foreign commerce. It is cause for regret, however, that the great number of such associations and the comparative lack of cooperation between them fails to secure an efficiency commensurate with the public interest. Through the agency of the Department of Commerce and Labor, and in some cases directly, the Department of State transmits to reputable business interests information of commercial opportunities, supplementing the regular published consular reports. Some central organization in touch with associations and chambers of commerce throughout the country and able to keep purely American interests in closer touch with different phases of commercial affairs would, I believe, be of great value. Such organization might be managed by a committee composed of a small number of those now actively carrying on the work of some of the larger associations, and there might be added to the committee, as members ex officio, one or two officials of the Department of State and one or two officials from the Department of Commerce and Labor and representatives of the appropriate committees of Congress. The authority and success of such an organization would evidently be enhanced if the Congress should see fit to prescribe its scope and organization through legislation which would give to it some such official standing as that, for example, of the National Red Cross.

With these factors and the continuance of the foreign-service establishment (departmental, diplomatic, and consular) upon the high plane where it has been placed by the recent reorganization this Government would be abreast of the times in fostering the interests of its foreign trade, and the rest must be left to the energy and enterprise of our business men.

Improvement of the Foreign Service

The entire foreign-service organization is being improved and developed with especial regard to the requirements of the commercial interests of the country. The rapid growth of our foreign trade makes it of the utmost importance that governmental agencies through which that trade is to be aided and protected should possess a high degree of efficiency. Not only should the foreign representatives be maintained upon a generous scale in so far as salaries and establishments are concerned, but the selection and advancement of officers should be definitely and permanently regulated by law so that the service shall not fail to attract men of high character and ability. The experience of the past few years with a partial application of civil-service rules to the Diplomatic and Consular Service leaves no doubt in my mind of the wisdom of a wider and more permanent extension of those principles to both branches of the foreign service. The men selected for appointment by means of the existing executive regulations have been of a far higher average of intelligence and ability than the men appointed before the regulations were promulgated. Moreover, the feeling that under the existing rules there is reasonable hope for permanence of tenure during good behavior and for promotion for meritorious service has served to bring about a zealous activity in the interests of the country, which never before existed or could exist. It is my earnest conviction that the enactment into law of the general principles of the existing regulations can not fail to effect further improvement in both branches of the foreign service by providing greater inducement for young men of character and ability to seek a career abroad in the service of the Government, and an incentive to those already in the service to put forth greater efforts to attain the high standards which the successful conduct of our international relations and commerce requires.

I therefore again commend to the favorable action of the Congress the enactment of a law applying to the diplomatic and consular service the principles embodied in section 1753 of the Revised Statutes of the United States, in the civil-service act of January 16, 1883, and the Executive orders of June 27, 1906, and of November 26, 1909. In its consideration of this important subject I desire to recall to the attention of the Congress the very favorable report made on the Lowden bill for the improvement of the foreign service by the Foreign Affairs Committee of the House of Representatives. Available statistics show the strictness with which the merit system has been applied to the foreign service during recent years and the absolute nonpartisan selection of consuls and diplomatic-service secretaries who, indeed, far from being selected with any view to political consideration, have actually been chosen to a disproportionate extent from States which would have been unrepresented in the foreign service under the system which it is to be hoped is now permanently obsolete. Some legislation for the perpetuation of the present system of examinations and promotions upon merit and efficiency would be of greatest value to our commercial and international interests.

Part III
[Transmitting report of the Tariff Board on Schedule K]
The White House, December 20, 1911

To the Senate and House of Representatives:

In my annual message to Congress, December, 1909, I stated that under section 2 of the act of August 5, 1909, I had appointed a Tariff Board of three members to cooperate with the State Department in the administration of the maximum and minimum clause of that act, to make a glossary or encyclopedia of the existing tariff so as to render its terms intelligible to the ordinary reader, and then to investigate industrial conditions and costs of production at home and abroad with a view to determining to what extent existing tariff rates actually exemplify the protective principle, viz., that duties should be made adequate, and only adequate, to equalize the difference in cost of production at home and abroad.

I further stated that I believed these investigations would be of great value as a basis for accurate legislation, and that I should from time to time recommend to Congress the revision of certain schedules in accordance with the findings of the Board.

In the last session of the Sixty-first Congress a bill creating a permanent Tariff Board of five members, of whom not more than three should be of the same political party, passed each House, but failed of enactment because of slight differences on which agreement was not reached before adjournment. An appropriation act provided that the permanent Tariff Board, if created by statute, should report to Congress on Schedule K in December, 1911.

Therefore, to carry out so far as lay within my power the purposes of this bill for a permanent Tariff Board, I appointed in March, 1911, a board of five, adding two members of such party affiliation as would have fulfilled the statutory requirement, and directed them to make a report to me on Schedule K of the tariff act in December of this year.

In my message of August 17, 1911, accompanying the veto of the wool bill, I said that, in my judgment, Schedule K should be revised and the rates reduced. My veto was based on the ground that, since the Tariff Board would make, in December, a detailed report on wool and wool manufactures, with special reference to the relation of the existing rates of duties to relative costs here and abroad, public policy and a fair regard to the interests of the producers and the manufacturers on the one hand and of the consumers on the other demanded that legislation should not be hastily enacted in the absence of such information; that I was not myself possessed at that time of adequate knowledge of the facts to determine whether or not the proposed act was in accord with my pledge to support a fair and reasonable protective policy; that such legislation might prove only temporary and inflict upon a great industry the evils of continued uncertainty.

I now herewith submit a report of the Tariff Board on Schedule K. The board is unanimous in its findings. On the basis of these findings I now recommend that the Congress proceed to a consideration of this schedule with a view to its revision and a general reduction of its rates.

The report shows that the present method of assessing the duty on raw wool—this is, by a specific rate on the grease pound (i. e., unscoured)—operates to exclude wools of high shrinkage in scouring but fine quality from the American market and thereby lessens the range of wools available to the domestic manufacturer; that the duty on scoured wool of 33 cents per pound is prohibitory and operates to exclude the importation of clean, low-priced foreign wools of inferior grades, which are nevertheless valuable material for manufacturing, and which can not be imported in the grease because of their heavy shrinkage. Such wools, if imported, might be used to displace the cheap substitutes now in use.

To make the preceding paragraph a little plainer, take the instance of a hundred pounds of first-class wool imported under the present duty, which is 11 cents a pound. That would make the duty on the hundred pounds $11. The merchantable part of the wool thus imported is the weight of the wool of this hundred pounds after scouring. If the wool shrinks 80 percent, as some wools do, then the duty in such a case would amount to $11 on 20 pounds of scoured wool. This, of course, would be prohibitory. If the wool shrinks only 50 percent, it would be $11 on 50 pounds of wool, and this is near to the average of the great bulk of wools that are imported from Australia, which is the principal source of our imported wool.

These discriminations could be overcome by assessing a duty in *ad valorem* terms, but this method is open to the objection, first, that it increases administrative difficulties and tends to decrease revenue through undervaluation; and, second, that as prices advance, the *ad valorem* rate increases the duty per pound at the time when the consumer most needs relief and the producer can best stand competition; while if prices decline the duty is decreased at the time when the consumer is least burdened by the price and the producer most needs protection.

Another method of meeting the difficulty of taxing the grease pound is to assess a specific duty on grease wool in terms of its scoured content. This obviates the chief evil of the present system, namely, the discrimination due to different shrinkages, and thereby tends greatly to equalize the duty. The board reports that this method is feasible in practice and could be administered without great expense. The scoured content of the wool is the basis on which users of wool make their calculations, and a duty of this kind would fit the usages of the trade. One effect of this method of assessment would be that, regardless of the rate of duty, there would be an increase in the supply and variety of wool by making available to the American market wools of both low and fine quality now excluded.

The report shows in detail the difficulties involved in attempting to state in categorical terms the cost of wool production and the great differences in cost as between different regions and different types of wool. It is found, however, that, taking all varieties in account, the average cost of production for the whole American clip is higher than the cost in the chief competing country by an amount somewhat less than the present duty.

The report shows that the duties on noils, wool wastes, and shoddy, which are adjusted to the rate of 33 cents on scoured wool are prohibitory in the same measure that the duty on scoured wool is prohibitory. In general, they are assessed at rates as high as, or higher than, the duties paid on the clean content of wools actually imported. They should be reduced and so adjusted to the rate on wool as to bear their proper proportion to the real rate levied on the actual wool imports.

The duties on many classes of wool manufacture are prohibitory and greatly in excess of the difference in cost of production here and abroad.

This is true of tops, of yarns (with the exception of worsted yarns of a very high grade), and of low and medium grade cloth of heavy weight.

On tops up to 52 cents a pound in value, and on yarns of 65 cents in value, the rate is 100 percent with correspondingly higher rates for lower values. On cheap and medium grade cloths, the existing rates frequently run to 150 percent and on some cheap goods to over 200 percent. This is largely due to that part of the duty which is levied ostensibly to compensate the manufacturer for the enhanced cost of his raw material due to the duty on wool. As a matter of fact, this compensatory duty, for numerous classes of goods, is much in excess of the amount needed for strict compensation.

On the other hand, the findings show that the duties which run to such high *ad valorem* equivalents are prohibitory, since the goods are not imported, but that the prices of domestic fabrics are not raised by the full amount of duty. On a set of 1-yard samples of 16 English fabrics, which are completely excluded by the present tariff rates, it was found that the total foreign value was $41.84; the duties which would have been assessed had these fabrics been imported, $76.90; the foreign value plus the amount of the duty, $118.74; or a nominal duty of 183 percent. In fact, however, practically identical fabrics of domestic make sold at the same time at $69.75, showing an enhanced price over the foreign market value of but 67 percent.

Although these duties do not increase prices of domestic goods by anything like their full amount, it is none the less true that such prohibitive duties eliminate the possibility of foreign competition, even in time of scarcity; that they form a temptation to monopoly and conspiracies to control domestic prices; that they are much in excess of the difference in cost of production here and abroad, and that they should be reduced to a point which accords with this principle.

The findings of the board show that in this industry the actual manufacturing cost, aside from the question of the price of materials, is much higher in this country than it is abroad; that in the making of yarn and cloth the domestic woolen or worsted manufacturer has in general no advantage in the form of superior machinery or more efficient labor to offset the higher wages paid in this country. The findings show that the cost of turning wool into yarn in this country is about double that in the leading competing country, and that the cost of turning yarn into cloth is somewhat more than double. Under the protective policy a great industry, involving the welfare of hundreds of thousands of people, has been established despite these handicaps.

In recommending revision and reduction, I therefore urge that action be taken with these facts in mind, to the end that an important and established industry may not be jeopardized.

The Tariff Board reports that no equitable method has been found to levy purely specific duties on woolen and worsted fabrics and that, excepting for a compensatory duty, the rate must be *ad valorem* on such manufactures. It is important to realize, however, that no flat *ad valorem* rate on such fabrics can be made to work fairly and effectively. Any single rate which is high enough to equalize the difference in manufacturing cost at home and abroad on highly finished goods involving such labor would be prohibitory on cheaper goods, in which the labor cost is a smaller proportion of the total value. Conversely, a rate only adequate to equalize this difference on cheaper goods would remove protection from the fine-goods manufacture, the increase in which has been one of the striking features of the trade's development in recent years. I therefore recommend that in any revision the importance of a graduated scale of *ad valorem* duties on cloths be carefully considered and applied.

I venture to say that no legislative body has ever had presented to it a more complete and exhaustive report than this on so difficult and complicated a subject as the relative costs of wool and woolens the world over. It is a monument to the thoroughness, industry, impartiality, and accuracy of the men engaged in its making. They were chosen from both political parties but have allowed no partisan spirit to prompt or control their inquiries. They are unanimous in their findings. I feel sure that after the report has been printed and studied the value of such a compendium of exact knowledge in respect to this schedule of the tariff will convince all of the wisdom of making such a board permanent in order that it may treat each schedule of the tariff as it has treated this, and then keep its bureau of information up to date with current changes in the economic world.

It is no part of the function of the Tariff Board to propose rates of duty. Their function is merely to present findings of fact on which rates of duty may be fairly determined in the light of adequate knowledge in accord with the economic policy to be followed. This is what the present report does.

The findings of fact by the board show ample reason for the revision downward of Schedule K, in accord with the protective principle, and present the data as to relative costs and prices from which may be determined what rates will fairly equalize the difference in production costs. I recommend that such revision be proceeded with at once.

Part IV

[On the financial condition of the treasury, needed banking and
currency reform, and departmental questions]

The White House, December 21, 1911

To the Senate and House of Representatives:

The financial condition of the Government, as shown at the close
of the last fiscal year, June 30, 1911, was very satisfactory. The ordinary receipts into the general fund, excluding postal revenues, amounted to
$701,372,374.99, and the disbursements from the general fund for cur-
rent expenses and capital outlays, excluding postal and Panama Canal disbursements, including the interest on the public debt, amounted to
$654,137,907.89, leaving a surplus of $47,234,377.10.

The postal revenue receipts amounted to $237,879,823.60, while the
payments made for the postal service from the postal revenues amounted
to $237,660,705.48, which left a surplus of postal receipts over disburse-
ments of $219,118.12, the first time in 27 years in which a surplus occurred.

The interest-bearing debt of the United States June 30,1911, amounted
to $915,353,190. The debt on which interest had ceased amounted to
$1,879,830.26, and the debt bearing no interest, including greenbacks, na-
tional bank notes to be redeemed, and fractional currency, amounted to

$386,751,917.43, or a total of interest and non-interest bearing debt amounting to $1,303,984,937.69.

The actual disbursements, exclusive of those for the Panama Canal and for the postal service for the year ending June 30, 1911, were $654,137,997.89. The actual disbursements for the year ending June 30, 1910, exclusive of the Panama Canal and the postal service disbursements, were $659,705,391.08, making a decrease of $5,567,393.19 in yearly expenditures in the year 1911 under that of 1910. For the year ending June 30, 1912, the estimated receipts, exclusive of the postal revenues, are $666,000,000, while the total estimates, exclusive of those for the Panama Canal and the postal expenditures payable from the postal revenues, amount to $645,842,799.34. This is a decrease in the 1912 estimates from that of the 1911 estimates of $1,534,367.22.

For the year ending June 30, 1913, the estimated receipts, exclusive of the postal revenues, are $667,000,000, while the total estimated appropriations, exclusive of the Panama Canal and postal disbursements payable from postal revenues, will amount to $637,920,803.35. This is a decrease in the 1913 estimates from that of the 1912 estimates of $7,921,995.99.

As to the postal revenues, the expansion of the business in that department, the normal increase in the Post Office and the extension of the service, will increase the outlay to the sum of $260,938,463; but as the department was self-sustaining this year the Postmaster General is assured that next year the receipts will at least equal the expenditures, and probably exceed them by more than the surplus of this year. It is fair and equitable, therefore, in determining the economy with which the Government has been run, to exclude the transactions of a department like the Post Office Department, which relies for its support upon its receipts. In calculations heretofore made for comparison of economy in each year, it has been the proper custom only to include in the statement the deficit in the Post Office Department which was paid out of the Treasury.

A calculation of the actual increase in the expenses of Government arising from the increase in the population and the general expansion of governmental functions, except those of the Post Office, for a number of years shows a normal increase of about 4 percent a year. By directing the exercise of great care to keep down the expenses and the estimates we have succeeded in reducing the total disbursements each year.

The Credit of the United States

The credit of this Government was shown to be better than that of any other Government by the sale of the Panama Canal 3 percent bonds. These bonds did not give their owners the privilege of using them as a basis for bank-note circulation, nor was there any other privilege extended to them which would affect their general market value. Their sale, therefore, measured the credit of the Government. The premium which was realized upon the bonds made the actual interest rate of the transaction 2.909 percent.

Efficiency and Economy in the Treasury Department

In the Treasury Department the efficiency and economy work has been kept steadily up. Provision is made for the elimination of 134 positions during the coming year. Two hundred and sixty-seven statutory positions were eliminated during the last year in the office of the Treasury in Washington, and 141 positions in the year 1910, making an elimination of 542 statutory positions since March 4, 1909; and this has been done without the discharge of anybody, because the normal resignations and deaths have been equal to the elimination of the places, a system of transfers having taken care of the persons whose positions were dropped out. In the field service of the department, too, 1,259 positions have been eliminated down to the present time, making a total net reduction of all Treasury positions to the number of 1,801. Meantime the efficiency of the work of the department has increased.

Monetary Reform

A matter of first importance that will come before Congress for action at this session is monetary reform. The Congress has itself arranged an early introduction of this great question through the report of its Monetary Commission. This commission was appointed to recommend a solution of the banking and currency problems so long confronting the Nation and to furnish the facts and data necessary to enable the Congress to take action. The commission was appointed when an impressive and urgent popular demand for legislative relief suddenly arose out of the distressing situation of the people caused by the deplorable panic of 1907. The Congress decided that while it could not give immediately the relief required, it would provide a commission to furnish the means for prompt action at a later date.

In order to do its work with thoroughness and precision this commission has taken some time to make its report. The country is undoubtedly hoping for as prompt action on the report as the convenience of the Congress can permit. The recognition of the gross imperfections and marked inadequacy of our banking and currency system even in our most quiet financial periods is of long standing; and later there has matured a recognition of the fact that our system is responsible for the extraordinary devastation, waste, and business paralysis of our recurring periods of panic. Though the members of the Monetary Commission have for a considerable time been working in the open, and while large numbers of the people have been openly working with them, and while the press has largely noted and discussed this work as it has proceeded, so that the report of the commission promises to represent a national movement, the details of the report are still being considered. I can not, therefore, do much more at this time than commend the immense importance of monetary reform, urge prompt consideration and action when the commission's report is received, and express my satisfaction that the plan to be proposed promises to embrace main features that, having met the approval of a great preponderance of the practical and professional opinion of the country, are likely to meet equal approval in Congress.

It is exceedingly fortunate that the wise and undisputed policy of maintaining unchanged the main features of our banking system rendered it at once impossible to introduce a central bank; for a central bank would certainly have been resisted, and a plan into which it could have been introduced would probably have been defeated. But as a central bank could not be a part of the only plan discussed or considered, that troublesome question is eliminated. And ingenious and novel as the proposed National Reserve Association appears, it simply is a logical outgrowth of what is best in our present system, and is, in fact, the fulfillment of that system.

Exactly how the management of that association should be organized is a question still open. It seems to be desirable that the banks which would own the association should in the main manage it. It will be an agency of the banks to act for them, and they can be trusted better than anybody else chiefly to conduct it. It is mainly bankers' work. But there must be some form of Government supervision and ultimate control, and I favor a reasonable representation of the Government in the management. I entertain no fear of the introduction of politics or of any undesirable influences from a properly measured Government representation.

I trust that all banks of the country possessing the requisite standards will be placed upon a footing of perfect equality of opportunity. Both the National system and the State system should be fairly recognized, leaving them eventually to coalesce if that shall prove to be their tendency. But such evolution can not develop impartially if the banks of one system are given or permitted any advantages of opportunity over those of the other system. And I trust also that the new legislation will carefully and completely protect and assure the individuality and the independence of each bank, to the end that any tendency there may ever be toward a consolidation of the money or banking power of the Nation shall be defeated.

It will always be possible, of course, to correct any features of the new law which may in practice prove to be unwise; so that while this law is sure to be enacted under conditions of unusual knowledge and authority, it also will include, it is well to remember, the possibility of future amendment.

With the present prospects of this long-awaited reform encouraging us, it would be singularly unfortunate if this monetary question should by any chance become a party issue. And I sincerely hope it will not. The exceeding amount of consideration it has received from the people of the Nation has been wholly nonpartisan; and the Congress set its nonpartisan seal upon it when the Monetary Commission was appointed. In commending the question to the favorable consideration of Congress, I speak for, and in the spirit of, the great number of my fellow citizens who without any thought of party or partisanship feel with remarkable earnestness that this reform is necessary to the interests of all the people.

The War Department

There is now before Congress a bill, the purpose of which is to increase the efficiency and decrease the expense of the Army. It contains four principal features: First, a consolidation of the General Staff with the Adjutant General's and the Inspector General's Departments; second, a consolidation of the Quartermaster's Department with the Subsistence and the Pay Departments; third, the creation of an Army Service Corps; and fourth, an extension of the enlistment period from three to five years.

With the establishment of an Army Service Corps, as proposed in the bill, I am thoroughly in accord and am convinced that the establishment of such a corps will result in a material economy and a very great increase of efficiency in the Army. It has repeatedly been recommended by me and my predecessors. I also believe that a consolidation of the Staff Corps can be made with a resulting increase in efficiency and economy, but not along the lines provided in the bill under consideration.

I am opposed to any plan the result of which would be to break up or interfere with the essential principles of the detail system in the Staff Corps established by the act of February 2, 1901, and I am opposed to any plan the result of which would be to give to the officer selected as Chief of Staff or to any other member of the General Staff Corps greater permanency of office than he now has. Under the existing law neither the Chief of Staff nor any other member of the General Staff Corps can remain in office for a period of more than four years, and there must be an interval of two years between successive tours of duty.

The bill referred to provides that certain persons shall become permanent members of the General Staff Corps, and that certain others are subject to redetail without an interval of two years. Such provision is fraught with danger to the welfare of the Army, and would practically nullify the main purpose of the law creating the General Staff.

In making the consolidations no reduction should be made in the total number of officers of the Army, of whom there are now too few to perform the duties imposed by law. I have in the past recommended an increase in the number of officers by 600 in order to provide sufficient officers to perform all classes of staff duty and to reduce the number of line officers detached from their commands. Congress at the last session increased the total number of officers by 200, but this is not enough. Promotion in the line of the Army is too slow. Officers do not attain command rank at an age early enough properly to exercise it. It would be a mistake further to retard this already slow promotion by throwing back into the line of the

Army a number of high-ranking officers to be absorbed as is provided in the proposed plan of consolidation.

Another feature of the bill which I believe to be a mistake is the proposed increase in the term of enlistment from three to five years. I believe it would be better to enlist men for six years, release them at the end of three years from active service, and put them in reserve for the remaining three years. Reenlistments should be largely confined to the noncommissioned officers and other enlisted men in the skilled grades. This plan, by the payment of a comparatively small compensation during the three years of reserve, would keep a large body of men at the call of the Government, trained and ready for service, and able to meet any exigency.

The Army of the United States is in good condition. It showed itself able to meet an emergency in the successful mobilization of an army division of from 15,000 to 20,000 men, which took place along the border of Mexico during the recent disturbances in that country. The marvelous freedom from the ordinary camp diseases of typhoid fever and measles is referred to in the report of the Secretary of War, and shows such an effectiveness in the sanitary regulations and treatment of the Medical Corps, and in the discipline of the Army itself, as to invoke the highest commendation.

Memorial Amphitheater at Arlington

I beg to renew my recommendation of last year that the Congress appropriate for a memorial amphitheater at Arlington, Virginia, the funds required to construct it upon the plans already approved.

The Panama Canal

The very satisfactory progress made on the Panama Canal last year has continued, and there is every reason to believe that the canal will be completed as early as the first of July, 1913, unless something unforeseen occurs. This is about 18 months before the time promised by the engineers.

We are now near enough the completion of the canal to make it imperatively necessary that legislation should be enacted to fix the method by which the canal shall be maintained and controlled and the zone governed.

The fact is that today there is no statutory law by authority of which the President is maintaining the government of the zone. Such authority was given in an amendment to the Spooner Act, which expired by the terms of its own limitation some years ago. Since that time the government has continued, under the advice of the Attorney General that in the absence of action by Congress, there is necessarily an implied authority on the part of the Executive to maintain a government in a territory in which he has to see that the laws are executed. The fact that we have been able thus to get along during the important days of construction without legislation expressly formulating the government of the zone, or delegating the creation of it to the President, is not a reason for supposing that we may continue the same kind of a government after the construction is finished. The implied authority of the President to maintain a civil government in the zone may be derived from the mandatory direction given him in the original Spooner Act, by which he was commanded to build the canal; but certainly, now that the canal is about to be completed and to be put under a permanent management, there ought to be specific statutory authority for its regulation and control and for the government of the zone, which we hold for the chief and main purpose of operating the canal.

I fully concur with the Secretary of War that the problem is simply the management of a great public work, and not the government of a local republic; that every provision must be directed toward the successful maintenance of the canal as an avenue of commerce, and that all provisions for the government of those who live within the zone should be subordinate to the main purpose.

The zone is 40 miles long and 10 miles wide. Now, it has a population of 50,000 or 60,000, but as soon as the work of construction is completed, the towns which make up this population will be deserted, and only comparatively few natives will continue their residence there. The control of them ought to approximate a military government. One judge and two justices of the peace will be sufficient to attend to all the judicial and litigated business there is. With a few fundamental laws of Congress, the zone should be governed by the orders of the President, issued through the War Department, as it is today. Provisions can be made for the guaranties of life, liberty, and property, but beyond those, the government should be that of a military reservation, managed in connection with this great highway of trade.

Furnishing Supplies and Repairs

In my last annual message I discussed at length the reasons for the Government's assuming the task of furnishing to all ships that use the canal, whether our own naval vessels or others, the supplies of coal and oil and other necessities with which they must be replenished either before or after passing through the canal, together with the dock facilities and repairs of every character. This it is thought wise to do through the Government, because the Government must establish for itself, for its own naval vessels, large depots and dry docks and warehouses, and these may easily be enlarged so as to secure to the world public using the canal reasonable prices and a certainty that there will be no discrimination between those who wish to avail themselves of such facilities.

Tolls

I renew my recommendation with respect to the tolls of the canal that within limits, which shall seem wise to Congress, the power of fixing tolls be given to the President. In order to arrive at a proper conclusion, there must be some experimenting, and this can not be done if Congress does not delegate the power to one who can act expeditiously.

Power Exists to Relieve American Shipping

I am very confident that the United States has the power to relieve from the payment of tolls any part of our shipping that Congress deems wise. We own the canal. It was our money that built it. We have the right to charge tolls for its use. Those tolls must be the same to everyone; but when we are dealing with our own ships, the practice of many Governments of subsidizing their own merchant vessels is so well established in general that a subsidy equal to the tolls, an equivalent remission of tolls, can not be held to be a discrimination in the use of the canal. The practice in the Suez Canal makes this clear. The experiment in tolls to be made by the President would doubtless disclose how great a burden of tolls the coastwise trade between the Atlantic and the Pacific coast could bear without preventing its usefulness in competition with the transcontinental railroads. One of the chief reasons for building the canal was to set up this competition and to bring the two shores closer together as a practical trade problem. It may be that the tolls will have to be wholly remitted. I do not think this is the best principle, because I believe that the cost of such a Government work as the Panama Canal ought to be imposed gradually but certainly upon the trade which it creates and makes possible. So far as we can, consistent with the development of the world's trade through the canal, and the benefit which it was intended to secure to the east and west coastwise trade, we ought to labor to secure from the canal tolls a sufficient amount ultimately to meet the debt which we have assumed and to pay the interest.

The Philippine Islands

In respect to the Philippines, I urgently join in the recommendation of the Secretary of War that the act of February 6, 1905, limiting the indebtedness that may be incurred by the Philippine Government for the construction of public works, be increased from $5,000,000 to $15,000,000. The finances of that Government are in excellent condition. The maximum sum mentioned is quite low as compared with the amount of indebtedness of other governments with similar resources, and the success which has attended the expenditure of the $5,000,000 in the useful improvements of the harbors and other places in the Islands justifies and requires additional expenditures for like purposes.

Naturalization

I also join in the recommendation that the legislature of the Philippine Islands be authorized to provide for the naturalization of Filipinos and others who by the present law are treated as aliens, so as to enable them to become citizens of the Philippine Islands.

Friars' Lands

Pending an investigation by Congress at its last session, through one of its committees, into the disposition of the friars' lands, Secretary Dickinson directed that the friars' lands should not be sold in excess of the limits fixed for the public lands until Congress should pass upon the subject or should have concluded its investigation. This order has been an obstruction to the disposition of the lands, and I expect to direct the Secretary of War to return to the practice under the opinion of the Attorney General which will enable us to dispose of the lands much more promptly, and to prepare a sinking fund with which to meet the $7,000,000 of bonds issued for the purchase of the lands. I have no doubt whatever that the Attorney General's construction was a proper one, and that it is in the interest of everyone that the land shall be promptly disposed of. The danger of creating a monopoly of ownership in lands under the statutes as construed is nothing. There are only two tracts of 60,000 acres each unimproved and in remote Provinces that are likely to be disposed of in bulk, and the rest of the lands are subject to the limitation that they shall be first offered to the present tenants and lessors who hold them in small tracts.

Rivers and Harbors

The estimates for the river and harbor improvements reach $32,000,000 for the coming year. I wish to urge that whenever a project has been adopted by Congress as one to be completed, the more money which can be economically expended in its construction in each year, the greater the ultimate economy. This has especial application to the improvement of the Mississippi River and its large branches. It seems to me that an increase in the amount of money now being annually expended in the improvement of the Ohio River which has been formally adopted by Congress would be in the interest of the public. A similar change ought to be made during the present Congress, in the amount to be appropriated for the Missouri River. The engineers say that the cost of the improvement of the Missouri River from Kansas City to St. Louis, in order to secure 6 feet as a permanent channel, will reach $20,000,000. There have been at least three recommendations from the Chief of Engineers that if the improvement be adopted, $2,000,000 should be expended upon it annually. This particular improvement is especially entitled to the attention of Congress, because a company has been organized in Kansas City, with a capital of $1,000,000, which has built steamers and barges, and is actually using the river for transportation in order to show what can be done in the way of affecting rates between Kansas City and St. Louis, and in order to manifest their good faith and confidence in respect of the improvement. I urgently recommend that the appropriation for this improvement be increased from $600,000, as recommended now in the completion of a contract, to $2,000,000 annually, so that the work may be done in 10 years.

Waterway from the Lakes to the Gulf

The project for a navigable waterway from Lake Michigan to the mouth of the Illinois River, and thence via the Mississippi to the Gulf of Mexico, is one of national importance. In view of the work already accomplished by the Sanitary District of Chicago, an agency of the State of Illinois, which has constructed the most difficult and costly stretch of this waterway and made it an asset of the Nation, and in view of the fact that the people of Illinois have authorized the expenditure of $20,000,000 to carry this waterway 62 miles farther to Utica, I feel that it is fitting that this work should be supplemented by the Government, and that the expenditures recommended by the special board of engineers on the waterway from Utica to the mouth of the Illinois River be made upon lines which while providing a waterway for the Nation should otherwise benefit that State to the fullest extent. I recommend that the term of service of said special board of engineers be continued, and that it be empowered to reopen the question of the treatment of the lower Illinois River, and to negotiate with a properly constituted commission representing the State of Illinois, and to agree upon a plan for the improvement of the lower Illinois River and upon the extent to which the United States may properly cooperate with the State of Illinois in securing the construction of a navigable waterway from Lockport to the mouth of the Illinois River in conjunction with the development of water power by that State between Lockport and Utica.

The Department of Justice

Removal of Clerks of Federal Courts

The report of the Attorney General shows that he has subjected to close examination the accounts of the clerks of the Federal courts; that he has found a good many which disclose irregularities or dishonesty; but that he has had considerable difficulty in securing an effective prosecution or removal of the clerks thus derelict. I am certainly not unduly prejudiced against the Federal courts, but the fact is that the long and confidential relations which grow out of the tenure for life on the part of the judge and the practical tenure for life on the part of the clerk are not calculated to secure the strictness of dealing by the judge with the clerk in respect to his fees and accounts which assures in the clerk's conduct a freedom from overcharges and carelessness. The relationship between the judge and the clerk makes it ungracious for members of the bar to complain of the clerk or for department examiners to make charges against him to be heard by the court, and an order of removal of a clerk and a judgment for the recovery of fees are in some cases reluctantly entered by the judge. For this reason I recommend an amendment to the law whereby the President shall be given power to remove the clerks for cause. This provision need not interfere with the right of the judge to appoint his clerk or to remove him.

French Spoliation Awards

In my last message, I recommended to Congress that it authorize the payment of the findings or judgments of the Court of Claims in the matter of the French spoliation cases. There has been no appropriation to pay these judgments since 1905. The findings and awards were obtained after a very bitter fight, the Government succeeding in about 75 percent of the cases. The amount of the awards ought, as a matter of good faith on the part of the Government, to be paid.

Employers' Liability and Workmen's Compensation Commission

The limitation of the liability of the master to his servant for personal injuries to such as are occasioned by his fault has been abandoned in most civilized countries and provision made whereby the employee injured in the course of his employment is compensated for his loss of working ability irrespective of negligence. The principle upon which such provision proceeds is that accidental injuries to workmen in modern industry, with its vast complexity and inherent dangers arising from complicated machinery and the use of the great forces of steam and electricity, should be regarded as risks of the industry and the loss borne in some equitable proportion by those who for their own profit engage therein. In recognition of this the last Congress authorized the appointment of a commission to investigate the subject of employers' liability and workmen's compensation and to report the result of their investigations, through the President, to Congress. This commission was appointed and has been at work, holding hearings, gathering data, and considering the subject, and it is expected will be able to report by the first of the year, in accordance with the provisions of the law. It is hoped and expected that the commission will suggest legislation which will enable us to put in the place of the present wasteful and sometimes unjust system of employers' liability a plan of compensation which will afford some certain and definite relief to all employees who are injured in the course of their employment in those industries which are subject to the regulating power of Congress.

Measures to Prevent Delay and Unnecessary Cost of Litigation

In promotion of the movement for the prevention of delay and unnecessary cost, in litigation, I am glad to say that the Supreme Court has taken steps to reform the present equity rules of the Federal courts, and that we may in the near future expect a revision of them which will be a long step in the right direction.

The American Bar Association has recommended to Congress several bills expediting procedure, one of which has already passed the House unanimously, February 6, 1911. This directs that no judgment should be set aside or reversed, or new trial granted, unless it appears to the court, after an examination of the entire cause, that the error complained of has injuriously affected the substantial rights of the parties, and also provides for the submission of issues of fact to a jury, reserving questions of law for subsequent argument and decision. I hope this bill will pass the Senate and become law, for it will simplify the procedure at law.

Another bill to amend chapter 11 of the Judicial Code, in order to avoid errors in pleading, was presented by the same association, and one enlarging the jurisdiction of the Supreme Court so as to permit that court to examine, upon a writ of error, all cases in which any right or title is claimed under the Constitution, or any statute or treaty of the United States, whether the decision in the court below has been against the right or title or in its favor. Both these measures are in the interest of justice and should be passed.

Post Office

At the beginning of the present administration in 1909 the postal service was in arrears to the extent of $17,479,770.47. It was very much the largest deficit on record. In the brief space of two years this has been turned into a surplus of $220,000, which has been accomplished without curtailment of the postal facilities, as may be seen by the fact that there have been established 3,744 new post offices; delivery by carrier has been added to the service in 186 cities; 2,516 new rural routes have been established, covering 60,000 miles; the force of postal employees has been increased in these two years by more than 8,000, and their average annual salary has had a substantial increase.

Postal-Savings System

On January 3, 1911, postal-savings depositories were established experimentally in 48 States and Territories. After three months' successful operation the system was extended as rapidly as feasible to the 7,500 post offices of the first, second, and third classes constituting the presidential grade. By the end of the year practically all of these will have been designated and then the system will be extended to all fourth-class post offices doing a money-order business.

In selecting post offices for depositories consideration was given to the efficiency of the postmasters and only those offices where the ratings were satisfactory to the department have been designated. Withholding designation from postmasters with unsatisfactory ratings has had a salutary effect on the service.

The deposits have kept pace with the extension of the system. Amounting to only $60,652 at the end of the first month's operation in the experimental offices, they increased to $679,310 by July, and now after 11 months of operation have reached a total of $11,000,000. This sum is distributed among 2,710 banks and protected under the law by bonds deposited with the Treasurer of the United States.

Under the method adopted for the conduct of the system certificates are issued as evidence of deposits, and accounts with depositors are kept by the post offices instead of by the department. Compared with the practice in other countries of entering deposits in pass books and keeping at the central office a ledger account with each depositor, the use of the certificate has resulted in great economy of administration.

The depositors thus far number approximately 150,000. They include 40 nationalities, native Americans largely predominating and English and Italians coming next.

The first conversion of deposits into United States bonds bearing interest at the rate of 2 1/2 percent occurred on July 1, 1911, the amount of deposits exchanged being $41,900, or a little more than 6 percent of the total outstanding certificates of deposit on June 30. Of this issue, bonds to the value of $6,120 were in coupon form and $35,780 in registered form.

Parcel Post

Steps should be taken immediately for the establishment of a rural parcel post. In the estimates of appropriations needed for the maintenance of the postal service for the ensuing fiscal year an item of $150,000 has been inserted to cover the preliminary expense of establishing a parcel post on rural mail routes, as well as to cover an investigation having for its object the final establishment of a general parcel post on all railway and steamboat transportation routes. The department believes that after the initial expenses of establishing the system are defrayed and the parcel post is in full operation on the rural routes it will not only bring in sufficient revenue to meet its cost, but also a surplus that can be utilized in paying the expenses of a parcel post in the City Delivery Service.

It is hoped that Congress will authorize the immediate establishment of a limited parcel post on such rural routes as may be selected, providing for the delivery along the routes of parcels not exceeding eleven pounds, which is the weight limit for the international parcel post, or at the post office from which such route emanates, or on another route emanating from the same office. Such preliminary service will prepare the way for the more thorough and comprehensive inquiry contemplated in asking for the appropriation mentioned, enable the department to gain definite information concerning the practical operation of a general system, and at the same time extend the benefit of the service to a class of people who, above all others, are specially in need of it.

The suggestion that we have a general parcel post has awakened great opposition on the part of some who think that it will have the effect to destroy the business of the country storekeeper. Instead of doing this, I think the change will greatly increase business for the benefit of all. The reduction in the cost of living it will bring about ought to make its coming certain.

The Navy Department

On the 2d of November last, I reviewed the fighting fleet of battleships and other vessels assembled in New York Harbor, consisting of 24 battleships, 2 armored cruisers, 2 cruisers, 22 destroyers, 12 torpedo boats, 8 submarines, and other attendant vessels, making 98 vessels of all classes, of a tonnage of 576,634 tons. Those who saw the fleet were struck with its preparedness and with its high military efficiency. All Americans should be proud of its personnel.

The fleet was deficient in the number of torpedo destroyers, in cruisers, and in colliers, as well as in large battleship cruisers, which are now becoming a very important feature of foreign navies, notably the British, German, and Japanese.

The building plan for this year contemplates two battleships and two colliers. This is because the other and smaller vessels can be built much more rapidly in case of emergency than the battleships, and we certainly ought to continue the policy of two battleships a year until after the Panama Canal is finished and until in our first line and in our reserve line we can number 40 available vessels of proper armament and size.

The reorganization of the Navy and the appointment of four aids to the Secretary have continued to demonstrate their usefulness. It would be difficult now to administer the affairs of the Navy without the expert counsel and advice of these aids, and I renew the recommendation which I made last year, that the aids be recognized by statute.

It is certain that the Navy, with its present size, should have admirals in active command higher than rear admirals. The recognized grades in order are: Admiral of the fleet, admiral, vice admiral, and rear admiral. Our great battleship fleet is commanded by a rear admiral, with four other rear admirals under his orders. This is not as it should be, and when questions of precedence arise between our naval officers and those of European navies, the American rear admiral, though in command of ten times the force of a foreign vice admiral, must yield precedence to the latter. Such an absurdity ought not to prevail, and it can be avoided by the creation of two or three positions of flag rank above that of rear admiral.

I attended the opening of the new training school at North Chicago, Ill., and am glad to note the opportunity which this gives for drawing upon young men of the country from the interior, from farms, stores, shops, and offices, which insures a high average of intelligence and character among them, and which they showed in the very wonderful improvement in discipline and drill which only a few short weeks' presence at the naval station had made.

I invite your attention to the consideration of the new system of detention and of punishment for Army and Navy enlisted men which has obtained in Great Britain, and which has made greatly for the better control of the men. We should adopt a similar system here.

Like the Treasury Department and the War Department, the Navy Department has given much attention to economy in administration, and has cut down a number of unnecessary expenses and reduced its estimates except for construction and the increase that that involves.

I urge upon Congress the necessity for an immediate increase of 2,000 men in the enlisted strength of the Navy, provided for in the estimates. Four thousand more are now needed to man all the available vessels.

There are in the service today about 47,750 enlisted men of all ratings.

Careful computation shows that in April, 1912, 49,166 men will be required for vessels in commission, and 3,000 apprentice seamen should be kept under training at all times.

Abolition of Navy Yards

The Secretary of the Navy has recommended the abolition of certain of the smaller and unnecessary navy yards, and in order to furnish a complete and comprehensive report has referred the question of all navy yards to the joint board of the Army and Navy. This board will shortly make its report and the Secretary of the Navy advises me that his recommendations on the subject will be presented early in the coming year. The measure of economy contained in a proper handling of this subject is so great and so important to the interests of the Nation that I shall present it to Congress as a separate subject apart from my annual message. Concentration of the nec-essary work for naval vessels in a few navy yards on each coast is a vital necessity if proper economy in Government expenditures is to be attained.

Amalgamation of Staff Corps in the Navy

The Secretary of the Navy is striving to unify the various corps of the Navy to the extent possible and thereby stimulate a Navy spirit as distinguished from a corps spirit. In this he has my warm support.

All officers are to be naval officers first and specialists afterwards. This means that officers will take up at least one specialty, such as ordnance, construction, or engineering. This is practically what is done now, only some of the specialists, like the pay officers and naval constructors, are not of the line. It is proposed to make them all of the line.

All combatant corps should obviously be of the line. This necessitates amalgamating the pay officers and also those engaged in the technical work of producing the finished ship. This is at present the case with the single exception of the naval constructors, whom it is now proposed to amalgam-ate with the line.

Council of National Defense

I urge again upon Congress the desirability of establishing the council of national defense. The bill to establish this council was before Congress last winter, and it is hoped that this legislation will pass during the present session. The purpose of the council is to determine the general policy of national defense and to recommend to Congress and to the President such measures relating to it as it shall deem necessary and expedient.

No such machinery is now provided by which the readiness of the Army and Navy may be improved and the programs of military and naval requirements shall be coordinated and properly scrutinized with a view of the necessities of the whole Nation rather than of separate departments.

Departments of Agriculture and Commerce and Labor

For the consideration of matters which are pending or have been disposed of in the Agricultural Department and in the Department of Commerce and Labor, I refer to the very excellent reports of the Secretaries of those departments. I shall not be able to submit to Congress until after the Christmas holidays the question of conservation of our resources arising in Alaska and the West and the question of the rate for second-class mail matter in the Post Office Department.

Commission on Efficiency and Economy

The law does not require the submission of the reports of the Commission on Economy and Efficiency until the thirty-first of December. I shall therefore not be able to submit a report of the work of that commission until the assembling of Congress after the holidays.

Civil Retirement and Contributory Pension System

I have already advocated, in my last annual message, the adoption of a civil-service retirement system, with a contributory feature to it so as to reduce to a minimum the cost to the Government of the pensions to be paid. After considerable reflection, I am very much opposed to a pension system that involves no contribution from the employees. I think the experience of other governments justifies this view; but the crying necessity for some such contributory system, with possibly a preliminary governmental outlay, in order to cover the initial cost and to set the system going at once while the contributions are accumulating, is manifest on every side. Nothing will so much promote the economy and efficiency of the Government as such a system.

Elimination of All Local Offices from Politics

I wish to renew again my recommendation that all the local offices throughout the country, including collectors of internal revenue, collectors of customs, postmasters of all four classes, immigration commissioners and marshals, should be by law covered into the classified service, the necessity for confirmation by the Senate be removed, and the President and the others, whose time is now taken up in distributing this patronage under the custom that has prevailed since the beginning of the Government in accordance with the recommendation of the Senators and Congressmen of the majority party, should be relieved from this burden. I am confident that such a change would greatly reduce the cost of administering the Government, and that it would add greatly to its efficiency. It would take away the power to use the patronage of the Government for political purposes. When officers are recommended by Senators and Congressmen from political motives and for political services rendered, it is impossible to expect that while in office the appointees will not regard their tenure as more or less dependent upon continued political service for their patrons, and no regulations, however stiff or rigid, will prevent this, because such regulations, in view of the method and motive for selection, are plainly inconsistent and deemed hardly worthy of respect.

10

Special Message

[On economy and efficiency in the Government services]
The White House, January 17, 1912

To the Senate and House of Representatives:

I submit for the information of the Congress this report of progress made in the inquiry into the efficiency and economy of the methods of transacting public business.

Efficiency and economy in the Government service have been demanded with increasing insistence for a generation. Real economy is the result of efficient organization. By perfecting the organization the same benefits may be obtained at less expense. A reduction in the total of the annual appropriations is not in itself a proof of economy, since it is often accompanied by a decrease in efficiency. The needs of the Nation may demand a large increase of expenditure, yet to keep the total appropriations within the expected revenue is necessary to the maintenance of public credit.

Upon the President must rest a large share of the responsibility for the demands made upon the Treasury for the current administration of the executive branch of the Government. Upon the Congress must rest responsibility for those grants of public funds which are made for other purposes.

Reason for the Inquiry

Recognizing my share of responsibility for efficient and economical administration, I have endeavored during the past two years, with the assistance of heads of departments, to secure the best results. As one of the means to this end I requested a grant from Congress to make my efforts more effective.

An appropriation of $100,000 was made June 25, 1910, "to enable the President to inquire into the methods of transacting the public business of the executive departments and other Government establishments and to recommend to Congress such legislation as may be necessary to carry into effect changes found to be desirable that can not be accomplished by Executive action alone." I have been given this fund to enable me to take action and to make specific recommendations with respect to the details of transacting the business of an organization whose activities are almost as varied as those of the entire business world. The operations of the Government affect the interest of every person living within the jurisdiction of the United States. Its organization embraces stations and centers of work located in every city and in many local subdivisions of the country. Its gross expenditures amount to nearly $1,000,000,000 annually. Including the personnel of the Military and Naval Establishments, more than 400,000 persons are required to do the work imposed by law upon the executive branch of the Government.

Magnitude of the Task

This vast organization has never been studied in detail as one piece of administrative mechanism. Never have the foundations been laid for a thorough consideration of the relations of all of its parts. No comprehensive effort has been made to list its multifarious activities or to group them in such a way as to present a clear picture of what the Government is doing. Never has a complete description been given of the agencies through which these activities are performed. At no time has the attempt been made to study all of these activities and agencies with a view to the assignment of each activity to the agency best fitted for its performance, to the avoidance of duplication of plant and work, to the integration of all administrative agencies of the Government, so far as may be practicable, into a unified organization for the most effective and economical dispatch of public business.

First Complete Investigation

Notwithstanding that voluminous reports are compiled annually and presented to the Congress, no satisfactory statement has ever been published of the financial transactions of the Government as a whole. Provision is made for due accountability for all moneys coming into the hands of officers of the Government, whether as collectors of revenue or disbursing agents, and for insuring that authorizations for expenditures as made by law shall not be exceeded. But no general system has ever been devised for reporting and presenting information regarding the character of the expenditures made, in such a way as to reveal the actual costs entailed in the operation of individual services and in the performance of particular undertakings; nor in such a way as to make possible the exercise of intelligent judgment regarding the discretion displayed in making expenditure and concerning the value of the results obtained when contrasted with the sacrifices required. Although earnest efforts have been put forth by administrative officers and though many special inquiries have been made by the Congress, no exhaustive investigation has ever before been instituted concerning the methods employed in the transaction of public business with a view to the adoption of the practices and procedure best fitted to secure the transaction of such business with maximum dispatch, economy, and efficiency.

With large interests at stake the Congress and the Administration have never had all the information which should be currently available if the most intelligent direction is to be given to the business in hand.

I am convinced that results which are really worth while can not be secured, or at least can be secured only in small part, through the prosecution at irregular intervals of special inquiries bearing on particular services or features of administration. The benefits thus obtained must be but temporary. The problem of good administration is not one that can be solved at one time. It is a continuously present one.

Plan of the Work

In accordance with my instructions, the Commission on Economy and Efficiency, which I organized to aid me in the inquiry, has directed its efforts primarily to the formulation of concrete recommendations looking to the betterment of the fundamental conditions under which governmental operations must be carried on. With a basis thus laid, it has proceeded to the prosecution of detailed studies of individual services and classes of work, and of particular practices and methods, pushing these studies as far, and covering as many points and services, as the resources and time at its disposal have permitted.

In approaching its task it has divided the work into five fields of inquiry having to do respectively with organization, personnel, business methods, accounting and reporting, and the budget.

Organization

I have stated that the Congress, the President, and the administrative officers are attempting to discharge the duties with which they are intrusted without full information as to the agencies through which the work of the Government is being performed. To provide more complete information on this point the commission has submitted to me a report on the organization of the Government as it existed July 1, 1911. This report, which is transmitted herewith, shows in great detail, by means of outlines, not only the departments, commissions, bureaus, and offices through which the Government performs its varied activities, but also the sections, shops, field stations, etc., constituting the subordinate divisions through which the work is actually done. It shows for the services at Washington each such final unit as a laboratory, library, shop, and administrative subdivision; and for the services outside of Washington each station and point at which any activity of the Government is carried on.

Outlines of Organization

From these outlines it is possible to determine not only how each department, bureau, and operating unit, such as a navy yard, is organized, but also, by classifying these units by character and geographical location, the number of units of a like character that exist at Washington, and the number and character of services of the Government in each city or other point in the United States. With this information available, it is possible to study any particular activity or the problem of maintaining services at any given city or point.

Information of this character has never before been available. Administrative officials have been called upon to discharge their duties without that full knowledge of the machinery under their direction which is so necessary to the exercise of effective control; much less have they had information regarding agencies in other services that might be made use of. Under such circumstances each service is compelled to rely upon itself, to build up its own organization, and to provide its own facilities regardless of those in existence elsewhere.

This outline has been prepared on the loose-leaf system, so that it is possible to keep it revised to date at little or no expense. The outline thus constitutes a work of permanent value.

Comprehensive Plan of Organization

With this outline as a basis, the commission has entered upon the preparation of three series of reports. The first series deals with the manner in which the services of the Government should be grouped in departments. This is a matter of fundamental importance. It is only after a satisfactory solution of this problem that many important measures of reform become possible. Only by grouping services according to their character can substantial progress be made in eliminating duplication of work and plant and proper working relations be established between services engaged in similar activities. Until the head of a department is called upon to deal exclusively with matters falling in but one or a very few distinct fields, effective supervision and control is impossible. As long as the same department embraces services so diverse in character as those of life saving and the management of public finances, standardization of accounting methods and of other business practices is exceedingly difficult of attainment.

So dependent are other reforms upon the proper grouping of services that I have instructed the commission to indicate in its report the changes which should be made in the existing organization and to proceed in the same way as would far-seeing architects or engineers in planning for the improvement and development of a great city. My desire is to secure and to furnish to the Congress a scheme of organization that can be used as a basis of discussion and action for years to come.

In the past services have been created one by one as exigencies have seemed to demand, with little or no reference to any scheme of organization of the Government as a whole. I am convinced that the time has come when the Government should take stock of all its activities and agencies and formulate a comprehensive plan with reference to which future changes may be made. The report of the commission is being prepared with this idea in mind. When completed it will be transmitted to the Congress. The recommendations will be of such a character that they can be acted upon one by one if they commend themselves to the Congress and as action in regard to any one of them is deemed to be urgent.

Reports on Particular Services

The second and third series of reports deal, respectively, with the organization and activities of particular services, and the form of organization for the performance of particular business operations.

One of the reports of the second series is upon the Revenue-Cutter Service, which costs the Government over two and a half million dollars each year. In the opinion of the commission its varied activities can be performed with equal, or greater, advantage by other services. The commission, therefore, recommends that it be abolished. It is estimated that by so doing a saving of not less than $1,000,000 a year can be made.

Another report illustrating the second series recommends that the Lighthouse and Life-Saving Services be administered by a single bureau instead of as at present by two bureaus located in different departments. These services have much in common. Geographically, they are similarly located; administratively, they have many of the same problems. It is estimated that consolidation would result in a saving of not less than $100,000 annually.

In a third report the commission has recommended the abolition of the Returns Office of the Department of the Interior. This action, in its opinion, will cause no loss in service to the public and will result in a direct saving of not less than $25,000 a year, in addition to a large indirect economy in the reduction of work to be performed in the several offices.

In another report the commission has recommended the consolidation of the six auditing offices of the Treasury and the inclusion in the auditing system of the seven naval officers who now audit customs accounts at the principal ports. The changes recommended will improve in many ways the auditing of public accounts and will result in an immediate saving of at least $135,000 annually.

General Technical Services

A third series of reports is being prepared on those branches of the organization which are technical in character and which exist for the service of the Government as a whole—branches which have to do with such matters as public printing, heating, lighting, the making of repairs, the providing of transportation, and the compilation of statistics where mechanical equipment is essential.

Abolition of Local Offices

Perhaps the part of the organization in which the greatest economy in public expenditure is possible is to be found in the numerous local offices of the Government. In some instances the establishment and the discontinuance of these local offices are matters of administrative discretion. In other instances they are established by permanent law in such a manner that their discontinuance is beyond the power of the President or that of any executive officer. In a number of services these laws were passed nearly a century ago. Changes in economic conditions have taken place which have had the effect of rendering certain offices not only useless but even worse than useless in that their very existence needlessly swells expenditures and complicates the administrative system.

The attention of the Congress has been called repeatedly to these conditions. In some instances the Congress has approved recommendations for the abolition of useless positions. In other cases not only do the recommendations of the Executive that useless positions be abolished remain unheeded, but laws are passed to establish new offices at places where they are not needed.

The responsibility for the maintenance of these conditions must naturally be divided between the Congress and the Executive. But that the Executive has performed his duty when he has called the attention of the Congress to the matter must also be admitted. Realizing my responsibility in the premises, I have directed the commission to prepare a report setting forth the positions in the local services of the Government which may be discontinued with advantage, the saving which would result from such action and the changes in law which are necessary to carry into effect changes in organization found to be desirable. On the coming in of the report, such offices as may be found useless and can be abolished will be so treated by Executive order.

Personnel

In my recent message to the Congress I urged consideration of the necessity of placing in the classified service all of the local officers under the Departments of the Treasury, the Interior, Post Office, and Commerce and Labor.

Classification of Local Officers

The importance of the existence of a competent and reasonably permanent civil service was not appreciated until the last quarter of the last century. At that time examinations were instituted as a means of ascertaining whether candidates for appointment possessed the requisite qualifications for Government positions. Since then it has come to be universally admitted that entrance to almost every subordinate position in the public service should be dependent upon the proof in some appropriate way of the ability of the appointee.

As yet, however, little if any attempt has been made by law to secure, either for the higher administrative positions in the service at Washington or for local offices, the qualifications which the incumbents of these positions must have if the business of the Government is to be conducted in the most efficient and economical manner. Furthermore, in the case of many of the local officers the law positively provides that the term of office shall be of four years' duration.

The next step which must be taken is to require of heads of bureaus in the departments at Washington, and of most of the local officers under the departments, qualifications of capacity similar to those now required of certain heads of bureaus and of local officers. The extension of the merit system to these officers and a needed readjustment of salaries will have important effects in securing greater economy and efficiency.

In the first place, the possession by the incumbents of these positions of the requisite qualifications must in itself promote efficiency.

In the second place, the removal of local officers from the realm of political patronage in many cases would reduce the pay roll of the field services. At the present time the incumbents of many of these positions leave the actual performance of many of their duties to deputies and assistants. The Government often pays two persons for doing work that could easily be done by one. What is the loss to the Government can not be stated, but that it is very large can not be denied, when it is remembered how numerous are the local officers in the postal, customs, internal revenue, public lands, and other field services of the Government.

In the third place, so long as local officers are within the sphere of political patronage it is difficult to consider the question of the establishment or discontinuance of local offices apart from the effect upon local political situations.

Finally, the view that these various offices are to be filled as a result of political considerations has for its consequence the necessity that the President and Members of Congress devote to matters of patronage time which they should devote to questions of policy and administration.

The greatest economy and efficiency, and the benefits which may accrue from the President's devoting his time to the work which is most worth while, may be assured only by treating all the distinctly administrative officers in the departments at Washington and in the field in the same way as inferior officers have been treated. The time has come when all these officers should be placed in the classified service. The time has also come when those provisions of law which give to these officers a fixed term of years should be repealed. So long as a fixed term is provided by law the question of reappointment of an officer, no matter how efficiently he may have performed his duties, will inevitably be raised periodically. So long as appointments to these offices must be confirmed by the Senate, and so long as appointments to them must be made every four years, just so long will it be impossible to provide a force of employees with a reasonably permanent tenure who are qualified by reason of education and training to do the best work.

Superannuation

Attention has been directed in recent years to the need of a suitable plan of retiring the superannuated employees in the executive civil service. In the belief that it is desirable that any steps toward the establishment of such a plan shall be taken with caution, I instructed the commission to make an inquiry first into the conditions at Washington. This inquiry has been directed to the ascertainment of the extent to which superannuation now exists and to the consideration of the availability of the various plans which either have been proposed for adoption in this country or have actually been adopted in other countries. I shall submit, in the near future, for the consideration of the Congress a plan for the retirement of aged employees in the civil service which will safeguard the interests of the Government and at the same time make reasonable provision for the needs of those who have given the best part of their lives to the service of the State.

Efficiency of Personnel

I have caused inquiry to be made into the character of the appointees from the point of view of efficiency and competence which has resulted from present methods of appointment; into the present relation of compensation to the character of work done; into the existing methods of promotion and the keeping of efficiency records in the various departments; and into the conditions of work in Government offices. This inquiry will help to determine to what extent conditions of work are uniform in the different departments and how far uniformity in such conditions will tend to improve the service. I have felt that satisfaction with the conditions in which they worked was a necessary prerequisite to an efficient personnel, and that satisfaction was not to be expected where conditions in one department were less favorable than in another.

This inquiry has not been completed. When it has been ascertained that evils exist which can be remedied through the exercise of the powers now vested in the President, I shall endeavor to remedy those evils. Where that is not the case, I shall present for the consideration of the Congress plans which, I believe, will be followed by great improvement in the service.

Business Methods

In every case where technical processes have been studied it has been demonstrated beyond question that large economies may be effected. The subjects first approached were those which lie close to each administrator, viz., office practices. An illustration of the possibilities within this field may be found in the results of the inquiry into the methods of handling and filing correspondence. Every office in the Government has reported its methods to the commission. These reports brought to light the fact that present methods were quite the reverse of uniform. Some offices follow the practice of briefing all correspondence; some do not. Some have flat files; others fold all papers before filing. Some use press copies; others retain only carbon copies.

Unnecessary Cost of Handling and Filing Correspondence

The reports also show not only a very wide range in the methods of doing this comparatively simple part of the Government business, but an extraordinary range in cost. For the handling of incoming mail the averages of cost by departments vary from $5.84 to $81.40 per 1,000. For the handling of outgoing mail the averages by departments vary from $5.94 to $69.89 per 1,000. This does not include the cost of preparation, but is confined merely to the physical side of the work. The variations between individual offices is many times greater than that shown for averages by departments.

It is at once evident either that it is costing some of the offices too little or that others are being run at an unwarranted expense. Nor are these variations explained by differences in character of work. For example, there are two departments which handle practically the same kind of business and in very large volume. The average cost of handling incoming mail to one was found to be over six times as great as the cost of handling incoming mail to the other.

It has been found that differences of average cost by departments closely follow differences in method and that the greatest cost is found in the department where the method is most involved. Another fact is of interest, viz., that in two departments, which already show low averages, orders have been issued which will lead to a large saving without impairing efficiency. It can not be said what the saving ultimately will be when the attention of officers in all of the departments has been focused on present methods with a view to changing them in such manner as to reduce cost to the lowest point compatible with efficient service. It, however, must be a considerable percentage of nearly $5,000,000, the total estimated cost of handling this part of the Government business at Washington.

Results have already been obtained which are noteworthy. Mention has been made of the orders issued by two departments. Of these the order of one is most revolutionary in character, since it requires flat filing, where before all correspondence was folded; the doing away with letterpress copies; and the discontinuance of indorsements on slips, one of the most expensive processes and one which in the other department has been carried to very great length.

Need for Labor-Saving Office Devices

The use of labor-saving office devices in the service has been made the subject of special inquiry. An impression prevails that the Government is not making use of mechanical devices for economizing labor to the same extent as are efficiently managed private enterprises. A study has been made of the extent to which devices of this character are now being employed in the several branches of the Government and the opportunities that exist for their more general use. In order to secure information as to the various kinds of labor-saving devices that are in existence and as to their adaptability to Government work, an exhibition of labor-saving office appliances was held in Washington from July 6 to 15, 1911. One hundred and ten manufacturers and dealers participated, and more than 10,000 officers and employees visited the exhibition. There is no doubt that the exhibition served the purpose of bringing to the attention of officers devices which can be employed by them with advantage. The holding of this exhibition was, however, but a step preparatory to the contemplated investigation.

Unnecessary Cost of Copy Work

The efforts of the commission resulted also in the adoption by several bureaus or departments of improved methods of doing copying. The amount of copy work heretofore done by hand each year in the many offices is estimated to aggregate several hundred thousand dollars. The commission exhibited, at its offices, appliances that were thought to be especially adapted to this kind of Government work. Following these demonstrations methods of copying were introduced which have brought about a saving of over 75 percent in offices where used for six months. This change in one small cross section of office practice will more than offset the whole cost of my inquiry.

Waste in the Distribution of Public Documents

Going outside the office, one of the business processes which have been investigated is the distribution of departmental documents. This is a subject with which both the Congress and Administration heads are familiar. The prevailing practice in handling departmental publications is to have them manufactured at the Government Printing Office; each job when completed is delivered to the department; here the books or pamphlets are wrapped and addressed; they are then sent to the post office; there they are assorted and prepared for shipment through the mails; from the post office they are sent to the railroad station, which is only a few steps from the Government Printing Office, whence they started. The results of this laborious and circuitous method is to make the use of the best mechanical equipment impracticable and to waste each year not less than a quarter of a million dollars of Government funds in useless handling, to say nothing of the indirect loss due to lack of proper coordination.

Wasteful Use of Properties and Equipment

The use of equipment is a matter which also has been investigated. Up to the present time this investigation has been in the main confined to the subject of electric lighting. The Government pays over $600,000 per year for electric current; it has made large capital outlays for wiring and fixtures. With the increasing demands in many buildings the present equipment is taxed to its limit and if the present methods are continued much of this wiring must be done over; in many places employees are working at a great physical disadvantage, due to inadequate and improper lighting, and thereby with reduced efficiency. In every place where the inquiry has been conducted it appears that there is large waste; that without the cost of re-wiring, simply by giving proper attention to location of lights and the use of proper lamps and reflectors, the light efficiency at points where needed may be much increased and the cost of current reduced from 30 to 60 percent. Other inquiries into the use which is being made of properties and equipment are contemplated which promise even larger results.

Unnecessary Cost of Insurance

It is the policy of the Government not to insure public property against fire and other losses. Question has been raised whether the Government might not apply the same principle to other forms of risk, including insurance of the fidelity of officials and employees. A report is now in preparation on the subject which will show opportunities for large savings. I believe that the present expense for insuring the faithful execution of contracts, which, though paid by the contractor, is more than covered in the added price to the Government, can be largely reduced without taking away any element of security.

Lack of Specifications

The importance of establishing and maintaining standard specifications is found not only in the possibility of very materially reducing the direct cost of Government trading, but also in insuring to the service materials, supplies, and equipment which are better adapted to its purposes. One of the results of indefiniteness of specifications is to impose contract conditions which make it extra-hazardous for persons to enter into contractual relations. This not only deprives the Government of the advantage of broad competition, but causes it to pay an added margin in price to vendors who must carry the risk. The specifications which may have been worked out in one department usually differ from specifications for the same article to be used in another department. Much progress has been made toward improving this condition through the schedules of the General Supply Committee, but there are many classes of supplies not on these lists which may be standardized, and the articles which are there listed may be specified with exactness.

In connection with standard specifications for purchasing, the subject of a standard form of contract has been given consideration. No one form or small number of forms will be applicable to all the agreements into which the Government enters. There can be standard conditions and provisions for such contracts, however, and the work in this connection is being prosecuted in an effort to simplify the forms of contracts and to do away with the great diversity of requirements which so often perplex and irritate those who wish to enter into a contract with the Government.

Excessive Cost of Travel

One of the first steps taken toward constructive work was the reclassification of the expenditures for the year 1910 by objects. The foundation was thus made for the investigation of Government trading practices. While it was recognized that this large field could not be covered within a year except at enormous cost, the subjects of "Transportation of persons" and "Subsistence while in travel status" were taken as concrete examples. The annual cost of travel to the Government was found to be about $12,000,000. It was also found that the Government employees were traveling in practically every way that was open to the public; it was further found that although the Government was the largest user of transportation, it was buying railroad tickets on a less favorable basis than would be possible if the subject of traveling expenditures were systematically handled from the point of view of the Government as a whole. The form of ticket most often used between such points as New York, Philadelphia, and Washington was the single-trip first-class ticket. In two departments definite tests have been made in the use of mileage books and in each practically the same result has been reported, viz., an average saving of a little over one-half of 1 cent per mile. What the possible saving to the Government by a more systematic handling of transportation may be, can not be estimated at this time. Upon inquiry it was found that an analysis of travel vouchers for the year would cost not less than $120,000. The investigation, therefore, was confined to the analysis of travel vouchers which came to departments during the month of April. A report of the result of this inquiry has been made and at an early date will be sent to the Congress with recommendations.

One of the results or by-products of this inquiry into travel expenses was the recommendation that the jurat or affidavit which is now required by order of the comptroller be discontinued. The jurat does not add to the value of the return, involves persons traveling in much annoyance and trouble in going before an officer competent to administer oaths, while every disciplinary result is obtained through certification under the law prescribing a penalty for the falsification of accounts. A discontinuance of the jurat in all cases would result in a direct saving of about $60,000 per annum.

Other Expenditures to Be Investigated

Before economy in Government trading can be adequately covered, such subjects as the following must be systematically inquired into, viz.: Subsistence and support of persons; subsistence and care for animals and the storage and care of vehicles; telephone, telegraph, and commercial messenger service; printing, engraving, lithographing, and binding; advertising and the publication of notices; heat, light, power, and electricity purchased; repairs by contract and open market order; building and other materials; drafting, scientific and stationery supplies; fuel; mechanics', engineering, and electricians' supplies; cleaning and toilet supplies; wearing apparel and hand-sewing supplies; forage and other supplies for animals; provisions; explosives and pyrotechnic supplies; heat, light, power, and electrical equipment; live stock; furniture and furnishings; educational and scientific equipment. From what has been already ascertained concerning certain of these different objects of Government expenditure, it is evident that large savings will result from such an examination.

Better Methods for Purchasing

Through a long period of years and by numerous laws and orders there has grown up a procedure governing public advertising and contracting that is more burdensome and expensive in some cases than is necessary. The procedure is not uniform in the various departments; it is not uniform in many cases for the different services in the same department. To make uniform the requirements so far as practicable will be in the interest of economy and efficiency and bring about that simplicity that will secure the largest opportunity for contractors to bid for Government work, and will secure for the Government the most favorable prices obtained by any purchaser.

Accounting and Reporting

In my message of March 3, 1911, attention was called to some of the defects in the present methods of accounting and reporting. I said:

> The condition under which legislators and administrators, both past and present, have been working may be summarized as follows: There have been no adequate means provided whereby either the President or his advisers may act with intelligence on current business before them; there has been no means for getting prompt, accurate, and correct information as to results obtained; * * * there have been practically no accounts showing what the Government owns and only a partial representation of what it owes; appropriations have been over encumbered without the facts being known; officers of Government have had no regular or systematic method of having brought to their attention the costs of governmental administration, operation, and maintenance, and therefore could not judge as to economy or waste; there has been inadequate means whereby those who served with fidelity and efficiency might make a record of accomplishment and be distinguished from those who were inefficient and wasteful; functions and establishments have been duplicated, even multiplied, causing conflict and unnecessary expense; lack of full information has made intelligent direction impossible and cooperation between different branches of the service difficult.

By reason of the confused character of records and reports and the lack of information which has been provided, this was one of the first subjects into which inquiry was made looking toward the issuing of Executive orders.

Character of Accounts Required

In laying the foundation for the revision of the present accounting methods it has been assumed that such information should be produced, and only such as is continuously needed by administrative heads or as will be of value to the Congress. The work has been prosecuted under the following heads: The character and form of expenditure documents that should be employed by the several departments; classification of objects of expenditure; the kind and character of accounts that should be kept by the Government; the character of reports giving information regarding revenues and expenditures that should be rendered to superior administrative officers and to the Congress, and which will enable them to lay before the Congress information which each Member should have in order that the legislative branch may be fully informed concerning the objects and purposes of governmental expenditures.

Uniformity in Classification and Methods

Upon these matters the commission has made extended studies. So far as the kind and character of accounts to be kept by the Government are concerned, not only have reports on methods of accounting and reporting been made by representatives of each of the departments, but for four of these services detailed descriptive reports have been prepared showing exactly what forms are used and what procedure is followed in keeping and recording accounts. Proceeding from these statements of fact, the purpose is to work out in collaboration with department representatives a unified procedure, and a uniform classification of facts which will enable accounting officers to present to administrative heads, to the President, and to the Congress complete, accurate, and prompt information, in any summary or detail that may be desired.

Constructive Results Obtained

The general basis for uniformity of accounting and reporting has already been laid in constructive reports with recommendations. The results of this work have been promulgated by the Comptroller of the Treasury with the approval of the Secretary of the Treasury in circulars issued in May and June last. These circulars prescribed the kind of accounts which shall be kept for the purpose of making available to the administrative head of each department, bureau, and office the information which is needed for directing the business of the Government.

In all of the work of the commission on these subjects emphasis has been laid upon cooperation with departmental committees composed of representatives appointed by the heads of departments for the express purpose of joining with the commission in the preliminary studies and in the conclusions and recommendations relating to the several departments and establishments.

Reports at Present Required by Congress

During the consideration of these subjects the commission has made a study of the present requirements of law relating to reports which are in whole or in part financial in character from the various departments and establishments. There are more than 90 acts of Congress which annually require reports of this character. These requirements of the law result in nearly 200 printed reports relating to financial matters, which must be submitted annually to the Congress by the various departments and establishments. Studies of these reports and comparisons of the classification of expenditures as set forth therein have been made by the commission to the end that, so far as practicable, uniformity of classification of objects of expenditure may be recommended and identical terminology adopted.

Recommendations and Modifications

In due time I shall transmit to the Congress such recommendations for changes in the present laws relating to these annual reports as appear to be pertinent and necessary.

Special consideration has been given by the commission to the annual reports relating to the financial transactions of the Government as a whole. In this connection the forms of the financial statements of the Government from early days to the present time have been examined. Further, in order that full information should be available, an investigation has been made of the forms of annual reports and budget statements, of the results of accounting, and of the terminology used by twenty or more foreign nations.

One of the consequences of this work is apparent in a modification of the form in which the gross receipts and disbursements of the Government have been exhibited heretofore by the Secretary of the Treasury in his annual reports to the Congress.

These modifications are important as illustrations of what may be expected in improvement in the annual statements of the Government as a whole when final recommendations are made, based upon these extended studies. Further results of this work will be apparent when standard forms for financial reports of departments and establishments, which are now in preparation through cooperation with the responsible officials of various departments, are completed and published. It will then be evident how far short of realizable ideals have been our annual statements and reports of the past.

The Budget

The United States is the only great Nation whose Government is operated without a budget. This fact seems to be more striking when it is considered that budgets and budget procedures are the outgrowth of democratic doctrines and have had an important part in the development of modern constitutional rights. The American Commonwealth has suffered much from irresponsibility on the part of its governing agencies. The constitutional purpose of a budget is to make government responsive to public opinion and responsible for its acts.

The Budget as an Annual Program

A budget should be the means for getting before the legislative branch, before the press, and before the people a definite annual program of business to be financed; it should be in the nature of a prospectus both of revenues and expenditures; it should comprehend every relation of the Government to the people, whether with reference to the raising of revenues or the rendering of service.

In many foreign countries the annual budget program is discussed with special reference to the revenue to be raised, the thought being that the raising of revenue bears more direct relation to welfare than does Government expenditure. Around questions of source of revenue political parties have been organized, and on such questions voters in the United States have taken sides since the first revenue law was proposed.

Citizen Interest in Expenditures

In political controversy it has been assumed generally that the individual citizen has little interest in what the Government spends. In my opinion, this has been a serious mistake, one which is becoming more serious each year. Now that population has become more dense, that large cities have developed, that people are required to live in congested centers, that the national resources frequently are the subject of private ownership and private control, and that transportation and other public-service facilities are held and operated by large corporations, what the Government does with nearly $1,000,000,000 each year is of as much concern to the average citizen as is the manner of obtaining this amount of money for public use. In the present inquiry special attention has been given to the expenditure side of the budget.

In prosecuting this inquiry, however, it has not been thought that arbitrary reductions should be made. The popular demand for economy has been to obtain the best service—the largest possible results for a given cost.

We want economy and efficiency; we want saving, and saving for a purpose. We want to save money to enable the Government to go into some of the beneficial projects which we are debarred from taking up now because we can not increase our expenditures. Projects affecting the public health, new public works, and other beneficial activities of government can be furthered if we are able to get a dollar of value for every dollar of the Government's money which we expend.

Public-Welfare Questions

The principal governmental objects in which the people of the United States are interested include:

The national defense; the protection of persons and property; the promotion of friendly relations and the protection of American interests abroad; the regulation of commerce and industry; the promotion of agriculture, fisheries, forestry, and mining; the promotion of manufacturing, commerce, and banking; the promotion of transportation and communication; the postal service, including postal savings and parcel post; the care for and utilization of the public domain; the promotion of education, art, science, and recreation; the promotion of the public health; the care and education of the Indians and other wards of the Nation.

These are public-welfare questions in which I assume every citizen has a vital interest. I believe that every Member of Congress, as an official representative of the people, each editor, as a nonofficial representative of public opinion, each citizen, as a beneficiary of the trust imposed on officers of the Government, should be able readily to ascertain how much has been spent for each of these purposes; how much has been appropriated for the current year; how much the administration is asking for each of these purposes for the next fiscal year.

Furthermore, each person interested should have laid before him a clear, well-digested statement showing in detail whether moneys appropriated have been economically spent and whether each division or office has been efficiently run. This is the information which should be available each year in the form of a budget and in detail accounts and reports supporting the budget.

Continuance of the Commission

I ask the continuance of this Commission on Economy and Efficiency because of the excellent beginning which has been made toward the reorganization of the machinery of this Government on business principles. I ask it because its work is entirely nonpartisan in character and ought to appeal to every citizen who wishes to give effectiveness to popular government, in which we feel a just pride. This work further commends itself for the reason that the cost of organization and work has been carefully considered at every point. Three months were taken in consideration of plans before the inquiry was begun; six months were then spent in preliminary investigations before the commission was organized; before March 3, 1911, when I asked for a continuation of the original appropriation for the current year, only $12,000 had been spent.

In organizing the commission my purpose was to obtain men eminently qualified for this character of work, and it may be said that it was found to be extremely difficult to find persons having such qualifications who would undertake the task. Several of the members of the commission were induced to take up the work as a personal sacrifice; in fact, considering the temporary character of the inquiry, it may be said that no member of the commission was moved by salary considerations. Only the public character of the work has made it possible for the Government to carry on such an inquiry except at a very much larger cost than has been incurred.

It is a matter of public record that the three largest insurance companies in New York, when under legislative investigation, spent more than $500,000 for expert services to assist the administration to put the business on a modern basis; but the economies the first year were more than tenfold the cost. I am informed that New York, Chicago, Boston, St. Louis, Cincinnati, Milwaukee, and other cities are prosecuting inquiries, the cost of which is largely disproportionate to the cost incurred by the Federal Government. Furthermore, these inquiries have the vigorous support and direct cooperation of citizen agencies which alone are spending not less than $200,000 per annum, and in several instances these combined agencies have been working not less than five years to put the cities on a businesslike basis, yet there is still much to be done.

The reason for bringing these facts to your attention is to suggest the magnitude of the task, the time necessary to its accomplishment, the professional skill which is essential to the successful handling of the work, the impossibility of carrying on such a work entirely with men who are at the same time engaged in the ordinary routine of administration. While in the nature of things the readjustment of organization and methods should continue indefinitely in order to adapt a great institution to the business in hand, ultimately this should be provided for as a part of the regular activities of some permanently organized agency. It is only after such a thorough inquiry has been made by experts who are not charged with the grinding details of official responsibility, however, that conclusions can be reached as to how this best can be done.

I sincerely hope that Congress will not, in its anxiety to reduce expenditures, economize by cutting off an appropriation which is likely to offer greater opportunity for real economy in the future than any other estimated for.

Vigorous Prosecution of the Inquiry

Economies actually realized have more than justified the total expenditure of the inquiry to date, and the economies which will soon be made by Executive action, based upon the information now in hand, will be many times greater than those already realized. Furthermore, the inquiry is in process of establishing a sound basis for recommendations relating to changes in law which will be necessary in order to make effective the economies which can not be provided by Executive action alone. Still further, it should be realized that the progress made by the inquiry has been notable when measured against the magnitude of the task undertaken. The principal function of the inquiry has been that of coordination. The commission has acted and should continue to act as a central clearing house for the committees in the various departments and establishments. By no other means can the cooperation which is essential be developed and continued throughout the Government service.

Helpful as legislative investigations may be in obtaining information as a basis for legislative action, changes which affect technical operations and which have to do with the details of method and procedure, necessarily followed in effectively directing and controlling the activities of the various services, can be successfully accomplished only by highly trained experts, whose whole time shall be given to the work, acting in cooperation with those who are charged with the handling of administrative details. The upbuilding of efficient service must necessarily be an educational process. With each advance made there will remain to those who conduct the details of the business an additional incentive to increase the efficiency and to realize true economy in all branches of the Government service.

As has been said, the changes which have already been made are resulting in economies greater than the cost of the inquiry; reports in my hands, with recommendations, estimate approximately $2,000,000 of possible annual economies; other subjects under investigation indicate much larger results. These represent only a few of the many services which should be subjected to a like painstaking inquiry. If this is done, it is beyond question that many millions of savings may be realized. Over and above the economy and increased efficiency which may be said to result from the work of the commission as such is an indirect result that can not well be measured. I refer to the influence which a vigorous, thoroughgoing executive inquiry has on each of the administrative units responsible to the Executive. The purpose being constructive, as soon as any subject is inquired into each of the services affected becomes at once alert to opportunities for improvement. So real is this that eagerness in many instances must be restrained. For example, when reports were requested on the subject of handling and filing correspondence, so many changes were begun that it became necessary to issue a letter to heads of departments requesting them not to permit further changes until the results had been reported and uniform plans of action had been agreed upon. To have permitted each of the hundreds of offices to undertake changes on their own initiative would merely have added to the confusion.

Much time and expense are necessary to get an inquiry of this kind started, to lay the foundation for sound judgment, and to develop the momentum required to accomplish definite results. This initial work has been done. The inquiry with its constructive measures is well under way. The work should now be prosecuted with vigor and receive the financial support necessary to make it most effective during the next fiscal year.

In this relation it may be said that the expenditure for the inquiry during the present fiscal year is at the rate of $130,000. The mass of information which must be collected, digested, and summarized pertaining to each subject of inquiry is enormous. From the results obtained it is evident that every dollar which is spent in the prosecution of the inquiry in the future will result in manifold savings. Every economy which has been or will be effected through changes in organization or method will inure to the benefit of the Government and of the people in increasing measure through the years which follow. It is clearly the part of wisdom to provide for the coming year means at least equal to those available during the current year, and in my opinion the appropriation should be increased to $200,000, and an additional amount of $50,000 should be provided for the publication of those results which will be of continuing value to officers of the Government and to the people.

11

Special Message

[Transmitting the report of the Employers' Liability and
Workmen's Compensation Commission]
The White House, February 20, 1912

To the Senate and House of Representatives:

I have the honor to transmit herewith the report of the Employers'
Liability and Workmen's Compensation Commission, authorized by joint
resolution No. 41, approved June 25, 1910, "To make a thorough investigation of the subject of Employers' Liability and Workmen's Compensation,
and to submit a report through the President to the Congress of the United
States."

The commission recommends a carefully drawn bill, entitled "A bill
to provide an exclusive remedy and compensation for accidental injuries
resulting in disability or death, to employees or common carriers by railroads engaged in interstate or foreign commerce, or in the District
of Columbia, and for other purposes." This bill works out in detail a
compensation for accidental injuries to employees of common carriers in
interstate railroad business, on the theory of insuring each employee
against the results of injury received in the course of the employment, without reference to his contributory negligence, and without any of the rules
obtaining in the common law limiting the liability of the employer in such

cases. The only case in which no compensation is to be allowed by the act is where the injury or death of the employee is occasioned by his willful intention to bring about the injury or death of himself or of another, or when the injury results from his intoxication while on duty.

It is unnecessary to go into the details of the bill. They are, however, most admirably worked out. They provide for a medical and hospital service for the injured man, for a notice of the injury to the employer, where such notice is not obviously given by the accident itself; for the fixing of the recovery by agreement; if not by agreement, by an official adjuster, to be confirmed by the court, and, if a jury is demanded, to be passed on by a jury. The amount of recovery is regulated in proportion to the wages received, and the more or less serious character of the injury where death does not ensue, specific provision being made for particular injuries in so far as they can be specified. The compensation is to be made in the form of annual payments for a number of years or for life. The fees to be paid to attorneys are specifically limited by the act. The remedies offered are exclusive of any other remedies. The statistical investigation seems to show that under this act the cost to the railroads would be perhaps 25 percent more than the total cost which they now incur.

The report of the commission has been very able and satisfactory, the investigations have been most thorough, and the discussion of the constitutional questions which have arisen in respect to the validity of the bill is of the highest merit.

Three objections to the validity of the bill of course occur:

In the first place, the question arises whether under the provisions of the commerce clause the bill could be considered to be a regulation of interstate and foreign commerce. That seems to be already settled by the decision of the Supreme Court in the employers' liability case.

The second question is whether the making of these remedies exclusive and the compelling of the railroad companies to meet obligations arising from injuries, for which the railroad would not be liable under the common law, is a denial of the due process of law which is enjoined upon Congress by the fifth amendment to the Constitution in dealing with the property rights. This question the report takes up, and in an exhaustive review of the authorities makes clear, as it seems to me, the validity of the act. This is the question which in the Court of Appeals of the State of New

York was decided adversely to the validity of the compensation act adopted by the legislature of that State. How far that act and the one here proposed differ it is unnecessary to state. It is sufficient to say that the argument of the commission is most convincing to show that the police power of the Government exercised in the regulation of interstate commerce is quite sufficient to justify the imposition upon the interstate railroad companies of the liability for the injuries to its employees on an insurance basis.

The third objection is that the right of trial by jury, guaranteed by the seventh amendment, is denied. As a matter of fact, the right is preserved in this act by permitting a jury to pass on the issue when duly demanded, in accordance with the limitation of the act.

I sincerely hope that this act will pass. I deem it one of the great steps of progress toward a satisfactory solution of an important phase of the controversies between employer and employee that has been proposed within the last two or three decades. The old rules of liability under the common law were adapted to a different age and condition and were evidently drawn by men imbued with the importance of preserving the employers from burdensome or unjust liability. It was treated as a personal matter of each employee, and the employer and the employee were put on a level of dealing, which, however it may have been in the past, certainly creates injustice to the employee under the present conditions.

One of the great objections to the old common-law method of settling questions of this character was the lack of uniformity in the recoveries made by injured employees, and by the representatives of those who suffered death. Frequently meritorious cases that appealed strongly to every sense of human justice were shut out by arbitrary rules limiting the liability of the employer. On the other hand, often by perjured evidence and the undue emotional generosity of the jury, recoveries were given far in excess of the real injury, and sometimes on facts that hardly justified recovery at all. Now, under this system the tendency will be to create as nearly a uniform system as can be devised; there will be recoveries in every case, and they will be limited by the terms of the law so as to be reasonable.

The great injustice of the present system, by which recoveries of verdicts of any size do not result in actual benefit to the injured person because of the heavy expense of the litigation and the fees charged by the counsel for the plaintiff, will disappear under this new law, by which the fees of the counsel are limited to a very reasonable amount. The cases will be disposed of most expeditiously under this system, and the money will be distributed for the support of the injured person over a number of years, so as to make its benefit greater and more secure.

Of course the great object of this act is to secure justice to the weaker party under existing modern conditions, but a result hardly less important will follow from this act that I can not fail to mention.

The administration of justice today is clogged in every court by the great number of suits for damages for personal injury. The settlement of such cases by this system will serve to reduce the burden of our courts one-half by taking the cases out of court and disposing of them by this short cut. The remainder of the business in the courts will thus have greater attention from the judges, and will be disposed of with much greater dispatch. In every way, therefore, the act demands your earnest consideration, and I sincerely hope that it may be passed before the adjournment of this session of Congress.

There accompanies the letter of transmittal of Senator Sutherland not only the report of the commission but also the hearings of witnesses by the commission, all of which is herewith submitted.

12

Special Message

[Transmitting the annual report of the Postmaster General for the
fiscal year ended June 30, 1911; and the report of the Commission on
Second-class Mail Matter]
The White House, February 22, 1912

To the Senate and House of Representatives:

In transmitting the annual report of the Postmaster General for the
fiscal year ended June 30, 1911, it gives me pleasure to call attention to the
fact that the revenues for the fiscal year ended June 30, 1911, amounted to
$237,879,823.60 and that the expenditures amounted to $237,660,705.48,
making a surplus of $219,118.12. For the year ended June 30, 1909, the
postal service was in arrears to the extent of $17,479,770.47. In the interval
this very large deficit has been changed into a surplus, and that without
the curtailment of postal facilities. Indeed, in the same time there have
been established 3,744 new post offices, delivery by carrier provided in 186
additional cities, and new rural routes established, 2,516 in number and
aggregating 60,679 miles in extent. The force of postal employees has been
increased by more than 8,000, and a liberal policy in the matter of salaries
has been followed, so that the amount expended for salaries is now
$14,000,000 more than two years ago. The average salary has been in-
creased from $869 to $967 for rural carriers, $979 to $1,082 for post office

clerks, $1,021 to $1,084 for city letter carriers, and $1,168 to $1,183 for railway postal clerks.

The report shows that the postal-savings system was begun experimentally in January, 1911, and that it has now been extended so as to include 7,500 presidential post offices, which includes practically all of the post offices of that class. Preparations are also being made to establish the system at about 40,000 fourth-class offices. The deposits in 11 months have reached a total of $11,000,000, distributed among 2,710 national and State banks.

The Postmaster General recommends, as I have done in previous messages, the adoption of a parcel post, and the beginning of this in the organization of such service on rural routes and in the City Delivery Service first.

The placing of assistant postmasters in the classified service has secured greater efficiency. It is hoped that the same thing may be done with all the postmasters.

The report of the Postmaster General is full of statements of the important improvements in the organization and methods of the postal service made since the last annual report, and of tentative drafts of legislation embodying certain recommendations of the department which need legislation to carry them out.

There is only one recommendation in which I can not agree—that is one which recommends that the telegraph lines in the United States should be made a part of the postal system and operated in conjunction with the mail system. This presents a question of Government ownership of public utilities which are now being conducted by private enterprise under franchises from the Government. I believe that the true principle is that private enterprise should be permitted to carry on such public utilities under due regulation as to rates by proper authority rather than that the Government should itself conduct them. This principle I favor because I do not think it in accordance with the best public policy thus greatly to increase the body of public servants. Of course, if it could be shown that telegraph service could be furnished to the public at a less price than it is now furnished to the public by telegraph companies, and with equal efficiency, the argument might be a strong one in favor of the adoption of the proposition. But I am not satisfied from any evidence that if these properties were taken over by the Government they could be managed any more economically or any more efficiently or that this would enable the Government to furnish service at any smaller rate than the public are now required to pay by private companies.

More than this, it seems to me that the consideration of the question ought to be postponed until after the postal savings banks have come into complete and smooth operation and after a parcels post has been established not only upon the rural routes and the city deliveries but also throughout the department. It will take some time to perfect these additions to the activities of the Post Office Department, and we may well await their complete and successful adoption before we take on a new burden in this very extended department.

I cannot speak with too great emphasis of the improvement in the Post Office Department under the present management. The cutting down of cost, the shortening of methods, and the increase in efficiency are shown by the statistics of the Annual Report.

One of the most important matters referred to by the Postmaster General is the proposed fixing of new rates of postage for second-class mail matter. In connection with this subject, I have the honor to transmit herewith the report of the Commission on Second-Class Mail Matter, appointed pursuant to a joint resolution of the Sixty-first Congress, approved March 4, 1911.

The commission consists of Hon. Charles E. Hughes, Associate Justice of the Supreme Court of the United States; President A. Lawrence Lowell, of Harvard University; and Mr. Harry A. Wheeler, president of the Association of Commerce of the city of Chicago, whose character, ability, and experience command for their findings and recommendations the respect and confidence of the Congress and the country.

The report discloses a most exhaustive and critical inquiry into the subject of second-class mail matter after adequate notice to all the parties in interest. Extensive hearings were held by the commission, at which the Postmaster General and the Second and Third Assistant Postmasters General appeared and submitted formal statements presenting the various contentions of the Post Office Department, together with all the relevant official data and evidence relating to the cost of handling and transporting

second-class mail matter. Certain of the leading magazines were represented by counsel, while various other publications appeared by representatives and were heard in oral argument or permitted to submit written
briefs setting forth their respective reasons for opposing a change in the
present postage rate on second-class mail. The Second and Third Assistant
Postmasters General, together with minor officers of the department, were
critically cross-examined by the counsel and representatives of the periodicals, and all the various phases of the second-class postage problem were
made the subject of a most painstaking investigation.

The findings of the commission confirm the view that the cost of handling and transporting second-class mail matter is greatly in excess of the
postage paid, and that an increase in the rate is not only justified by the
facts, but is desirable.

The commission reports that the evidence submitted for its consideration is sufficient to warrant a finding of the approximate cost of handling
and transporting the several classes of second-class mail known as paid-at-
the-pound rate, free-in-county, and transient matter, in so far as relates to
the services of transportation, post-office cars, railway distribution, rural
delivery, and certain other items of cost, but that it is without adequate
data to determine the cost of the general post-office service and also what
portion of the cost of certain other aggregate services is properly assignable
to second-class mail matter. It finds that in the fiscal year 1908, the period
for which the statistics for the Post Office Department were compiled, the
cost of handling and transporting second-class mail, in the items of transportation, post-office cars, railway distribution, rural delivery, and certain
miscellaneous charges, was approximately 6 cents a pound for paid-at-the-
pound-rate matter, and for free-in-county and transient matter each approximately 5 cents a pound, and that upon this basis, as modified by subsequent reductions in the cost of railroad transportation, the cost of paid-
at-the-pound-rate matter, for the services mentioned, is now approximately 5½ cents a pound, while the cost of free-in-county and transient
matter remains as formerly, namely, each at approximately 5 cents a pound.

Since the commission has determined that the cost of handling and
transporting second-class mail is approximately 5½ cents for paid-at-the-
pound-rate matter and approximately 5 cents each for free-in-county and

transient matter, without taking into account the cost of the general post-office service and certain unassignable items of expense, it is apparent that the aggregate cost of all service performed by the postal establishment in connection with this class of mail matter is considerably above that amount.

The postal service is now, for the first time in years, operated upon a self-sustaining basis, and in my judgment this is a wise policy; but it should not be carried out at the expense of certain classes of mail matter that pay revenue largely in excess of their cost. It is not just that some classes of mail should be exorbitantly taxed to meet a deficiency caused by other classes, the revenue from which is much below their cost of handling and carriage. Where such inequalities exist they should be removed as early as practicable. The business enterprises of the publishers of periodicals, however, have been built up on the basis of the present second-class rate, and therefore it would be manifestly unfair to put into immediate effect a large increase in postage. That newspapers and magazines have been potent agencies for the dissemination of public intelligence and have consequently borne a worthy part in the development of the country all must admit; but it is likewise true that the original purpose of Congress in providing for them a subvention by way of nominal postal charges in consideration of their value as mediums of public information ought not to prevent an increase, because they are now not only educational but highly profitable. There is no warrant for the great disparity between existing postage rates on periodicals and the cost of the service the Government performs for them. The aggregate postal revenues for the fiscal year 1911 were $237,879,823.60, derived mainly from the postage collected on the four classes of mail matter. It is carefully estimated by the Post Office Department that the revenue derived from mail matter of the first class is approximately one and one-half times the cost of handling and carriage; that the returns from third and fourth class matter are slightly in excess of their cost of handling and carriage; and that while second-class matter embraces over 65 percent of the entire weight of all the mail carried, it, nevertheless, yields little more than 5 percent of the postal revenues.

The recommendations of the commission as to the postage rates on second-class mail are as follows:

1. The rate of 2 cents a pound on copies mailed by publishers to subscribers, to news agents, and as sample copies, and by news agents
to their subscribers or to other news agents.
2. The rate of 1 cent for each 4 ounces for copies mailed by other than
publishers and news agents; that is, the present transient rate.
3. The present free-in-county privilege retained, but not extended.

The commission also recommended that the cent-a-copy rate for
newspapers other than weeklies and for periodicals not exceeding 2 ounces
in weight, and the 2-cent-a-copy rate for periodicals exceeding 2 ounces
in weight, when mailed at a city letter-carrier office for local delivery, be
abolished.

As to the effect and adequacy of the proposed increase of 1 cent a
pound in postage the commission says:

> Such an increase will not, in the opinion of the commission, bring
> distress upon the publishers of newspapers and periodicals, or seriously
> interfere with the dissemination of useful news or information. A rea-
> sonable time should be allowed, after the rate is fixed, before it is put
> into effect. While the new rate will be very far from compensating the
> Government for the carriage and handling of second-class matter, it will
> to some extent relieve the existing burden and result in a more equitable
> adjustment of rates.

The commission suggests that the department "maintain an adequate
cost system, so that the effect of the new rates may be closely observed and a
proper basis may be secured for the consideration of any future proposals."

In these recommendations the Postmaster General and I heartily concur and commend them to the early attention of Congress. The proposed
increase of 1 cent a pound in the second-class postage rate, I believe, to be
most reasonable, and if sufficient time is allowed before the change goes
into effect it should work little serious injury to the business of the periodi-
cal publishers, while equalizing, at least in a measure, the burdens of postal
taxation.

13

Special Message

[On economy and efficiency in the Government services]
The White House, April 4, 1912

To the Senate and House of Representatives:

On the seventeenth of January last I sent a message to the Congress describing the work of the commission appointed by me under authority of the acts of June 25, 1910, and March 3, 1911, granting appropriations to enable me to inquire into the methods of transacting the public business of the various executive departments and other governmental establishments, and to make report as to improved efficiency and greater economy to be obtained in the expenditure of money for the maintenance of the Government. By way of illustrating the utility of the commission, and the work which they were engaged upon, I referred to a number of reports which they had filed, recommending changes in organization of the departments and bureaus of the Government, the avoidance of duplication of functions and services, and the installation of labor-saving devices and improved office methods. All of the recommendations looked to savings of considerable amounts. With the message of February 5, 1912, I transmitted to the Congress the reports on the centralization of distribution of Government documents, on the use of window envelopes, and on the use of a photographic process for copying records.

A number of the reports of the commission had not then been commented on by the heads of the departments that would be affected by the changes recommended, and therefore I did not feel justified at that time in recommending to the Congress the statutory amendments necessary to carry out the recommendations of the commission. Since then, however, I have received the recommendations of the heads of departments, and I transmit this message for the purpose of expressing my approval of the changes recommended by the commission and of laying before the Congress the reports prepared by the commission.

Local Offices Should Be in the Classified Service

Post Offices

I have several times called attention to the advantages to be derived from placing in the classified service the local officers under the Departments of the Treasury, of the Post Office, of Justice, of the Interior, and of Commerce and Labor. In my message submitted to the Congress on January seventeenth I referred to the loss occasioned to the Government because of the fact that in many cases two persons are paid for doing work that could easily be done by one. In the meantime I have caused an inquiry to be made as to the amount in money of this loss. The results of this inquiry are that the loss amounts to at least $10,000,000 annually. For example, it appears that a very substantial economy would result from putting experienced and trained officers in charge of the first and second class post offices instead of selecting the postmasters in accordance with the present practice. As the annual operating expenses of the first and second class offices aggregate the enormous sum of more than $80,000,000, undoubtedly if the postmasters of these offices were embraced in the classified service, and required to devote all their time to the public service, the annual savings would eventually represent many millions of dollars. The saving in salaries alone, not taking into account any saving due to increased efficiency of operation, would amount to about $4,500,000. At the present time the salaries of postmasters of the first and second class amount to $6,076,900, while the salaries of assistant postmasters of the same classes amount to $2,820,000. If the position of postmaster were placed in the classified service and those officers were given salaries equal to 20 percent more than the salaries now given to the assistant postmasters, the latter position being no longer required, there would be a saving in salaries to the Government of $4,512,900. In the case of postmasters at offices of the third class a large annual saving could be made.

Pension Agencies

An annual saving of nearly $62,000 could be made if the position of pension agent were placed in the classified service, since the work now done by a pension agent at a salary of $4,000 and a chief clerk at a salary ranging between $1,400 and $2,250 could easily be done by one person in the permanent classified service at a salary varying from $2,100 to $3,000. Greater economy and efficiency would result from the abolition of the pension agencies and from the adoption of a plan in accordance with which pensions would be paid by the Pension Office in Washington.

District Land Offices

What is true in the matter of payment of pensions is also true in the service under the General Land Office. The field service of this office could be more efficiently and economically operated if it were provided by law that the office of receiver of district land offices be abolished and the duties transferred to the register, assisted by a bonded clerk, and the register placed in the classified service. It has several times been estimated that more than $200,000 would be saved annually and the efficiency of the service greatly increased by the adoption of such a plan.

Internal-Revenue and Customs Offices

Large expenditures are made for salaries of political appointees in the internal-revenue and customs services. In both services a direct saving in salaries, and an indirect economy through increased efficiency, would follow a transfer of such offices to the classified service.

Other Local Offices

In the other field services the saving which would result from the classification of the local officers under the departments is not as marked or probably capable of as exact estimation as in those mentioned, but there is no doubt that substantial savings would follow. It is not to be doubted that where no saving would result the classification of the local officers would increase the efficiency of the service. It would be desirable also to place all marshals, deputy marshals, and assistant attorneys in the classified service, although but little direct economy would result. Supervising inspectors in the Steamboat Inspection Service and the members of the field service in the Bureau of Fisheries should be placed in the classified service.

Commission's Report on Local Offices

The report on methods of appointment submitted to me by the commission, which covers fully the subject of appointments by the President by and with the advice and consent of the Senate, and recommends that various local officers, such as postmasters, collectors of internal revenue, etc., and heads of bureaus in the departmental service, be included in the classified service, is transmitted herewith (Appendix No. 1.) The report and recommendations are approved by me.

Legislation Needed to Establish the Merit System

In the interest of an efficient and economical administration of the vast business of the Government, I urge the necessity for the inauguration of this important reform, and recommend that the necessary amendments be made to the laws governing appointments, such amendments to take effect not later than July 1, 1913, so that there may be secured to the people the benefits to be derived from a conduct of their affairs by officers selected on a merit basis and devoting their time and talents solely to the duties of their offices.

Consolidation of Lighthouse and Life-Saving Services

The commission's report (Appendix No. 2) recommends that the Life-Saving Service of the Department of the Treasury be discontinued as a separate organization and that the maintenance and operation of the life-saving stations of the country be made one of the duties of the Bureau of Lighthouses of the Department of Commerce and Labor. I concur in this recommendation and urge that the necessary legislation for carrying it into effect be enacted.

Both of these services are organized and maintained for the same general purpose—the protection of life and property endangered along the coasts and other navigable waters. Both maintain stations along the coast, which are located for the most part in close proximity. Both have substantially the same business problems to meet in locating, constructing, and maintaining these stations; in recruiting the personnel; in manufacturing or purchasing equipment; in purchasing, housing in depots, and distributing supplies; in operating a field-inspection service; in maintaining telephonic and other means of communication; in disbursing funds; in keeping proper books of accounts; and in rendering reports showing financial and other transactions. The maintenance of two separate services, as at present, means a duplication of organization in respect to all of these operations. The recommendation of the commission does not contemplate any essential change in the work of the life-saving stations; it is for the transfer of the business management of these institutions to the Bureau of Lighthouses. That bureau being fully organized for the administration of stations of this character will be able to direct and manage these stations with comparatively little addition to its present force and equipment. The commission estimates that, in addition to the advantage that will be obtained through having these two services operated by the same organization, a direct economy will be secured of at least $100,000 annually, and that the saving will greatly exceed this sum after the first year.

Revenue-Cutter Service

The report of the commission on the Revenue-Cutter Service (Appendix No. 3) represents a detailed investigation of the history, organization, and activities of this branch of the Government service and its relations to other services. The conclusion is reached that all of the duties now being performed by this service can be performed with equal efficiency by other services and that a great economy will result by having these duties so performed. The commission accordingly recommends that the service be abolished as a distinct organization; that its equipment be distributed among other services requiring the use of marine craft; and that provision be made for the performance of the work now being done by it by such other services.

With these fundamental recommendations of the commission I am in full accord, and I recommend that the necessary legislation be enacted to put them into effect.

At the present time the Revenue-Cutter Service is organized as a Naval Establishment. The country is, in effect, maintaining two navies, and is using one of these navies for the performance of duties of a civil character. The maintenance of two separate naval establishments entails unnecessary expense and is not in the interest of either efficiency or economy. In so far as the duties of the Revenue-Cutter Service are of a naval character, or are such as can readily be performed by the regular Naval Establishment, they should be performed by such establishment; in so far as they are of a purely civil character, use should be made of services organized and conducted upon a civil basis.

In respect to the distribution of the equipment and duties of the Revenue-Cutter Service among other branches of the Government, the recommendation of the commission looks to the transfer to the Navy Department of the vessels which are adapted to deep-sea cruising and the discharge by the Naval Establishment of most of the duties now performed by the Revenue-Cutter Service upon the high seas. In memoranda submitted on the report of the commission, copies of which are submitted with such report, on the one hand the Secretary of the Navy raises the question as to whether these duties can be performed by the regular Naval Establishment without detracting from its military efficiency, while on the other hand the Secretary of Commerce and Labor raises the question whether certain of these duties can not be performed by the Lighthouse Service if that service is provided with vessels suitable for the purpose.

In view of these suggestions I recommend that, in the enactment of legislation providing for the abolition of the Revenue-Cutter Service, provision be made for the transfer of all the vessels and equipment of the Revenue-Cutter Service from the Treasury Department to the Department of Commerce and Labor; that the Secretary of Commerce and Labor be directed to assign such vessels and equipment to the Lighthouse Establishment, Bureau of Fisheries, and other services under his jurisdiction requiring the use of vessels, as, in his judgment, is for the best interest of the public service, and that authority be given to him to turn over to the Navy such vessels as he may find, upon investigation, not to be required by his department and which by their character are fitted to serve as useful auxiliaries to the Naval Establishment.

In thus recommending that the Revenue-Cutter Service as a separate establishment be abolished, I desire to make plain that such action does not carry with it the discontinuance of the rendering of any valuable and proper service now being rendered by that organization. On the contrary, I am persuaded that all such services will continue to be performed under the system recommended by me with equal or greater efficiency.

It should be noted that the adoption of the recommendation here made will result in bringing under one general administration all of the work of the Government having to do with the protection of life and property at sea. This will result not only in greatly increased efficiency, but in a large saving. The Lighthouse Establishment is compelled by the nature of the work to maintain and operate a large fleet of vessels and supplementary administrative divisions, depots, inspection services, etc., to attend to matters pertaining to their business management. It is thus fully prepared to take over and operate the additional vessels that may be assigned to it and to perform the additional duties with which it may be intrusted at an added expense that will be small in comparison with that now entailed in maintaining an independent service on a military basis.

A further benefit of no little importance that will also be secured will be that of relieving the Department of the Treasury of duties which are in no ways germane to the primary function of that department.

The Consolidation of Auditing Offices

The report upon the organization and methods of work of the accounting offices of the Treasury (Appendix No. 4) recommends that the offices of the six auditors be consolidated under one auditor, and that the auditors of customs accounts located at the principal ports, and known as naval officers, be made assistants to the auditors. An increase in the efficiency of the Treasury audit will be one result of the carrying out of these recommendations, and the saving of expense when the consolidation has been fully completed will amount to at least $200,000 a year, based upon current appropriations. The present organization, under which six independent auditors are engaged in the one work of final audit of the Government accounts, is certainly one that can produce only diversity of practice and procedure, inefficient use of personnel and equipment, and delay and uncertainty of requirements from which the public as well as officers of the Government must suffer.

In my opinion a change in law to carry into effect these recommendations of the commission, which have my approval, will be in the interest of the public service.

The Returns Office

The report upon the "Returns Office" of the Department of the Interior (Appendix No. 5) recommends the abolition of that office and that provision for public inspection of Government contracts be made through the office of the auditors of the Treasury, in which offices the originals of all contracts are filed. It also recommends the substitution of a certificate for the affidavit required to be attached to the contracts of the Departments of War, the Navy, and the Interior, and an amendment of the statute which now requires all the contracts of those departments to be in writing. I transmit letters from the secretaries of the departments referred to, concurring in the conclusions and recommendations of the commission. I approve the report and commend it to the favorable consideration of the Congress.

Government Expenses for Travel

The report upon "Travel expenditures" of officers and employees of the Government (Appendix No. 6) presents a view of existing conditions that can lead to but one conclusion—that under the existing laws, and regulations and practices pursuant thereto, the allowances for travel are as varied as there are executive departments. The same classes of officers and employees are receiving different rates of allowances, depending only upon the department or bureau in which they are employed. Under similar conditions there should be uniformity. The report recommends that all allowances in the form of mileage be discontinued and that actual cost of transportation be paid; that in lieu of payment of actual cost of other expenses, commonly known as subsistence, which would include lodging, a scale of per diem allowances be established by the President for the several classes of officers and employees. It is also recommended by the commission that all accounts for reimbursement of traveling expenses shall be certified as to correctness in lieu of the requirement of law in many cases that the verification be by affidavit. The latter procedure is troublesome and expensive, and the penalty for a false certification is fully as valuable in its deterrent effect as the penalty for making a false affidavit.

With the report are the comments of the War and the Navy Departments, made at my request. The report of the commission has my approval, and the suggestions therein for a change in the law on the subject are submitted with a request for action in accordance therewith.

Handling and Filing of Correspondence

The handling and filing of correspondence constitutes one of the business processes of the Government to which, as pointed out in my message of January 17, the commission has paid especial attention. The investigations of existing conditions have brought out clearly that, in many cases, present methods are inefficient and entail large, unnecessary costs. The features of present practices which stand out most prominently as entailing large, unnecessary labor and expense pertain to the briefing, press-copying, and recording and indexing of communications. A statement has been prepared giving the results of an investigation of the salary cost entailed in performing these operations in the several departments at Washington. It is the opinion of the commission that the operations of briefing and press-copying letters can be entirely eliminated, and that the recording and indexing of incoming and outgoing letters can be reduced at least 50 percent.

Though the commission is making independent investigations of methods followed in handling and filing correspondence in certain bureaus and services, the results of which will be embodied in reports describing such methods, pointing out wherein they are defective, and recommending changes to make them conform to the most approved practices, the general policy pursued is that of working in close cooperation with the departments and services through the means of joint committees. To the end that these committees might all work as nearly as possible along uniform lines, and that the departments and establishments might have before them the conclusions reached by the commission relative to fundamental principles and the best practices in respect to the performance of this class of work, the commission has prepared, and I have sent to the heads of departments a memorandum setting forth the principles which should govern in the matter of handling and filing of correspondence. This memorandum also contains suggestions for the use of labor-saving devices in preparing and mailing letters. I am transmitting herewith a copy of this memorandum (Appendix No. 7).

On the basis of this memorandum active efforts are now being made in all of the departments for the improvement of the methods of handling and filing of correspondence. These efforts have resulted in radical changes in existing methods and the effecting of large economies. The flat-filing system has been substituted for the old cumbrous folded and indorsement system. Carbon copies of letters have been substituted for press copies. The briefing of documents has been entirely discontinued in a number of services, and in others the maintenance of book records of incoming and outgoing communications has been discontinued. The effort is being made to make correspondence files self-indexing, and thus avoid the necessity for making and using secondary finding devices. This work can only be intelligently prosecuted as the result of painstaking and detail investigation of the special conditions to be met in each particular service. Many months will, therefore, be required to carry out this work throughout the entire Government. It is of the utmost importance that the work should be prosecuted under a general supervision or direction such as is furnished by the present commission.

Distribution of Government Documents

Attention is called to the report of the commission, transmitted to the Congress with my message of February fifth and to the supplementary statement sent herewith (Appendix No. 8) on the centralization of distribution of Government publications. By adopting this recommendation it is conservatively estimated that $242,000 can be saved. This is exclusive of the saving which could be made by handling the congressional documents in the same manner. An account kept for 31 days with the volume of this business of handling congressional documents showed an average of 21 tons per day. These documents were first taken from the Printing Office to the Capitol, then from the Capitol to the post office, then hauled back to the Union Station, the latter being but a short distance from the Printing Office. An up-to-date plant at the Printing Office which could handle all this would entail an increased capital outlay for permanent equipment of only about $75,000. The recommendation for centralizing the distribution of documents from the departments, if acted on, will affect the appropriations of seven departments, five independent establishments, and the Washington post office.

I may say in connection with this report and recommendation that the House of Representatives, in passing the agricultural appropriation bill for the fiscal year 1913, instead of reducing the cost of distributing Government publications in the Department of Agriculture by $137,000, has increased to the extent of $13,260 the amount appropriated for salaries for the Division of Publications over the appropriation for the current year.

Outlines of Organization

The outlines of organization of the Government, which were transmitted with the message of January seventeenth, have been sent to each of the departments, with a request that orders issue which will require that the outline be kept up to date (Appendix No. 9). This will not only make available at all times the information needed by Congress or the administration when called for, and assist materially in the preparation of estimates of appropriations, but will make unnecessary the publication of the official register, thereby saving approximately $45,000 for each issue.

Conclusion

In submitting these reports, with recommendations, I will state that in my opinion each of the foregoing recommendations, if acted on, will contribute largely to increase efficiency. Directly and indirectly the changes proposed will result in the saving of many millions of dollars of public funds. This will leave the Congress free to determine whether the amount thus saved shall be utilized to reduce taxation or to provide funds with which to extend activities already carried on and to enter on beneficial projects which otherwise could not be undertaken for lack of funds.

Again I urge upon the Congress the desirability of providing whatever funds can be used effectively to carry forward with all possible vigor the work now well begun. The $200,000 required for the prosecution of the inquiry during the ensuing year, and the $50,000 estimated for the publication of results, are inconsiderable in comparison with the economies which can be realized.

14

Veto Message

[Returning to the House of Representatives, without approval, H.R.
22195, "An Act to Reduce the Duties on Wool and the Manufactures
of Wool," and stating certain objections thereto]
The White House, August 9, 1912

To the House of Representatives:

On December 20, 1911, I sent a message to the Congress, recommending a prompt revision of the tariff on wool and woolens. I urged a reduction of duties which should remove all the excesses and inequalities of the schedule, but should leave a degree of protection adequate to maintain the continued employment of machinery and labor already established in that great industry. With that message I transmitted a report of the Tariff Board, which furnished for the first time the information needed to frame a revision bill of this character, and recommended that legislation should be at once undertaken in the light of this information.

Despite the efforts which have been made to discredit the work of the Tariff Board, their report on this schedule has been accepted, with scarcely a dissenting voice, by all those familiar with the problems discussed, including active representatives of organizations formed in the interest of the public and the consumer. Importers and merchants, as well as producers and manufacturers, have testified to the accuracy and impartiality of these findings of fact. For the first time in the history of American tariffs the opportunity has been afforded of securing a revision based on established facts, independent both of the *ex parte* statements of interested persons and the guesswork of political theorists.

My position has been made perfectly plain. I shall stand by my pledges to maintain a degree of protection necessary to offset the difference in cost of production here and abroad, and will heartily approve of any bill reducing duties to this level. Bills have been introduced into Congress, carefully framed and based on the findings of the Tariff Board, which, while maintaining the principle of protection, have provided for sweeping reductions. Such a bill was presented by the minority members of the Ways and Means Committee, which, while providing protection to the woolgrower, reduces the duty on most wools 20 percent, and the duties on manufactures by from 20 to more than 50 percent, and gives in many instances less net protection to the manufacturer than was granted by the Gorman-Wilson free-wool act of 1894.

Instead of such a measure of thorough and genuine revision, based on full information of the facts, and with rates properly adjusted to all the different stages of the industry, there is now presented for my approval H.R. 22195, "An act to reduce the duties on wool and the manufactures of wool," a bill identical with the one which I vetoed in August, 1911, before the report of the Tariff Board had been made. The Tariff Board's report fully and completely justifies my veto of that date. The amount of *ad valorem* duty necessary to offset the difference in the cost of production of raw wool here and abroad varies with every grade of wool. Consequently, an *ad valorem* rate of duty adjusted to meet the difference in the cost of production of high-priced wools is not protective to low-priced wools. In any case, the report of the Tariff Board shows that the *ad valorem* duty of 29 percent on raw wool, imposed in the bill now submitted to me, is inadequate to meet this difference in cost in the case of four-fifths of our total wool clip. The disastrous effect upon the business of our farmers engaged in wool raising can not be more clearly stated. To maintain the status quo in the wool-growing industry, the minimum *ad valorem* rate necessary, even for high-grade wool in years of high prices, would be 35 percent.

The rate provided in this bill on cloths of all kinds is 49 percent. The amount of net protection given by this rate, in addition to proper compensation for the duty on wool, depends on the ratio between the cost of the raw material and the cost of making the cloth. The cost of the raw material in woolen and worsted fabrics varies in general from 50 percent to 70 percent of the total value of the fabric. Consequently, the net protective duty, with wool at 29 percent, would vary from 28.7 percent to 34.5 percent. In the great majority of cases these rates are inadequate to equalize the difference in the cost of manufacture here and abroad. This is especially true of the finest goods involving a high proportion of labor cost. One of the striking developments of the last few years has been the growth in this country of a fine goods industry. The rates provided in this bill, inadequate as they are for most of the cloths produced in this country, would make the continuance here of the manufacture of fine goods an impossibility.

Even more dangerous in their effects are the rates proposed on tops and yarns. Tops are the result of the first stage in the making of raw wool into cloth. Yarn is the result of the second stage. Taken in connection with a rate of 29 percent on wool, and 49 percent on cloths, the rates of 32 percent on tops and 35 percent on yarn, fixed in this bill, seem impossible of justification. They would disrupt, and to no purpose, the existing adjustment, within the industry, of all its different branches. It is improbable in the highest degree that raw wool would be imported in great quantities when the cloth maker can import his tops at a duty of 32 percent and yarns at a duty of 35 percent. The report of the Tariff Board shows the difference in relative costs to be uniformly greater than the amount of protection on yarns given by this bill. In a year of low prices, the net protection granted by the proposed rates would not be more than half the difference in costs. The free wool act of 1894 gave a protective rate of 40 percent on all yarns over 40 cents a pound in value, with free raw material. The present bill gives only 35 percent on such yarns with a duty of 29 percent on the raw material. The great increase in the imports of tops and yarns which would result from the rates in the bill now submitted to me, would destroy the effect of the protection to raw wool and at the same time would be at the cost of widespread disaster to the wool-combing and spinning branches of the industry. The last 15 years has witnessed a great growth of top making and worsted spinning in this country, and the capacity of the plants is now equal to domestic requirements. Under the rates proposed such plants could be continued, if at all, only by writing off most of the investment as a net loss and by a reduction of wages. To sum up, then, most of the rates in the submitted bill are so low in themselves that if enacted into law the inevitable result would be the irretrievable injury to the wool-growing industry, the enforced idleness of much of our wool-combing and spinning machinery, and of thousands of looms, and the consequent throwing out of employment of thousands of workmen.

In view of these facts, in view of the platform upon which I was elected, in view of my promise to follow and maintain the protective policy, no course is open to me but to withhold my approval from this bill. I am very much disappointed that such a bill is a second time presented to me. I have inferred from the speeches made in both the House and the Senate that the members of the majority in both Houses are deeply impressed with the necessity of reducing the tariff under the present act on wool and woolens; that they do not propose to stand on the question of the amount of reduction or to insist that it must be enough necessarily to satisfy the principle of tariff for revenue only, but that they are willing to accept a substantial reduction in the present rates in order that the people might be relieved from the possibility of oppressive prices due to excessive rates, I strongly desire to reduce duties, provided only the protection system be maintained, and that industries now established be not destroyed. It now appears from the Tariff Board's report, and from bills which have been introduced into the House and the Senate, that a bill may be drawn so as to be within the requirements of protection and still offer a reduction of 20 percent on most wool and of from 20 percent to 50 percent on cloths. I can not act upon the assumption that the controlling majority in either House will refuse to pass a bill of this kind, if in fact it accomplishes so substantial a reduction, merely because members of the opposing party and the Executive unite in its approval. I, therefore, urge upon Congress that it do not adjourn without taking advantage of the plain opportunity thus substantially to reduce unnecessary existing duties. I appeal to Congress to reconsider the measure, which I now return, without my approval, and to adopt a substitute therefor making substantial reductions below the rates of the present act, which the Tariff Board shows possible, without destroying any established industry or throwing any wage earners out of employment, and which I will promptly approve.

15

Memorandum

[To accompany the Panama Canal Act]
The White House, August 24, 1912

In signing the Panama Canal bill, I wish to leave this memorandum. The bill is admirably drawn for the purpose of securing the proper maintenance, operation, and control of the canal, and the government of the Canal Zone, and for the furnishing to all the patrons of the canal, through the Government, of the requisite docking facilities and the supply of coal and other shipping necessities. It is absolutely necessary to have the bill passed at this session in order that the capital of the world engaged in the preparation of ships to use the canal may know in advance the conditions under which the traffic is to be carried on through this waterway.

I wish to consider the objections to the bill in the order of their importance.

First. The bill is objected to because it is said to violate the Hay-Pauncefote Treaty in discriminating in favor of the coastwise trade of the United States by providing that no tolls shall be charged to vessels engaged in that trade passing through the canal. This is the subject of a protest by the British Government.

The British protest involves the right of the Congress of the United

States to regulate its domestic and foreign commerce in such manner as to the Congress may seem wise, and specifically the protest challenges the right of the Congress to exempt American shipping from the payment of tolls for the use of the Panama Canal or to refund to such American ships the tolls which they may have paid, and this without regard to the trade in which such ships are employed, whether coastwise or foreign. The protest states "the proposal to exempt all American shipping from the payment of the tolls would, in the opinion of His Majesty's Government, involve an infraction of the treaty (Hay-Pauncefote), nor is there, in their opinion, any difference in principle between charging tolls only to refund them and remitting tolls altogether. The result is the same in either case and the adoption of the alternative method of refunding tolls in preference of re-mitting them, while perhaps complying with the letter of the treaty, would still controvert its spirit." The provision of the Hay-Pauncefote Treaty in-volved is contained in article 3, which provides:

The United States adopts, as the basis of the neutralization of such ship canal, the following rules, substantially as embodied in the convention of Constantinople, signed the twenty-eighth October, 1888, for the free navigation of the Suez Canal—that is to say:

> 1. The canal shall be free and open to the vessels of commerce and of war of all nations observing these rules, on terms of entire equality, so that there shall be no discrimination against any such nation, or its citi-zens or subjects, in respect of the conditions or charges of traffic, or otherwise. Such conditions and charges of traffic shall be just and equi-table.

Then follows five other rules to be observed by other nations to make neutralization effective, the observance of which is the condition for the privilege of using the canal.

In view of the fact that the Panama Canal is being constructed by the United States wholly at its own cost, upon territory ceded to it by the Republic of Panama for that purpose, and that, unless it has restricted it-self, the United States enjoys absolute rights of ownership and control, including the right to allow its own commerce the use of the canal upon such terms as it sees fit, the sole question is, Has the United States, in the language above quoted from the Hay-Pauncefote Treaty, deprived itself of the exercise of the right to pass its own commerce free or to remit tolls collected for the use of the Canal?

It will be observed that the rules specified in article 3 of the treaty were adopted by the United States for a specific purpose, namely, as the basis of the neutralization of the canal, and for no other purpose. The article is a declaration of policy by the United States that the canal shall be neutral; that the attitude of this Government toward the commerce of the world is that all nations will be treated alike and no discrimination made by the United States against any one of them observing the rules adopted by the United States. The right to the use of the canal and to equality of treatment in the use depends upon the observance of the conditions of the use by the nations to whom we extended that privilege. The privileges of all nations to whom we extended the use upon the observance of these conditions were to be equal to that extended to any one of them which observed the conditions. In other words, it was a conditional favored-nation treatment, the measure of which, in the absence of express stipulation to that effect, is not what the country gives to its own nationals, but the treatment it extends to other nations.

Thus it is seen that the rules are but a basis of neutralization, intended to effect the neutrality which the United States was willing should be the character of the canal and not intended to limit or hamper the United States in the exercise of its sovereign power to deal with its own commerce, using its own canal in whatsoever manner it saw fit.

If there is no "difference in principle between the United States charging tolls to its own shipping only to refund them and remitting tolls altogether," as the British protest declares, then the irresistible conclusion is that the United States, although it owns, controls, and has paid for the canal, is restricted by treaty from aiding its own commerce in the way that all the other nations of the world may freely do. It would scarcely be claimed that the setting out in a treaty between the United States and Great Britain of certain rules adopted by the United States as the basis of the neutralization of the canal would bind any Government to do or refrain from doing anything other than the things required by the rules to insure the privilege of use and freedom from discrimination. Since the rules do not provide as a condition for the privilege of use upon equal terms with other nations that other nations desiring to build up a particular trade involving the use of the canal shall not either directly agree to pay the tolls or to refund to its ships the tolls collected for the use of the canal, it is evident that the treaty does not affect that inherent, sovereign right, unless, which is not likely, it be claimed that the promulgation by the United States of these rules insuring all nations against its discrimination, would authorize the United States to pass upon the action of other nations and require that no one of them should grant to its shipping larger subsidies or more liberal inducement for the use of the canal than were granted by others; in other words, that the United States has the power to equalize the practice of other nations in this regard.

If it is correct, then, to assume that there is nothing in the Hay-Pauncefote Treaty preventing Great Britain and the other nations from extending such favors as they may see fit to their shipping using the canal, and doing it in the way they see fit, and if it is also right to assume that there is nothing in the treaty that gives the United States any supervision over, or right to complain of, such action, then the British protest leads to the absurd conclusion that this Government in constructing the canal, maintaining the canal, and defending the canal, finds itself shorn of its right to deal with its own commerce in its own way, while all other nations using the canal in competition with American commerce enjoy that right and power unimpaired.

The British protest, therefore, is a proposal to read into the treaty a surrender by the United States of its right to regulate its own commerce in its own way and by its own methods—a right which neither Great Britain herself, nor any other nation that may use the canal, has surrendered or proposes to surrender. The surrender of this right is not claimed to be in terms. It is only to be inferred from the fact that the United States has conditionally granted to all the nations the use of the canal without discrimination by the United States between the grantees; but as the treaty leaves all nations desiring to use the canal with full right to deal with their own vessels as they see fit, the United States would only be discriminating against itself if it were to recognize the soundness of the British contention.

The bill here in question does not positively do more than to discriminate in favor of the coastwise trade, and the British protest seems to recognize a distinction between such exemption and the exemption of American vessels engaged in foreign trade. In effect, of course, there is a substantial and practical difference. The American vessels in foreign trade come into competition with vessels of other nations in that same trade, while foreign vessels are forbidden to engage in the American coastwise trade. While the bill here in question seems to vest the President with discretion to discriminate in fixing tolls in favor of American ships and against foreign ships engaged in foreign trade, within the limitation of the range from 50 cents a ton to $1.25 a net ton, there is nothing in the act to compel the President to make such a discrimination. It is not, therefore, necessary to discuss the policy of such discrimination until the question may arise in the exercise of the President's discretion.

The policy of exempting the coastwise trade from all tolls really involves the question of granting a Government subsidy for the purpose of encouraging that trade in competition with the trade of the transcontinental railroads. I approve this policy. It is in accord with the historical course of the Government in giving Government aid to the construction of the transcontinental roads. It is now merely giving Government aid to a means of transportation that competes with those transcontinental roads.

Second. The bill permits the registry of foreign-built vessels as vessels of the United States for foreign trade, and it also permits the admission without duty of materials for the construction and repair of vessels in the United States. This is objected to on the ground that it will interfere with the shipbuilding interests of the United States. I can not concur in this view. The number of vessels of the United States engaged in foreign trade is so small that the work done by the present shipyards is almost wholly that of constructing vessels for the coastwise trade or Government vessels. In other words, there is substantially no business for building ships in the foreign trade in the shipyards of the United States which will be injured by this new provision. It is hoped that this registry of foreign-built ships in American foreign trades will prove to be a method of increasing our foreign shipping. The experiment will hurt no interest of ours, and we can observe its operation. If it proves to extend our commercial flag to the high seas, it will supply a long-felt want.

Third. Section 5 of the interstate commerce act is amended by forbidding railroad companies to own, lease, operate, control, or have any interest in any common carrier by water operated through the Panama Canal with which such railroad or other carrier does or may compete for traffic. I have twice recommended such restriction as to the Panama Canal. It was urged upon me that the Interstate Commerce Commission might control the trade so as to prevent an abuse from the joint ownership of railroads and of Panama steamships competing with each other, and therefore that this radical provision was not necessary. Conference with the Interstate Commerce Commission, however, satisfied me that such control would not be as effective as this restriction. The difficulty is that the interest of the railroad company is so much larger in its railroad and in the maintenance of its railroad rates than in making a profit out of the steamship line that it can afford temporarily to run its vessels for nearly nothing in order to drive out the business independent steamship lines, and thus obtain complete control of the shipping in the trade through the canal and regulate the rates according to the interest of the railroad company. Jurisdiction is conferred on the Interstate Commerce Commission finally to determine the question of fact as to the competition or possibility of competition of the water carrier with the railroad, and this may be done in advance of any investment of capital.

Fourth. The effect of the amendment of section 5 of the interstate-commerce act also is extended so as to make it unlawful for railroad companies owning or controlling lines of steamships in any other part of the jurisdiction of the United States to continue to do so, and as to such railroad companies and such water carriers the Interstate Commerce Commission is given the duty and power not only finally to determine the question of competition or possibility of competition, but also to determine "that the specified service by water is being operated in the interest of the public and is of advantage to the convenience and commerce of the people, and that such extension will neither exclude, prevent, nor reduce competition on the route by water under consideration"; and, if it finds this to be the case, to extend the time during which such service by water may continue beyond the date fixed in-the act for its first operation—to wit, July l, 1914. Whenever the time is extended, then the water carrier, its rates and schedules, and practices are brought within the control of the Interstate Commerce Commission. How far it is within the power of Congress to delegate to the Interstate Commerce Commission such wide discretion it is unnecessary now to discuss. There is ample time between now and the time of this provision of the act's going into effect to have the matter examined by the Supreme Court, or to change the form of the legislation, should it be deemed necessary. Certainly the suggested invalidity of this section, if true, would not invalidate the entire act, the remainder of which may well stand without regard to this provision.

Fifth. The final objection is to a provision which prevents the owner of any steamship who is guilty of violating the antitrust law from using the canal. It is quite evident that this section applies only to those vessels engaged in the trade in which there is a monopoly contrary to our Federal statute, and it is a mere injunctive process against the continuance of such monopolistic trade. It adds the penalty of denying the use of the canal to a person or corporation violating the antitrust law. It may have some practical operation where the business monopolized is transportation by ships, but it does not become operative to prevent the use of the canal until the decree of the court shall have established the fact of the guilt of the owner of the vessel. While the penalties of rise antitrust law seem to me to be quite sufficient already, I do not know that this new remedy against a particular kind of a trust may not sometimes prove useful.

In a message sent to Congress after this bill had passed both Houses I ventured to suggest a possible amendment by which all persons, and especially all British subjects who felt aggrieved by the provisions of the bill on the ground that they are in violation of the Hay-Pauncefote Treaty, might try that question out in the Supreme Court of the United States. I think this would have satisfied those who oppose the view which Congress evidently entertains of the treaty and might avoid the necessity for either diplomatic negotiation or further decision by an arbitral tribunal. Congress, however, has not thought it wise to accept the suggestion, and therefore I must proceed in the view which I have expressed, and am convinced is the correct one, as to the proper construction of the treaty and the limitations which it imposes upon the United States. I do not find that the bill here in question violates those limitations.

On the whole, I believe the bill to be one of the most beneficial that has passed this or any other Congress, and I find no reason in the objections made to the bill which should lead me to delay, until another session of Congress, provisions that are imperatively needed now in order that due preparation by the world may be made for the opening of the canal.

16

Annual Message

Part I
[On our foreign relations]
The White House, December 3, 1912

To the Senate and House of Representatives:

The foreign relations of the United States actually and potentially affect the state of the Union to a degree not widely realized and hardly surpassed by any other factor in the welfare of the whole Nation. The position of the United States in the moral, intellectual, and material relations of the family of nations should be a matter of vital interest to every patriotic citizen. The national prosperity and power impose upon us duties which we can not shirk if we are to be true to our ideals. The tremendous growth of the export trade of the United States has already made that trade a very real factor in the industrial and commercial prosperity of the country. With the development of our industries the foreign commerce of the United States must rapidly become a still more essential factor in its economic welfare. Whether we have a farseeing and wise diplomacy and are not recklessly plunged into unnecessary wars, and whether our foreign policies are based upon an intelligent grasp of present-day world conditions and a clear view of the potentialities of the future, or are governed by a temporary and timid expediency or by narrow views befitting an infant nation, are questions in the alternative consideration of which must convince any thoughtful citizen that no department of national polity offers greater opportunity for promoting the interests of the whole people on the one hand, or greater chance on the other of permanent national injury, than that which deals with the foreign relations of the United States.

The fundamental foreign policies of the United States should be raised high above the conflict of partisanship and wholly dissociated from differences as to domestic policy. In its foreign affairs the United States should present to the world a united front. The intellectual, financial, and industrial interests of the country and the publicist, the wage earner, the farmer, and citizen of whatever occupation must cooperate in a spirit of high patriotism to promote that national solidarity which is indispensable to national efficiency and to the attainment of national ideals.

The relations of the United States with all foreign powers remain upon a sound basis of peace, harmony, and friendship. A greater insistence upon justice to American citizens or interests wherever it may have been denied and a stronger emphasis of the need of mutuality in commercial and other relations have only served to strengthen our friendships with foreign countries by placing those friendships upon a firm foundation of realities as well as aspirations.

Before briefly reviewing the more important events of the last year in our foreign relations, which it is my duty to do as charged with their conduct and because diplomatic affairs are not of a nature to make it appropriate that the Secretary of State make a formal annual report, I desire to touch upon some of the essentials to the safe management of the foreign relations of the United States and to endeavor, also, to define clearly certain concrete policies which are the logical modern corollaries of the undisputed and traditional fundamentals of the foreign policy of the United States.

Reorganization of the State Department

At the beginning of the present administration the United States, having fully entered upon its position as a world power, with the responsibilities thrust upon it by the results of the Spanish-American War, and already engaged in laying the groundwork of a vast foreign trade upon which it should one day become more and more dependent, found itself without the machinery for giving thorough attention to, and taking effective action upon, a mass of intricate business vital to American interests in every country in the world.

The Department of State was an archaic and inadequate machine lacking most of the attributes of the foreign office of any great modern power. With an appropriation made upon my recommendation by the Congress on August 5, 1909, the Department of State was completely reorganized. There were created Divisions of Latin-American Affairs and of Far Eastern, Near Eastern, and Western European Affairs. To these divisions were called from the foreign service diplomatic and consular officers possessing experience and knowledge gained by actual service in different parts of the world and thus familiar with political and commercial conditions in the regions concerned. The work was highly specialized. The result is that where previously this Government from time to time would emphasize in its foreign relations one or another policy, now American interests in every quarter of the globe are being cultivated with equal assiduity. This principle of politico-geographical division possesses also the good feature of making possible rotation between the officers of the departmental, the diplomatic, and the consular branches of the foreign service, and thus keeps the whole diplomatic and consular establishments under the Department of State in close touch and equally inspired with the aims and policy of the Government. Through the newly created Division of Information the foreign service is kept fully informed of what transpires from day to day in the international relations of the country, and contemporary foreign comment affecting American interests is promptly brought to the attention of the department. The law offices of the department were greatly strengthened. There were added foreign-trade advisers to cooperate with the diplomatic and consular bureaus and the politico-geographical divisions in the innumerable matters where commercial diplomacy or consular work calls for such special knowledge. The same officers, together with the rest of the new organization, are able at all times to give to American citizens accurate information as to conditions in foreign countries with which they have business and likewise to cooperate more effectively with the Congress and also with the other executive departments.

Merit System in Consular and Diplomatic Corps

Expert knowledge and professional training must evidently be the essence of this reorganization. Without a trained foreign service there would not be men available for the work in the reorganized Department of State. President Cleveland had taken the first step toward introducing the merit system in the foreign service. That had been followed by the application of the merit principle, with excellent results, to the entire consular branch. Almost nothing, however, had been done in this direction with regard to the Diplomatic Service. In this age of commercial diplomacy it was evidently of the first importance to train an adequate personnel in that branch of the service. Therefore, on November 26, 1909, by an Executive order I placed the Diplomatic Service up to the grade of secretary of embassy, inclusive, upon exactly the same strict nonpartisan basis of the merit system, rigid examination for appointment and promotion only for efficiency, as had been maintained without exception in the Consular Service.

Statistics as to Merit and Nonpartisan Character of Appointments

How faithful to the merit system and how nonpartisan has been the conduct of the Diplomatic and Consular Services in the last four years may be judged from the following: Three ambassadors now serving held their present rank at the beginning of my administration. Of the ten ambassadors whom I have appointed, five were by promotion from the rank of minister. Nine ministers now serving held their present rank at the beginning of my administration. Of the thirty ministers whom I have appointed, eleven were promoted from the lower grades of the foreign service or from the Department of State. Of the nineteen missions in Latin America where our relations are close and our interest is great, fifteen chiefs of mission are serving, three having entered the service during this administration. Thirty-seven secretaries of embassy or legation who have received their initial appointments after passing successfully the required examination were chosen for ascertained fitness, without regard to political affiliations. A dearth of candidates from Southern and Western States has alone made it impossible thus far completely to equalize all the States' representations in the foreign service. In the effort to equalize the representation of the various States in the Consular Service I have made sixteen of the twenty-nine new appointments as consul which have occurred during my administration from the Southern States. This is 55 percent. Every other consular appointment made, including the promotion of eleven young men from the consular assistant and student interpreter corps, has been by promotion or transfer, based solely upon efficiency shown in the service.

In order to assure to the business and other interests of the United States a continuance of the resulting benefits of this reform, I earnestly renew my previous recommendations of legislation making it permanent along some such lines as those of the measure now pending in Congress.

Larger Provision for Embassies and Legations and for Other Expenses of our Foreign Representatives Recommended

In connection with legislation for the amelioration of the foreign service, I wish to invite attention to the advisability of placing the salary appropriations upon a better basis. I believe that the best results would be obtained by a moderate scale of salaries, with adequate funds for the expense of proper representation, based in each case upon the scale and cost of living at each post, controlled by a system of accounting, and under the general direction of the Department of State.

In line with the object which I have sought of placing our foreign service on a basis of permanency, I have at various times advocated provision by Congress for the acquisition of Government-owned buildings for the residence and offices of our diplomatic officers, so as to place them more nearly on an equality with similar officers of other nations and to do away with the discrimination which otherwise must necessarily be made, in some cases, in favor of men having large private fortunes. The act of Congress which I approved on February 17, 1911, was a right step in this direction. The Secretary of State has already made the limited recommendations permitted by the act for any one year, and it is my hope that the bill introduced in the House of Representatives to carry out these recommendations will be favorably acted on by the Congress during its present session.

In some Latin-American countries the expense of government-owned legations will be less than elsewhere, and it is certainly very urgent that in such countries as some of the Republics of Central America and the Caribbean, where it is peculiarly difficult to rent suitable quarters, the representatives of the United States should be justly and adequately provided with dignified and suitable official residences. Indeed, it is high time that the dignity and power of this great Nation should be fittingly signalized by proper buildings for the occupancy of the Nation's representatives everywhere abroad.

Diplomacy a Hand Maid of Commercial Intercourse and Peace

The diplomacy of the present administration has sought to respond to modern ideas of commercial intercourse. This policy has been characterized as substituting dollars for bullets. It is one that appeals alike to idealistic humanitarian sentiments, to the dictates of sound policy and strategy, and to legitimate commercial aims. It is an effort frankly directed to the increase of American trade upon the axiomatic principle that the Government of the United States shall extend all proper support to every legitimate and beneficial American enterprise abroad. How great have been the results of this diplomacy, coupled with the maximum and minimum provision of the tariff law, will be seen by some consideration of the wonderful increase in the export trade of the United States. Because modern diplomacy is commercial, there has been a disposition in some quarters to attribute to it none but materialistic aims. How strikingly erroneous is such an impression may be seen from a study of the results by which the diplomacy of the United States can be judged.

Successful Efforts in Promotion of Peace

In the field of work toward the ideals of peace this Government negotiated, but to my regret was unable to consummate, two arbitration treaties which set the highest mark of the aspiration of nations toward the substitution of arbitration and reason for war in the settlement of international disputes. Through the efforts of American diplomacy several wars have been prevented or ended. I refer to the successful tripartite mediation of the Argentine Republic, Brazil, and the United States between Peru and Ecuador;

the bringing of the boundary dispute between Panama and Costa Rica to peaceful arbitration; the staying of warlike preparations when Haiti and the Dominican Republic were on the verge of hostilities; the stopping of a war in Nicaragua; the halting of internecine strife in Honduras. The Government of the United States was thanked for its influence toward the restoration of amicable relations between the Argentine Republic and Bolivia. The diplomacy of the United States is active in seeking to assuage the remaining ill-feeling between this country and the Republic of Colombia. In the recent civil war in China the United States successfully joined with the other interested powers in urging an early cessation of hostilities. An agreement has been reached between the Governments of Chile and Peru whereby the celebrated Tacna-Arica dispute, which has so long embittered international relations on the west coast of South America, has at last been adjusted. Simultaneously came the news that the boundary dispute between Peru and Ecuador had entered upon a stage of amicable settlement. The position of the United States in reference to the Tacna-Arica dispute between Chile and Peru has been one of nonintervention, but one of friendly influence and pacific counsel throughout the period during which the dispute in question has been the subject of interchange of views between this Government and the two Governments immediately concerned. In the general easing of international tension on the west coast of South America the tripartite mediation, to which I have referred, has been a most potent and beneficent factor.

China

In China the policy of encouraging financial investment to enable that country to help itself has had the result of giving new life and practical application to the open-door policy. The consistent purpose of the present administration has been to encourage the use of American capital in the development of China by the promotion of those essential reforms to which China is pledged by treaties with the United States and other powers. The hypothecation to foreign bankers in connection with certain industrial enterprises, such as the Hukuang railways, of the national revenues upon which these reforms depended, led the Department of State early in the administration to demand for American citizens participation in such enterprises, in order that the United States might have equal rights and an equal voice in all questions pertaining to the disposition of the public revenues concerned. The same policy of promoting international accord among the powers having similar treaty rights as ourselves in the matters of reform, which could not be put into practical effect with out the common consent of all, was likewise adopted in the case of the loan desired by China for the reform of its currency. The principle of international cooperation in matters of common interest upon which our policy had already been based in all of the above instances has admittedly been a great factor in that concert of the powers which has been so happily conspicuous during the perilous period of transition through which the great Chinese nation has been passing.

Central America Needs our help in Debt Adjustment

In Central America the aim has been to help such countries as Nicaragua and Honduras to help themselves. They are the immediate beneficiaries. The national benefit to the United States is twofold. First, it is obvious that the Monroe doctrine is more vital in the neighborhood of the Panama Canal and the zone of the Caribbean than anywhere else. There, too, the maintenance of that doctrine falls most heavily upon the United States. It is therefore essential that the countries within that sphere shall be removed from the jeopardy involved by heavy foreign debt and chaotic national finances and from the ever-present danger of international complications due to disorder at home. Hence the United States has been glad to encourage and support American bankers who were willing to lend a helping hand to the financial rehabilitation of such countries because this financial rehabilitation and the protection of their customhouses from being the prey of would-be dictators would remove at one stroke the menace of foreign creditors and the menace of revolutionary disorder.

The second advantage of the United States is one affecting chiefly all the southern and Gulf ports and the business and industry of the South. The Republics of Central America and the Caribbean possess great natural wealth. They need only a measure of stability and the means of financial regeneration to enter upon an era of peace and prosperity, bringing profit and happiness to themselves and at the same time creating conditions sure to lead to a flourishing interchange of trade with this country.

I wish to call your especial attention to the recent occurrences in Nicaragua, for I believe the terrible events recorded there during the revolution of the past summer—the useless loss of life, the devastation of property, the bombardment of defenseless cities, the killing and wounding of women and children, the torturing of noncombatants to exact contributions, and the suffering of thousands of human beings—might have been averted had the Department of State, through approval of the loan convention by the Senate, been permitted to carry out its now well-developed policy of encouraging the extending of financial aid to weak Central American States with the primary objects of avoiding just such revolutions by assisting those Republics to rehabilitate their finances, to establish their currency on a stable basis, to remove the customhouses from the danger of revolutions by arranging for their secure administration, and to establish reliable banks.

During this last revolution in Nicaragua, the Government of that Republic having admitted its inability to protect American life and property against acts of sheer lawlessness on the part of the malcontents, and having requested this Government to assume that office, it became necessary to land over 2,000 marines and bluejackets in Nicaragua. Owing to their presence the constituted Government of Nicaragua was free to devote its attention wholly to its internal troubles, and was thus enabled to stamp out the rebellion in a short space of time. When the Red Cross supplies sent to Granada had been exhausted, 8,000 persons having been given food in one day upon the arrival of the American forces, our men supplied other unfortunate, needy Nicaraguans from their own haversacks. I wish to congratulate the officers and men of the United States navy and Marine Corps who took part in reestablishing order in Nicaragua upon their splendid conduct, and to record with sorrow the death of seven American marines and bluejackets. Since the reestablishment of peace and order, elections have been held amid conditions of quiet and tranquility. Nearly all the American marines have now been withdrawn. The country should soon be on the road to recovery. The only apparent danger now threatening Nicaragua arises from the shortage of funds. Although American bankers have already rendered assistance, they may naturally be loath to advance a loan adequate to set the country upon its feet without the support of some such convention as that of June, 1911, upon which the Senate has not yet acted.

Enforcement of Neutrality Laws

In the general effort to contribute to the enjoyment of peace by those Republics which are near neighbors of the United States, the administration has enforced the so-called neutrality statutes with a new vigor, and those statutes were greatly strengthened in restricting the exportation of arms and munitions by the joint resolution of last March. It is still a regrettable fact that certain American ports are made the rendezvous of professional revolutionists and others engaged in intrigue against the peace of those Republics. It must be admitted that occasionally a revolution in this region is justified as a real popular movement to throw off the shackles of a vicious and tyrannical government. Such was the Nicaraguan revolution against the Zelaya regime. A nation enjoying our liberal institutions can not escape sympathy with a true popular movement, and one so well justified. In very many cases, however, revolutions in the Republics in question have no basis in principle, but are due merely to the machinations of conscienceless and ambitious men, and have no effect but to bring new suffering and fresh burdens to an already oppressed people. The question whether the use of American ports as *foci* of revolutionary intrigue can be best dealt with by a further amendment to the neutrality statutes or whether it would be safer to deal with special cases by special laws is one worthy of the careful consideration of the Congress.

Visit of Secretary Knox to Central America and the Caribbean

Impressed with the particular importance of the relations between the United States and the Republics of Central America and the Caribbean region, which of necessity must become still more intimate by reason of the mutual advantages which will be presented by the opening of the Panama Canal, I directed the Secretary of State last February to visit these Republics for the purpose of giving evidence of the sincere friendship and good will which the Government and people of the United States bear toward them. Ten Republics were visited. Everywhere he was received with a cordiality of welcome and a generosity of hospitality such as to impress me deeply and to merit our warmest thanks. The appreciation of the Governments and people of the countries visited, which has been appropriately shown in various ways, leaves me no doubt that his visit will conduce to that closer union and better understanding between the United States and those Republics which I have had it much at heart to promote.

Our Mexican Policy

For two years revolution and counter-revolution has distraught the neighboring Republic of Mexico. Brigandage has involved a great deal of depredation upon foreign interests. There have constantly recurred questions of extreme delicacy. On several occasions very difficult situations have arisen on our frontier. Throughout this trying period, the policy of the United States has been one of patient nonintervention, steadfast recognition of constituted authority in the neighboring nation, and the exertion of every effort to care for American interests. I profoundly hope that the Mexican nation may soon resume the path of order, prosperity, and progress. To that nation in its sore troubles, the sympathetic friendship of the United States has been demonstrated to a high degree. There were in Mexico at the beginning of the revolution some thirty or forty thousand American citizens engaged in enterprises contributing greatly to the prosperity of that Republic and also benefiting the important trade between the two countries. The investment of American capital in Mexico has been estimated at $1,000,000,000. The responsibility of endeavoring to safeguard those interests and the dangers inseparable from propinquity to so turbulent a situation have been great, but I am happy to have been able to adhere to the policy above outlined—a policy which I hope may be soon justified by the complete success of the Mexican people in regaining the blessings of peace and good order.

Agricultural Credits

A most important work, accomplished in the past year by the American diplomatic officers in Europe, is the investigation of the agricultural credit system in the European countries. Both as a means to afford relief to the consumers of this country through a more thorough development of agricultural resources and as a means of more sufficiently maintaining the agricultural population, the project to establish credit facilities for the farmers is a concern of vital importance to this Nation. No evidence of prosperity among well-established farmers should blind us to the fact that lack of capital is preventing a development of the Nation's agricultural resources and an adequate increase of the land under cultivation; that agricultural production is fast falling behind the increase in population; and that, in fact, although these well-established farmers are maintained in increasing prosperity because of the natural increase in population, we are not developing the industry of agriculture. We are not breeding in proportionate numbers a race of independent and independence-loving landowners, for a lack of which no growth of cities can compensate. Our farmers have been our mainstay in times of crisis, and in future it must still largely be upon their stability and common sense that this democracy must rely to conserve its principles of self-government.

The need of capital which American farmers feel today had been experienced by the farmers of Europe, with their centuries-old farms, many years ago. The problem had been successfully solved in the Old World and it was evident that the farmers of this country might profit by a study of their systems. I therefore ordered, through the Department of State, an investigation to be made by the diplomatic officers in Europe, and I have laid the results of this investigation before the governors of the various States with the hope that they will be used to advantage in their forthcoming meeting.

Increase of Foreign Trade

In my last annual message I said that the fiscal year ended June 30, 1911, was noteworthy as marking the highest record of exports of American products to foreign countries. The fiscal year 1912 shows that this rate of advance has been maintained, the total domestic exports having a valuation approximately of $2,200,000,000, as compared with a fraction over $2,000,000,000 the previous year. It is also significant that manufactured and partly manufactured articles continue to be the chief commodities forming the volume of our augmented exports, the demands of our own people for consumption requiring that an increasing proportion of our abundant agricultural products be kept at home. In the fiscal year 1911 the exports of articles in the various stages of manufacture, not including food-stuffs partly or wholly manufactured, amounted approximately to $907,500,000. In the fiscal year 1912 the total was nearly $1,022, 000,000, a gain of $114,000,000.

Advantage of Maximum and Minimum Tariff Provision

The importance which our manufactures have assumed in the commerce of the world in competition with the manufactures of other countries again draws attention to the duty of this Government to use its utmost endeavors to secure impartial treatment for American products in all markets. Healthy commercial rivalry in international intercourse is best assured by the possession of proper means for protecting and promoting our foreign trade. It is natural that competitive countries should view with some concern this steady expansion of our commerce. If in some instance the measures taken by them to meet it are not entirely equitable, a remedy should be found. In former messages I have described the negotiations of the Department of State with foreign Governments for the adjustment of the maximum and minimum tariff as provided in section 2 of the tariff law of 1909. The advantages secured by the adjustment of our trade relations under this law have continued during the last year, and some additional cases of discriminatory treatment of which we had reason to complain have been removed. The Department of State has for the first time in the history of this country obtained substantial most-favored-nation treatment from all the countries of the world. There are, however, other instances which, while apparently not constituting undue discrimination in the sense of section 2, are nevertheless exceptions to the complete equity of tariff treatment for American products that the Department of State consistently has sought to obtain for American commerce abroad.

Necessity for Supplementary Legislation

These developments confirm the opinion conveyed to you in my annual message of 1911, that while the maximum and minimum provision of the tariff law of 1909 has been fully justified by the success achieved in removing previously existing undue discriminations against American products, yet experience has shown that this feature of the law should be amended in such way as to provide a fully effective means of meeting the varying degrees of discriminatory treatment of American commerce in foreign countries still encountered, as well as to protect against injurious treatment on the part of foreign Governments, through either legislative or administrative measures, the financial interests abroad of American citizens whose enterprises enlarge the market for American commodities.

I can not too strongly recommend to the Congress the passage of some such enabling measure as the bill which was recommended by the Secretary of State in his letter of December 13, 1911. The object of the proposed legislation is, in brief, to enable the Executive to apply, as the case may require, to any or all commodities, whether or not on the free list from a country which discriminates against the United States, a graduated scale of duties up to the maximum of 25 percent *ad valorem* provided in the present law. Flat tariffs are out of date. Nations no longer accord equal tariff treatment to all other nations irrespective of the treatment from them received. Such a flexible power at the command of the Executive would serve to moderate any unfavorable tendencies on the part of those countries from which the importations into the United States are substantially confined to articles on the free list as well as of the countries which find a lucrative market in the United States for their products under existing customs rates. It is very necessary that the American Government should be equipped with weapons of negotiation adapted to modern economic conditions, in order that we may at all times be in a position to gain not only technically just but actually equitable treatment for our trade, and also for American enterprise and vested interests abroad.

Business Secured to Our Country by Direct Official Effort

As illustrating the commercial benefits of the Nation derived from the new diplomacy and its effectiveness upon the material as well as the more ideal side, it may be remarked that through direct official efforts alone there have been obtained in the course of this administration, contracts from foreign Governments involving an expenditure of $50,000,000 in the factories of the United States. Consideration of this fact and some reflection upon the necessary effects of a scientific tariff system and a foreign service alert and equipped to cooperate with the business men of America carry the conviction that the gratifying increase in the export trade of this country is, in substantial amount, due to our improved governmental methods of protecting and stimulating it. It is germane to these observations to remark that in the two years that have elapsed since the successful negotiation of our new treaty with Japan, which at the time seemed to present so many practical difficulties, our export trade to that country has increased at the rate of over $1,000,000 a month. Our exports to Japan for the year ended June 30, 1910, were $21,959,310, while for the year ended June 30, 1912, the exports were $53,478,046, a net increase in the sale of American products of nearly 150 percent.

Special Claims Arbitration With Great Britain

Under the special agreement entered into between the United States and Great Britain on August 18, 1910, for the arbitration of outstanding pecuniary claims, a schedule of claims and the terms of submission have been agreed upon by the two Governments, and together with the special agreement were approved by the Senate on July 19, 1911, but in accordance with the terms of the agreement they did not go into effect until confirmed by the two Governments by an exchange of notes, which was done on April 26 last. Negotiations are still in progress for a supplemental schedule of claims to be submitted to arbitration under this agreement, and meanwhile the necessary preparations for the arbitration of the claims included in the first schedule have been undertaken and are being carried on under the authority of an appropriation made for that purpose at the last session of Congress. It is anticipated that the two Governments will be prepared to call upon the arbitration tribunal, established under this agreement, to meet at Washington early next year to proceed with this arbitration.

Fur Seal Treaty and Need for Amendment of Our Statute

The act adopted at the last session of Congress to give effect to the fur-seal convention of July 7, 1911, between Great Britain, Japan, Russia, and the

United States provided for the suspension of all land killing of seals on the Pribilof Islands for a period of five years, and an objection has now been presented to this provision by the other parties in interest, which raises the issue as to whether or not this prohibition of land killing is inconsistent with the spirit, if not the letter, of the treaty stipulations. The justification of establishing this close season depends, under the terms of the convention, upon how far, if at all, it is necessary for protecting and preserving the American fur-seal herd and for increasing its number. This is a question requiring examination of the present condition of the herd and the treatment which it needs in the light of actual experience and scientific investigation. A careful examination of the subject is now being made, and this Government will soon be in possession of a considerable amount of new information about the American seal herd, which has been secured during the past season and will be of great value in determining this question; and if it should appear that there is any uncertainty as to the real necessity for imposing a close season at this time I shall take an early opportunity to address a special message to Congress on this subject, in the belief that this Government should yield on this point rather than give the slightest ground for the charge that we have been in any way remiss in observing our treaty obligations.

Final Settlement of North Atlantic Fisheries Dispute

On the twentieth of July last an agreement was concluded between the United States and Great Britain adopting, with certain modifications, the rules and method of procedure recommended in the award rendered by the North Atlantic Coast Fisheries Arbitration Tribunal on September 7, 1910, for the settlement hereafter, in accordance with the principles laid down in the award, of questions arising with reference to the exercise of the American fishing liberties under Article I of the treaty of October 20, 1818, between the United States and Great Britain. This agreement received the approval of the Senate on August 1 and was formally ratified by the two Governments on November 15 last. The rules and a method of procedure embodied in the award provided for determining by an impartial tribunal the reasonableness of any new fishery regulations on the treaty coasts of Newfoundland and Canada before such regulations could be enforced against American fishermen exercising their treaty liberties on those coasts, and also for determining the delimitation of bays on such coasts more than 10 miles wide, in accordance with the definition adopted by the tribunal of the meaning of the word "bays" as used in the treaty. In the subsequent negotiations between the two Governments, undertaken for the purpose of giving practical effect to these rules and methods of procedure, it was found that certain modifications therein were desirable from the point of view of both Governments, and these negotiations have finally resulted in the agreement above mentioned by which the award recommendations as modified by mutual consent of the two Governments are finally adopted and made effective, thus bringing this century-old controversy to a final conclusion, which is equally beneficial and satisfactory to both Governments.

Imperial Valley and Mexico

In order to make possible the more effective performance of the work necessary for the confinement in their present channel of the waters of the lower Colorado River, and thus to protect the people of the Imperial Valley, as well as in order to reach with the Government of Mexico an understanding regarding the distribution of the waters of the Colorado River, in which both Governments are much interested, negotiations are going forward with a view to the establishment of a preliminary Colorado River commission, which shall have the powers necessary to enable it to do the needful work and with authority to study the question of the equitable distribution of the waters. There is every reason to believe that an understanding upon this point will be reached and that an agreement will be signed in the near future.

Chamizal Dispute

In the interest of the people and city of El Paso this Government has been assiduous in its efforts to bring to an early settlement the long-standing Chamizal dispute with Mexico. Much has been accomplished, and while the final solution of the dispute is not immediate, the favorable attitude lately assumed by the Mexican Government encourages the hope that this troublesome question will be satisfactorily and definitively settled at an early day.

International Commission of Jurists

In pursuance of the convention of August 23, 1906, signed at the Third Pan American Conference, held at Rio de Janeiro, the International Commission of Jurists met at that capital during the month of last June. At this meeting 16 American Republics were represented, including the United States, and comprehensive plans for the future work of the commission were adopted. At the next meeting fixed for June, 1914, committees already appointed are instructed to report regarding topics assigned to them.

Opium Conference—Unfortunate Failure of Our Government to Enact Recommended Legislation

In my message on foreign relations communicated to the two Houses of Congress December 7, 1911, I called especial attention to the assembling of the Opium Conference at The Hague, to the fact that that conference was to review all pertinent municipal laws relating to the opium and allied evils, and certainly all international rules regarding these evils, and to the fact that it seemed to me most essential that the Congress should take immediate action on the antinarcotic legislation before the Congress, to which I had previously called attention by a special message.

The international convention adopted by the conference conforms almost entirely to the principles contained in the proposed antinarcotic legislation which has been before the last two Congresses. It was most unfortunate that this Government, having taken the initiative in the international action which eventuated in the important international opium convention, failed to do its share in the great work by neglecting to pass the necessary legislation to correct the deplorable narcotic evils in the United States as well as to redeem international pledges upon which it entered by virtue of the above-mentioned convention. The Congress at its present session should enact into law those bills now before it which have been so carefully drawn up in collaboration between the Department of

State and the other executive departments, and which have behind them not only the moral sentiment of the country, but the practical support of all the legitimate trade interests likely to be affected. Since the international convention was signed, adherence to it has been made by several European States not represented at the conference at The Hague and also by seventeen Latin-American Republics.

Europe and the Near East

The war between Italy and Turkey came to a close in October last by the signature of a treaty of peace, subsequently to which the Ottoman Empire renounced sovereignty over Cyrenaica and Tripolitania in favor of Italy. During the past year the Near East has unfortunately been the theater of constant hostilities. Almost simultaneously with the conclusion of peace between Italy and Turkey and their arrival at an adjustment of the complex questions at issue between them, war broke out between Turkey on the one hand and Bulgaria, Greece, Montenegro, and Serbia on the other. The United States has happily been involved neither directly nor indirectly with the causes or questions incident to any of these hostilities and has maintained in regard to them an attitude of absolute neutrality and of complete political disinterestedness. In the second war in which the Ottoman Empire has been engaged the loss of life and the consequent distress on both sides have been appalling, and the United States has found occasion, in the interest of humanity, to carry out the charitable desires of the American people, to extend a measure of relief to the sufferers on either side through the impartial medium of the Red Cross. Beyond this the chief care of the Government of the United States has been to make due provision for the protection of its national resident in belligerent territory. In the exercise of my duty in this matter I have dispatched to Turkish waters a special-service squadron, consisting of two armored cruisers, in order that this Government may if need be bear its part in such measures as it may be necessary for the interested nations to adopt for the safeguarding of foreign lives and property in the Ottoman Empire in the event that a dangerous situation should develop. In the meanwhile the several interested European powers have promised to extend to American citizens the benefit of such precautionary or protective measures as they might adopt, in the same manner in which it has been the practice of this Government to extend its protection to all foreign residents in those countries of the Western Hemisphere in which it has from time to time been the task of the United States to act in the interest of peace and good order. The early appearance of a large fleet of European warships in the Bosphorus apparently assured the protection of foreigners in that quarter, where the presence of the American *stationnaire* the USS *Scorpion* sufficed, under the circumstances, to represent the United States. Our cruisers were thus left free to act if need be along the Mediterranean coasts should any unexpected contingency arise affecting the numerous American interests in the neighborhood of Smyrna and Beirut.

Spitzbergen

The great preponderance of American material interests in the subarctic island of Spitzbergen, which has always been regarded politically as "no man's land," impels this Government to a continued and lively interest in the international dispositions to be made for the political governance and administration of that region. The conflict of certain claims of American citizens and others is in a fair way to adjustment, while the settlement of matters of administration, whether by international conference of the interested powers or otherwise, continues to be the subject of exchange of views between the Governments concerned.

Liberia

As a result of the efforts of this Government to place the Government of Liberia in position to pay its outstanding indebtedness and to maintain a stable and efficient government, negotiations for a loan of $1,700,000 have been successfully concluded, and it is anticipated that the payment of the old loan and the issuance of the bonds of the 1912 loan for the rehabilitation of the finances of Liberia will follow at an early date, when the new receivership will go into active operation. The new receivership will consist of a general receiver of customs designated by the Government of the United States and three receivers of customs designated by the Governments of

Germany, France, and Great Britain, which countries have commercial interests in the Republic of Liberia.

In carrying out the understanding between the Government of Liberia and that of the United States, and in fulfilling the terms of the agreement between the former Government and the American bankers, three competent ex-army officers are now effectively employed by the Liberian Government in reorganizing the police force of the Republic, not only to keep in order the native tribes in the hinterland but to serve as a necessary police force along the frontier. It is hoped that these measures will assure not only the continued existence but the prosperity and welfare of the Republic of Liberia. Liberia possesses fertility of soil and natural resources, which should insure to its people a reasonable prosperity. It was the duty of the United States to assist the Republic of Liberia in accordance with our historical interest and moral guardianship of a community founded by American citizens, as it was also the duty of the American Government to attempt to assure permanence to a country of much sentimental and perhaps future real interest to a large body of our citizens.

Morocco

The legation at Tangier is now in charge of our consul general, who is acting as *chargé d'affaires,* as well as caring for our commercial interests in that country. In view of the fact that many of the foreign powers are now represented by *chargés d'affaires* it has not been deemed necessary to appoint at the present time a minister to fill a vacancy occurring in that post.

The Far East

The political disturbances in China in the autumn and winter of 1911–12 resulted in the abdication of the Manchu rulers on February 12, followed by the formation of a provisional republican government empowered to conduct the affairs of the nation until a permanent government might be regularly established. The natural sympathy of the American people with the assumption of republican principles by the Chinese people was appropriately expressed in a concurrent resolution of Congress on April 17, 1912. A constituent assembly, composed of representatives duly chosen by the people of China in the elections that are now being held, has been called to meet in January next to adopt a permanent constitution and organize the Government of the nascent Republic. During the formative constitutional stage and pending definite action by the assembly, as expressive of the popular will, and the hoped-for establishment of a stable republican form of government, capable of fulfilling its international obligations, the United States is, according to precedent, maintaining full and friendly *de facto* relations with the provisional Government.

The new condition of affairs thus created has presented many serious and complicated problems, both of internal rehabilitation and of international relations, whose solution it was realized would necessarily require much time and patience. From the beginning of the upheaval last autumn it was felt by the United States, in common with the other powers having large interests in China, that independent action by the foreign Governments in their own individual interests would add further confusion to a situation already complicated. A policy of international cooperation was accordingly adopted in an understanding, reached early in the disturbances, to act together for the protection of the lives and property of foreigners if menaced, to maintain an attitude of strict impartiality as between the contending factions, and to abstain from any endeavor to influence the Chinese in their organization of a new form of government. In view of the seriousness of the disturbances and their general character, the American minister at Peking was instructed at his discretion to advise our nationals in the affected districts to concentrate at such centers as were easily accessible to foreign troops or men of war. Nineteen of our naval vessels were stationed at various Chinese ports, and other measures were promptly taken for the adequate protection of American interests.

It was further mutually agreed, in the hope of hastening an end to hostilities, that none of the interested powers would approve the making of loans by its nationals to either side. As soon, however, as a united provisional Government of China was assured, the United States joined in a favorable consideration of that Government's request for advances needed for immediate administrative necessities and later for a loan to effect a permanent national reorganization. The interested Governments had already, by common consent, adopted, in respect to the purposes, expenditure, and security of any loans to China made by their nationals, certain conditions which were held to be essential, not only to secure reasonable protection for the foreign investors, but also to safeguard and strengthen China's credit by discouraging indiscriminate borrowing and by insuring the application of the funds toward the establishment of the stable and effective government necessary to China's welfare. In June last representative banking groups of the United States, France, Germany, Great Britain, Japan, and Russia formulated, with the general sanction of their respective governments, the guaranties that would be expected in relation to the expenditure and security of the large reorganization loan desired by China, which, however, have thus far proved unacceptable to the provisional Government.

Special Mission of Condolence to Japan

In August last I accredited the Secretary of State as special ambassador to Japan, charged with the mission of bearing to the imperial family, the Government, and the people of that Empire the sympathetic message of the American Commonwealth on the sad occasion of the death of His Majesty the Emperor Mutsuhito, whose long and benevolent reign was the greater part of Japan's modern history. The kindly reception everywhere accorded to Secretary Knox showed that his mission was deeply appreciated by the Japanese nation and emphasized strongly the friendly relations that have for so many years existed between the two peoples.

South America

Our relations with the Argentine Republic are most friendly and cordial. So, also, are our relations with Brazil, whose Government has accepted the invitation of the United States to send two army officers to study at the Coast Artillery School at Fort Monroe. The long-standing Alsop claim, which had been the only hindrance to the healthy growth of the most friendly relations between the United States and Chile, having been eliminated through the submission of the question to His Britannic Majesty King George V as "amiable compositeur," it is a cause of much gratification to me that our relations with Chile are now established upon a firm basis of growing friendship. The Chilean Government has placed an officer of the United States Coast Artillery in charge of the Chilean Coast Artillery School, and has shown appreciation of American methods by confiding to an American firm important work for the Chilean coast defenses.

Last year a revolution against the established Government of Ecuador broke out at the principal port of that Republic. Previous to this occurrence the chief American interest in Ecuador, represented by the Guayaquil & Quito Railway Co., incorporated in the United States, had rendered extensive transportation and other services on account to the Ecuadorian Government, the amount of which ran into a sum which was steadily increasing and which the Ecuadorian Government had made no provision to pay, thereby threatening to crush out the very existence of this American enterprise. When tranquility had been restored to Ecuador as a result of the triumphant progress of the Government forces from Quito, this Government interposed its good offices to the end that the American interests in Ecuador might be saved from complete extinction. As a part of the arrangement which was reached between the parties, and at the request of the Government of Ecuador, I have consented to name an arbitrator, who, acting under the terms of the railroad contract, with an arbitrator named by the Ecuadorian Government, will pass upon the claims that have arisen since the arrangement reached through the action of a similar arbitral tribunal in 1908.

In pursuance of a request made some time ago by the Ecuadorian Government, the Department of State has given much attention to the problem of the proper sanitation of Guayaquil. As a result a detail of officers of the Canal Zone will be sent to Guayaquil to recommend measures that will lead to the complete permanent sanitation of this plague and fever infected region of that Republic, which has for so long constituted a menace to health conditions on the Canal Zone. It is hoped that the report which this mission will furnish will point out a way whereby the modicum of assistance which the United States may properly lend the Ecuadorian Government may be made effective in ridding the west coast of South America of a focus of contagion to the future commercial current passing through the Panama Canal.

In the matter of the claim of John Celestine Landreau against the Government of Peru, which claim arises out of certain contracts and transactions in connection with the discovery and exploitation of guano, and which has been under discussion between the two Governments since 1874, I am glad to report that as the result of prolonged negotiations, which have been characterized by the utmost friendliness and good will on both sides, the Department of State has succeeded in securing the consent of Peru to the arbitration of the claim, and that the negotiations attending the drafting and signature of a protocol submitting the claim to an arbitral tribunal are proceeding with due celerity.

An officer of the American Public Health Service and an American sanitary engineer are now on the way to Iquitos, in the employ of the Peruvian Government, to take charge of the sanitation of that river port. Peru is building a number of submarines in this country, and continues to show every desire to have American capital invested in the Republic.

In July the United States sent undergraduate delegates to the Third International Students Congress held at Lima, American students having been for the first time invited to one of these meetings.

The Republic of Uruguay has shown its appreciation of American agricultural and other methods by sending a large commission to this country and by employing many American experts to assist in building up agricultural and allied industries in Uruguay.

Venezuela is paying off the last of the claims the settlement of which was provided for by the Washington protocols, including those of American citizens. Our relations with Venezuela are most cordial, and the trade of that Republic with the United States is now greater than with any other country.

Central America and the Caribbean

During the past summer the revolution against the administration which followed the assassination of President Caceres a year ago last November brought the Dominican Republic to the verge of administrative chaos, without offering any guaranties of eventual stability in the ultimate success of either party. In pursuance of the treaty relations of the United States with the Dominican Republic, which were threatened by the necessity of suspending the operation under American administration of the customhouses on the Haitian frontier, it was found necessary to dispatch special commissioners to the island to reestablish the customhouses and with a guard sufficient to insure needed protection to the customs administration. The efforts which have been made appear to have resulted in the restoration of normal conditions throughout the Republic. The good offices which the commissioners were able to exercise were instrumental in bringing the contending parties together and in furnishing a basis of adjustment which it is hoped will result in permanent benefit to the Dominican people.

Mindful of its treaty relations, and owing to the position of the Government of the United States as mediator between the Dominican Republic and Haiti in their boundary dispute, and because of the further fact that the revolutionary activities on the Haitian-Dominican frontier had become so active as practically to obliterate the line of demarcation that had been heretofore recognized pending the definitive settlement of the boundary in controversy, it was found necessary to indicate to the two island Governments a provisional *de facto* boundary line. This was done without prejudice to the rights or obligations of either country in a final settlement to be reached by arbitration. The tentative line chosen was one which, under the circumstances brought to the knowledge of this Government, seemed to conform to the best interests of the disputants. The border patrol which it had been found necessary to reestablish for customs purposes between the two countries was instructed provisionally to observe this line.

The Republic of Cuba last May was in the throes of a lawless uprising that for a time threatened the destruction of a great deal of valuable property—much of it owned by Americans and other foreigners—as well as the existence of the Government itself. The armed forces of Cuba being inadequate to guard property from attack and at the same time properly to operate against the rebels, a force of American marines was dispatched from our naval station at Guantanamo into the Province of Oriente for the protection of American and other foreign life and property. The Cuban Government was thus able to use all its forces in putting down the outbreak, which it succeeded in doing in a period of six weeks. The presence of two American warships in the harbor of Havana during the most critical period of this disturbance contributed in great measure to allay the fears of the inhabitants, including a large foreign colony.

There has been under discussion with the Government of Cuba for some time the question of the release by this Government of its leasehold rights at Bahia Honda, on the northern coast of Cuba, and the enlargement, in exchange therefor, of the naval station which has been established at Guantanamo Bay, on the south. As the result of the negotiations thus carried on an agreement has been reached between the two Governments providing for the suitable enlargement of the Guantanamo Bay station upon terms which are entirely fair and equitable to all parties concerned.

At the request alike of the Government and both political parties in Panama, an American commission undertook supervision of the recent presidential election in that Republic, where our treaty relations, and, indeed, every geographical consideration, make the maintenance of order and satisfactory conditions of peculiar interest to the Government of the United States. The elections passed without disorder, and the new administration has entered upon its functions.

The Government of Great Britain has asked the support of the United States for the protection of the interests of British holders of the foreign bonded debt of Guatemala. While this Government is hopeful of an arrangement equitable to the British bondholders, it is naturally unable to view the question apart from its relation to the broad subject of financial stability in Central America, in which the policy of the United States does not permit it to escape a vital interest. Through a renewal of negotiations between the Government of Guatemala and American bankers, the aim of which is a loan for the rehabilitation of Guatemalan finances, a way appears to be open by which the Government of Guatemala could promptly satisfy any equitable and just British claims, and at the same time so improve its whole financial position as to contribute greatly to the increased prosperity of the Republic and to redound to the benefit of foreign investments and foreign trade with that country. Failing such an arrangement, it may become impossible for the Government of the United States to escape its obligations in connection with such measures as may become necessary to exact justice to legitimate foreign claims.

In the recent revolution in Nicaragua, which, it was generally admitted, might well have resulted in a general Central American conflict but for the intervention of the United States, the Government of Honduras was especially menaced; but fortunately peaceful conditions were maintained within the borders of that Republic. The financial condition of that country remains unchanged, no means having been found for the final adjustment of pressing outstanding foreign claims. This makes it the more regrettable that the financial convention between the United States and Honduras has thus far failed of ratification. The Government of the United States continues to hold itself ready to cooperate with the Government of Honduras, which it is believed, can not much longer delay the meeting of its foreign obligations, and it is hoped at the proper time American bankers will be willing to cooperate for this purpose.

Necessity for Greater Governmental Effort in Retention and Expansion of our Foreign Trade

It is not possible to make to the Congress a communication upon the present foreign relations of the United States so detailed as to convey an adequate impression of the enormous increase in the importance and activities of those relations. If this Government is really to preserve to the American people that free opportunity in foreign markets which will soon be indispensable to our prosperity, even greater efforts must be made. Otherwise the American merchant, manufacturer, and exporter will find many a field in which American trade should logically predominate preempted through the more energetic efforts of other governments and other commercial nations.

There are many ways in which through hearty cooperation the legislative and executive branches of this Government can do much. The absolute essential is the spirit of united effort and singleness of purpose. I will allude only to a very few specific examples of action which ought then to result. America can not take its proper place in the most important fields for its commercial activity and enterprise unless we have a merchant marine. American commerce and enterprise can not be effectively fostered in those fields unless we have good American banks in the countries referred to. We need American newspapers in those countries and proper means for public information about them. We need to assure the permanency of a trained foreign service. We need legislation enabling the members of the foreign service to be systematically brought in direct contact with the industrial, manufacturing, and exporting interests of this country in order that American business men may enter the foreign field with a clear perception of the exact conditions to be dealt with and the officers themselves may prosecute their work with a clear idea of what American industrial and manufacturing interests require.

Conclusion

Congress should fully realize the conditions which obtain in the world as we find ourselves at the threshold of our middle age as a Nation. We have emerged full grown as a peer in the great concourse of nations. We have passed through various formative periods. We have been self-centered in the struggle to develop our domestic resources and deal with our domestic questions. The Nation is now too matured to continue in its foreign relations those temporary expedients natural to a people to whom domestic affairs are the sole concern. In the past our diplomacy has often consisted, in normal times, in a mere assertion of the right to international existence. We are now in a larger relation with broader rights of our own and obligations to others than ourselves. A number of great guiding principles were laid down early in the history of this Government. The recent task of our diplomacy has been to adjust those principles to the conditions of today, to develop their corollaries, to find practical applications of the old principles expanded to meet new situations. Thus are being evolved bases upon which can rest the superstructure of policies which must grow with the destined progress of this Nation. The successful conduct of our foreign relations demands a broad and a modern view. We can not meet new questions nor build for the future if we confine ourselves to outworn dogmas of the past and to the perspective appropriate at our emergence from colonial times and conditions. The opening of the Panama Canal will mark a new era in our international life and create new and world-wide conditions which, with their vast correlations and consequences, will obtain for hundreds of years to come. We must not wait for events to overtake us unawares. With continuity of purpose we must deal with the problems of our external relations by a diplomacy modern, resourceful, magnanimous, and fittingly expressive of the high ideals of a great nation.

Part II
[On fiscal, judicial, military, and insular affairs]
The White House, December 6, 1912

To the Senate and House of Representatives:

On the third of December I sent a message to the Congress, which was confined to our foreign relations. The Secretary of State makes no report to the President or to Congress, and a review of the history of the transactions of the State Department in one year must therefore be included by the President in his annual message or Congress will not be fully informed of them. A full discussion of all the transactions of the Government, with a view to informing the Congress of the important events of the year and recommending new legislation, requires more space than one message of reasonable length affords. I have therefore adopted the course of sending three or four messages during the first ten days of the session, so as to include reference to the more important matters that should be brought to the attention of the Congress.

Business Conditions

The condition of the country with reference to business could hardly be better. While the four years of the administration now drawing to a close have not developed great speculative expansion or a wide field of new investment, the recovery and progress made from the depressing conditions following the panic of 1907 have been steady and the improvement has been clear and easily traced in the statistics. The business of the country is now on a solid basis. Credits are not unduly extended, and every phase of the situation seems in a state of preparedness for a period of unexampled prosperity. Manufacturing concerns are running at their full capacity and the demand for labor was never so constant and growing. The foreign trade of the country for this year will exceed $4,000,000,000, while the balance in our favor—that of the excess of exports over imports—will exceed $500,000,000. More than half our exports are manufactures or partly manufactured material, while our exports of farm products do not show the same increase because of domestic consumption. It is a year of bumper crops; the total money value of farm products will exceed $9,500,000,000. It is a year when the bushel or unit price of agricultural products has gradually fallen, and yet the total value of the entire crop is greater by over $1,000,000,000 than we have known in our history.

Condition of the Treasury

The condition of the Treasury is very satisfactory. The total interest-bearing debt is $963,777,770, of which $134,631,980 constitute the Panama Canal loan. The non-interest-bearing debt is $378,301,284.90, including $346,681,016 of greenbacks. We have in the Treasury $150,000,000 in gold coin as a reserve against the outstanding greenbacks; and in addition we have a cash balance in the Treasury as a general fund of $167,152,478.99, or an increase of $26,975,552 over the general fund last year.

Receipts and Expenditures

For three years the expenditures of the Government have decreased under the influence of an effort to economize. This year presents an apparent exception. The estimate by the Secretary of the Treasury of the ordinary receipts, exclusive of postal revenues, for the year ending June 30, 1914, indicates that they will amount to $710,000,000. The sum of the estimates of the expenditures for that same year, exclusive of Panama Canal disbursements and postal disbursements payable from postal revenues, is $732,000,000, indicating a deficit of $22,000,000. For the year ending June 30, 1913, similarly estimated receipts were $667,000,000, while the total corresponding estimate of expenditures for that year, submitted through the Secretary of the Treasury to Congress, amounted to $656,000,000. This shows an increase of $76,000,000 in the estimates for 1914 over the total estimates of 1913. This is due to an increase of $25,000,000 in the estimate for rivers and harbors for the next year on projects and surveys authorized by Congress; to an increase under the new pension bill of $32,500,000; and to an increase in the estimates for expenses of the Navy Department of $24,000,000. The estimate for the Navy Department for the year 1913 included two battleships. Congress made provision for only one battleship, and therefore the Navy Department has deemed it necessary and proper to make an estimate which includes the first year's expenditure for three battleships in addition to the amount required for work on the uncompleted ships now under construction. In addition to the natural increase in the expenditures for the uncompleted ships, and the additional battleship estimated for, the other increases are due to the pay required for 4,000 or more additional enlisted men in the Navy; and to this must be added the additional cost of construction imposed by the change in the eight-hour law which makes it applicable to ships built in private shipyards.

With the exceptions of these three items, the estimates show a reduction this year below the total estimates for 1913 of more than $5,000,000.

The estimates for Panama Canal construction for 1914 are $17,000,000 less than for 1913.

Our Banking and Currency System

A time when panics seem far removed is the best time for us to prepare our financial system to withstand a storm. The most crying need this country has is a proper banking and currency system. The existing one is inadequate, and everyone who has studied the question admits it.

It is the business of the National Government to provide a medium, automatically contracting and expanding in volume, to meet the needs of trade. Our present system lacks the indispensable quality of elasticity.

The only part of our monetary medium that has elasticity is the bank-note currency. The peculiar provisions of the law requiring national banks to maintain reserves to meet the call of the depositors operates to increase the money stringency when it arises rather than to expand the supply of currency and relieve it. It operates upon each bank and furnishes a motive for the withdrawal of currency from the channels of trade by each bank to save itself, and offers no inducement whatever for the use of the reserve to expand the supply of currency to meet the exceptional demand.

After the panic of 1907 Congress realized that the present system was not adapted to the country's needs and that under it panics were possible that might properly be avoided by legislative provision. Accordingly a monetary commission was appointed which made a report in February, 1912. The system which they recommended involved a National Reserve Association, which was, in certain of its faculties and functions, a bank, and which was given through its governing authorities the power, by issuing circulating notes for approved commercial paper, by fixing discounts, and by other methods of transfer of currency, to expand the supply of the monetary medium where it was most needed to prevent the export or hoarding of gold and generally to exercise such supervision over the supply of money in every part of the country as to prevent a stringency and a panic. The stock in this association was to be distributed to the banks of the whole United States, State and National, in a mixed proportion to bank units and to capital stock paid in. The control of the association was vested in a board of directors to be elected by representatives of the banks, except certain ex-officio directors, three Cabinet officers, and the Comptroller of the Currency. The President was to appoint the governor of the association from three persons to be selected by the directors, while the two deputy governors were to be elected by the board of directors. The details of the plan were worked out with great care and ability, and the plan in general seems to me to furnish the basis for a proper solution of our present difficulties. I feel that the Government might very properly be given a greater voice in the executive committee of the board of directors without danger of injecting politics into its management, but I think the federation system of banks is a good one, provided proper precautions are taken to prevent banks of large capital from absorbing power through ownership of stock in other banks. The objections to a central bank it seems to me are obviated if the ownership of the reserve association is distributed among all the banks of a country in which banking is free. The earnings of the reserve association are limited in percentage to a reasonable and fixed amount, and the profits over and above this are to be turned into the Government Treasury. It is quite probable that still greater security against control by money centers may be worked into the plan.

Certain it is, however, that the objections which were made in the past history of this country to a central bank as furnishing a monopoly of financial power to private individuals, would not apply to an association whose ownership and control is so widely distributed and is divided between all the banks of the country, State and National, on the one hand, and the Chief Executive through three department heads and his Comptroller of the Currency, on the other. The ancient hostility to a national bank, with its branches, in which is concentrated the privilege of doing a banking business and carrying on the financial transactions of the Government, has prevented the establishment of such a bank since it was abolished in the Jackson Administration. Our present national banking law has obviated objections growing out of the same cause by providing a free banking system in which any set of stockholders can establish a national bank if they comply with the conditions of law. It seems to me that the National Reserve Association meets the same objection in a similar way; that is, by giving to each bank, State and National, in accordance with its size, a certain share in the stock of the reserve association, nontransferable and only to be held by the bank while it performs its functions as a partner in the reserve association.

The report of the commission recommends provisions for the imposition of a graduated tax on the expanded currency of such a character as to furnish a motive for reducing the issue of notes whenever their presence in the money market is not required by the exigencies of trade. In other words, the whole system has been worked out with the greatest care. Theoretically it presents a plan that ought to command support. Practically it may require modification in various of its provisions in order to make the security against abuses by combinations among the banks impossible. But in the face of the crying necessity that there is for improvement in our present system, I urgently invite the attention of Congress to the proposed plan and the report of the commission, with the hope that an earnest consideration may suggest amendments and changes within the general plan which will lead to its adoption for the benefit of the country. There is no class in the community more interested in a safe and sane banking and currency system, one which will prevent panics and automatically furnish in each trade center the currency needed in the carrying on of the business at that center, than the wage earner. There is no class in the community whose experience better qualifies them to make suggestions as to the sufficiency of a currency and banking system than the bankers and business men. Ought we, therefore, to ignore their recommendations and reject their financial judgment as to the proper method of reforming our financial system merely because of the suspicion which exists against them in the minds of many of our fellow citizens? Is it not the duty of Congress to take up the plan suggested, examine it from all standpoints, give impartial consideration to the testimony of those whose experience ought to fit them to give the best advice on the subject, and then to adopt some plan which will secure the benefits desired?

A banking and currency system seems far away from the wage earner and the farmer, but the fact is that they are vitally interested in a safe system of currency which shall graduate its volume to the amount needed and which shall prevent times of artificial stringency that frighten capital, stop employment, prevent the meeting of the pay roll, destroy local markets, and produce penury and want.

The Tariff

I have regarded it as my duty in former messages to the Congress to urge the revision of the tariff upon principles of protection. It was my judgment that the customs duties ought to be revised downward, but that the reduction ought not to be below a rate which would represent the difference in the cost of production between the article in question at home and abroad, and for this and other reasons I vetoed several bills which were presented to me in the last session of this Congress. Now that a new Congress has been elected on a platform of a tariff for revenue only rather than a protective tariff, and is to revise the tariff on that basis, it is needless for me to occupy the time of this Congress with arguments or recommendations in favor of a protective tariff.

Before passing from the tariff law, however, known as the Payne tariff law of August 5, 1909, I desire to call attention to section 38 of that act, assessing a special excise tax on corporations. It contains a provision requiring the levy of an additional 50 percent to the annual tax in cases of neglect to verify the prescribed return or to file it before the time required by law. This additional charge of 50 percent operates in some cases as a harsh penalty for what may have been a mere inadvertence or unintentional oversight, and the law should be so amended as to mitigate the severity of the charge in such instances. Provision should also be made for the refund of additional taxes heretofore collected because of such infractions in those cases where the penalty imposed has been so disproportionate to the offense as equitably to demand relief.

Budget

The estimates for the next fiscal year have been assembled by the Secretary of the Treasury and by him transmitted to Congress. I purpose at a later day to submit to Congress a form of budget prepared for me and recommended by the President's Commission on Economy and Efficiency, with a view of suggesting the useful and informing character of a properly framed budget.

War Department

The War Department combines within its jurisdiction functions which in other countries usually occupy three departments. It not only has the management of the Army and the coast defenses, but its jurisdiction extends to the government of the Philippines and of Puerto Rico and the control of the receivership of the customs revenues of the Dominican Republic; it also includes the recommendation of all plans for the improvement of harbors and waterways and their execution when adopted; and, by virtue of an Executive order, the supervision of the construction of the Panama Canal.

Army Reorganization

Our small Army now consists of 83,809 men, excluding the 5,000 Philippine scouts. Leaving out of consideration the Coast Artillery force, whose position is fixed in our various seacoast defenses, and the present garrisons of our various insular possessions, we have today within the continental United States a mobile Army of only about 35,000 men. This little force must be still further drawn upon to supply the new garrisons for the great naval base which is being established at Pearl Harbor, in the Hawaiian Islands, and to protect the locks now rapidly approaching completion at Panama. The forces remaining in the United States are now scattered in nearly 50 posts, situated for a variety of historical reasons in 24 States. These posts contain only fractions of regiments, averaging less than 700 men each. In time of peace it has been our historical policy to administer these units separately by a geographical organization. In other words, our Army in time of peace has never been a united organization but merely scattered groups of companies, battalions, and regiments, and the first task in time of war has been to create out of these scattered units an Army fit for effective teamwork and cooperation.

To the task of meeting these patent defects, the War Department has been addressing itself during the past year. For many years we had no officer or division whose business it was to study these problems and plan remedies for these defects. With the establishment of the General Staff nine years ago a body was created for this purpose. It has, necessarily, required time to overcome, even in its own personnel, the habits of mind engendered by a century of lack of method, but of late years its work has become systematic and effective, and it has recently been addressing itself vigorously to these problems.

A comprehensive plan of Army reorganization was prepared by the War College Division of the General Staff. This plan was thoroughly discussed last summer at a series of open conferences held by the Secretary of War and attended by representatives from all branches of the Army and from Congress. In printed form it has been distributed to Members of Congress and throughout the Army and the National Guard, and widely through institutions of learning and elsewhere in the United States. In it, for the first time, we have a tentative chart for future progress.

Under the influence of this study definite and effective steps have been taken toward Army reorganization so far as such reorganization lies within the Executive power. Hitherto there has been no difference of policy in the treatment of the organization of our foreign garrisons from those of troops within the United States. The difference of situation is vital, and the foreign garrison should be prepared to defend itself at an instant's notice against a foe who may command the sea. Unlike the troops in the United States, it can not count upon reinforcements or recruitment. It is an outpost upon which will fall the brunt of the first attack in case of war. The historical policy of the United States of carrying its regiments during time of peace at half strength has no application to our foreign garrisons. During the past year this defect has been remedied as to the Philippines garrison. The former garrison of 12 reduced regiments has been replaced by a garrison of 6 regiments at full strength, giving fully the same number of riflemen at an estimated economy in cost of maintenance of over $1,000,000 per year. This garrison is to be permanent. Its regimental units, instead of being transferred periodically back and forth from the United States, will remain in the islands. The officers and men composing these units will, however, serve a regular tropical detail as usual, thus involving no greater hardship upon the personnel and greatly increasing the effectiveness of the garrison. A similar policy is proposed for the Hawaiian and Panama garrisons as fast as the barracks for them are completed. I strongly urge upon Congress that the necessary appropriations for this purpose should be promptly made. It is, in my opinion, of first importance that these national outposts, upon which a successful home defense will, primarily, depend, should be finished and placed in effective condition at the earliest possible day.

The Home Army

Simultaneously with the foregoing steps the War Department has been proceeding with the reorganization of the Army at home. The formerly disassociated units are being united into a tactical organization of three divisions, each consisting of two or three brigades of Infantry and, so far as practicable, a proper proportion of divisional Cavalry and Artillery. Of course, the extent to which this reform can be carried by the Executive is practically limited to a paper organization. The scattered units can be brought under a proper organization, but they will remain physically scattered until Congress supplies the necessary funds for grouping them in more concentrated posts. Until that is done the present difficulty of drilling our scattered groups together, and thus training them for the proper team play, can not be removed. But we shall, at least, have an Army which will know its own organization and will be inspected by its proper commanders, and to which, as a unit, emergency orders can be issued in time of war or other emergency. Moreover, the organization, which in many respects is necessarily a skeleton, will furnish a guide for future development. The separate regiments and companies will know the brigades and divisions to which they belong. They will be maneuvered together whenever maneuvers are established by Congress, and the gaps in their organization will show the pattern into which can be filled new troops as the Nation grows and a larger Army is provided.

Regular Army Reserve

One of the most important reforms accomplished during the past year has been the legislation enacted in the Army appropriation bill of last summer, providing for a Regular Army reserve. Hitherto our national policy has assumed that at the outbreak of war our regiments would be immediately raised to full strength. But our laws have provided no means by which this could be accomplished, or by which the losses of the regiments when once sent to the front could be repaired. In this respect we have neglected the lessons learned by other nations. The new law provides that the soldier, after serving four years with colors, shall pass into a reserve for three years. At his option he may go into the reserve at the end of three years, remaining there for four years. While in the reserve he can be called to active duty only in case of war or other national emergency, and when so called and only in such case will receive a stated amount of pay for all of the period in which he has been a member of the reserve. The legislation is imperfect, in my opinion, in certain particulars, but it is a most important step in the right direction, and I earnestly hope that it will be carefully studied and perfected by Congress.

The National Guard

Under existing law the National Guard constitutes, after the Regular Army, the first line of national defense. Its organization, discipline, training, and equipment, under recent legislation, have been assimilated, as far as possible, to those of the Regular Army, and its practical efficiency, under the effect of this training, has very greatly increased. Our citizen soldiers under present conditions have reached a stage of development beyond which they can not reasonably be asked to go without further direct assistance in the form of pay from the Federal Government. On the other hand, such pay from the National Treasury would not be justified unless it produced a proper equivalent in additional efficiency on the part of the National Guard. The Organized Militia today can not be ordered outside of the limits of the United States, and thus can not lawfully be used for general military purposes. The officers and men are ambitious and eager to make themselves thus available and to become an efficient national reserve of citizen soldiery. They are the only force of trained men, other than the Regular Army, upon which we can rely. The so-called militia pay bill, in the form agreed on between the authorities of the War Department and the representatives of the National Guard, in my opinion adequately meets these conditions and offers a proper return for the pay which it is proposed to give to the National Guard. I believe that its enactment into law would be a very long step toward providing this Nation with a first line of citizen soldiery, upon which its main reliance must depend in case of any national emergency. Plans for the organization of the National Guard into tactical divisions, on the same lines as those adopted for the Regular Army, are being formulated by the War College Division of the General Staff.

National Volunteers

The National Guard consists of only about 110,000 men. In any serious war in the past it has always been necessary, and in such a war in the future it doubtless will be necessary, for the Nation to depend, in addition to the Regular Army and the National Guard, upon a large force of volunteers. There is at present no adequate provision of law for the raising of such a force. There is now pending in Congress, however, a bill which makes such provision, and which I believe is admirably adapted to meet the exigencies which would be presented in case of war. The passage of the bill would not entail a dollar's expense upon the Government at this time or in the future until war comes. But if war comes the methods therein directed are in accordance with the best military judgment as to what they ought to be, and the act would prevent the necessity for a discussion of any legislation and the delays incident to its consideration and adoption. I earnestly urge its passage.

Consolidation of the Supply Corps

The Army appropriation act of 1912 also carried legislation for the consolidation of the Quartermaster's Department, the Subsistence Department, and the Pay Corps into a single supply department, to be known as the Quartermaster's Corps. It also provided for the organization of a special force of enlisted men, to be known as the Service Corps, gradually to replace many of the civilian employees engaged in the manual labor necessary in every army. I believe that both of these enactments will improve the administration of our military establishment. The consolidation of the supply corps has already been effected, and the organization of the service corps is being put into effect.

All of the foregoing reforms are in the direction of economy and efficiency. Except for the slight increase necessary to garrison our outposts in Hawaii and Panama, they do not call for a larger Army, but they do tend to produce a much more efficient one. The only substantial new appropriations required are those which, as I have pointed out, are necessary to complete the fortifications and barracks at our naval bases and outposts beyond the sea.

Puerto Rico

Puerto Rico continues to show notable progress, both commercially and in the spread of education. Its external commerce has increased 17 percent over the preceding year, bringing the total value up to $92,631,886, or more than five times the value of the commerce of the island in 1901. During the year 160,657 pupils were enrolled in the public schools, as against 145,525 for the preceding year, and as compared with 26,000 for the first year of American administration. Special efforts are under way for the promotion of vocational and industrial training, the need of which is particularly pressing in the island. When the bubonic plague broke out last June, the quick and efficient response of the people of Puerto Rico to the demands of modern sanitation was strikingly shown by the thorough campaign which was instituted against the plague and the hearty public opinion which supported the Government's efforts to check its progress and to prevent its recurrence.

The failure thus far to grant American citizenship continues to be the only ground of dissatisfaction. The bill conferring such citizenship has passed the House of Representatives and is now awaiting the action of the Senate. I am heartily in favor of the passage of this bill. I believe that the demand for citizenship is just, and that it is amply earned by sustained loyalty on the part of the inhabitants of the island. But it should be remembered that the demand must be, and in the minds of most Puerto Ricans is, entirely disassociated from any thought of statehood. I believe that no substantial approved public opinion in the United States or in Puerto Rico contemplates statehood for the island as the ultimate form of relations between us. I believe that the aim to be striven for is the fullest possible allowance of legal and fiscal self-government, with American citizenship as to the bond between us; in other words, a relation analogous to the present relation between Great Britain and such self-governing colonies as Canada and Australia. This would conduce to the fullest and most self-sustaining development of Puerto Rico, while at the same time it would grant her the economic and political benefits of being under the American flag.

Philippines

A bill is pending in Congress which revolutionizes the carefully worked out scheme of government under which the Philippine Islands are now governed and which proposes to render them virtually autonomous at once and absolutely independent in eight years. Such a proposal can only be founded on the assumption that we have now discharged our trusteeship to the Filipino people and our responsibility for them to the world, and that they are now prepared for self-government as well as national sovereignty. A thorough and unbiased knowledge of the facts clearly shows that these assumptions are absolutely without justification. As to this, I believe that there is no substantial difference of opinion among any of those who have had the responsibility of facing Philippine problems in the administration of the islands, and I believe that no one to whom the future of this people is a responsible concern can countenance a policy fraught with the direst consequences to those on whose behalf it is ostensibly urged.

In the Philippine Islands we have embarked upon an experiment unprecedented in dealing with dependent people. We are developing there conditions exclusively for their own welfare. We found an archipelago containing 24 tribes and races, speaking a great variety of languages, and with a population over 80 percent of which could neither read nor write. Through the unifying forces of a common education, of commercial and economic development, and of gradual participation in local self-government we are endeavoring to evolve a homogeneous people fit to determine, when the time arrives, their own destiny. We are seeking to arouse a national spirit and not, as under the older colonial theory, to suppress such a spirit. The character of the work we have been doing is keenly recognized in the Orient, and our success thus far followed with not a little envy by those who, initiating the same policy, find themselves hampered by conditions grown up in earlier days and under different theories of administration. But our work is far from done. Our duty to the Filipinos is far from discharged. Over half a million Filipino students are now in the Philippine schools helping to mold the men of the future into a homogeneous people, but there still remain more than a million Filipino children of school age yet to be reached. Freed from American control the integrating forces of a common education and a common language will cease and the educational system now well started will slip back into inefficiency and disorder.

An enormous increase in the commercial development of the islands has been made since they were virtually granted full access to our markets three years ago, with every prospect of increasing development and diversified industries. Freed from American control such development is bound to decline. Every observer speaks of the great progress in public works for the benefit of the Filipinos, of harbor improvements, of roads and railways, of irrigation and artesian wells, public buildings, and better means of communication. But large parts of the islands are still unreached, still even unexplored, roads and railways are needed in many parts, irrigation systems are still to be installed, and wells to be driven. Whole villages and towns are still without means of communication other than almost impassable roads and trails. Even the great progress in sanitation, which has successfully suppressed smallpox, the bubonic plague, and Asiatic cholera, has found the cause of and a cure for beriberi, has segregated the lepers, has helped to make Manila the most healthful city in the Orient, and to free life throughout the whole archipelago from its former dread diseases, is nevertheless incomplete in many essentials of permanence in sanitary policy. Even more remains to be accomplished. If freed from American control sanitary progress is bound to be arrested and all that has been achieved likely to be lost.

Concurrent with the economic, social, and industrial development of the islands has been the development of the political capacity of the people. By their progressive participation in government the Filipinos are being steadily and hopefully trained for self-government. Under Spanish control they shared in no way in the government. Under American control they have shared largely and increasingly. Within the last dozen years they have gradually been given complete autonomy in the municipalities, the right to elect two-thirds of the provincial governing boards and the lower house of the insular legislature. They have four native members out of nine members of the commission, or upper house. The chief justice and two justices of the supreme court, about one-half of the higher judicial positions, and all of the justices of the peace are natives. In the classified civil service the proportion of Filipinos increased from 51 percent in 1904 to 67 percent in 1911. Thus today all the municipal employees, over 90 percent of the provincial employees, and 60 percent of the officials and employees of the central government are Filipinos. The ideal which has been kept in mind in our political guidance of the islands has been *real* popular self-government and not mere paper independence. I am happy to say that the Filipinos have done well enough in the places they have filled and in the discharge of the political power with which they have been intrusted to warrant the belief that they can be educated and trained to complete self-government. But the present satisfactory results are due to constant support and supervision at every step by Americans.

If the task we have undertaken is higher than that assumed by other nations, its accomplishment must demand even more patience. We must not forget that we found the Filipinos wholly untrained in government. Up to our advent all other experience sought to repress rather than encourage political power. It takes long time and much experience to ingrain political habits of steadiness and efficiency. Popular self-government ultimately must rest upon common habits of thought and upon a reasonably developed public opinion. No such foundations for self-government, let alone independence, are now present in the Philippine Islands. Disregarding even their racial heterogeneity and the lack of ability to think as a nation, it is sufficient to point out that under liberal franchise privileges only about 3 percent of the Filipinos vote and only 5 percent of the people are said to read the public press. To confer independence upon the Filipinos now is, therefore, to subject the great mass of their people to the dominance of an oligarchical and, probably, exploiting minority. Such a course will be as cruel to those people as it would be shameful to us.

Our true course is to pursue steadily and courageously the path we have thus far followed; to guide the Filipinos into self-sustaining pursuits; to continue the cultivation of sound political habits through education and political practice; to encourage the diversification of industries, and to realize the advantages of their industrial education by conservatively approved cooperative methods, at once checking the dangers of concentrated wealth and building up a sturdy, independent citizenship. We should do all this with a disinterested endeavor to secure for the Filipinos economic independence and to fit them for complete self-government, with the power to decide eventually, according to their own largest good, whether such self-government shall be accompanied by independence. A present declaration even of future independence would retard progress by the dissension and disorder it would arouse. On our part it would be a disingenuous attempt, under the guise of conferring a benefit on them, to relieve ourselves from the heavy and difficult burden which thus far we have been bravely and consistently sustaining. It would be a disguised policy of scuttle. It would make the helpless Filipino the football of oriental politics, under the protection of a guaranty of their independence, which we would be powerless to enforce.

Regulation of Water Power

There are pending before Congress a large number of bills proposing to grant privileges of erecting dams for the purpose of creating water power in our navigable rivers. The pendency of these bills has brought out an important defect in the existing general dam act. That act does not, in my opinion, grant sufficient power to the Federal Government in dealing with the construction of such dams to exact protective conditions in the interest of navigation. It does not permit the Federal Government, as a condition of its permit, to require that a part of the value thus created shall be applied to the further general improvement and protection of the stream. I believe this to be one of the most important matters of internal improvement now confronting the Government. Most of the navigable rivers of this country are comparatively long and shallow. In order that they may be made fully useful for navigation there has come into vogue a method of improvement known as canalization, or the slack-water method, which consists in building a series of dams and locks, each of which will create a long pool of deep navigable water. At each of these dams there is usually created also water power of commercial value. If the water power thus created can be made available for the further improvement of navigation in the stream, it is manifest that the improvement will be much more quickly effected on the one hand, and, on the other, that the burden on the general taxpayers of the country will be very much reduced. Private interests seeking permits to build water-power dams in navigable streams usually urge that they thus improve navigation, and that if they do not impair navigation they should be allowed to take for themselves the entire profits of the water-power development. Whatever they may do by way of relieving the Government of the expense of improving navigation should be given due consideration, but it must be apparent that there may be a profit beyond a reasonably liberal return upon the private investment which is a potential asset of the Government in carrying out a comprehensive policy of waterway development. It is no objection to the retention and use of such an asset by the Government that a comprehensive waterway policy will include the protection and development of the other public uses of water, which can not and should not be ignored in making and executing plans for the protection and development of navigation. It is also equally clear that inasmuch as the water power thus created is or may be an incident of a general scheme of waterway improvement within the constitutional jurisdiction of the Federal Government, the regulation of such water power lies also within that jurisdiction. In my opinion constructive statesmanship requires that legislation should be enacted which will permit the development of navigation in these great rivers to go hand in hand with the utilization of this by-product of water power, created in the course of the same improvement, and that the general dam act should be so amended as to make this possible. I deem it highly important that the Nation should adopt a consistent and harmonious treatment of these water-power projects, which will preserve for this purpose their value to the Government, whose right it is to grant the permit. Any other policy is equivalent to throwing away a most valuable national asset.

The Panama Canal

During the past year the work of construction upon the canal has progressed most satisfactorily. About 87 percent of the excavation work has been completed, and more than 93 percent of the concrete for all the locks is in place. In view of the great interest which has been manifested as to some slides in the Culebra Cut, I am glad to say that the report of Colonel Goethals should allay any apprehension on this point. It is gratifying to note that none of the slides which occurred during this year would have interfered with the passage of the ships had the canal, in fact, been in operation, and when the slope pressures will have been finally adjusted and the growth of vegetation will minimize erosion in the banks of the cut, the slide problem will be practically solved and an ample stability assured for the Culebra Cut.

Although the official date of the opening has been set for January 1, 1915, the canal will, in fact, from present indications, be opened for shipping during the latter half of 1913. No fixed date can as yet be set, but shipping interests will be advised as soon assurances can be given that vessels can pass through without unnecessary delay.

Recognizing the administrative problem in the management of the canal, Congress in the act of August 24, 1912, has made admirable provisions for executive responsibility in the control of the canal and the government of the Canal Zone. The problem of most efficient organization is receiving careful consideration, so that a scheme of organization and control best adapted to the conditions of the canal may be formulated and put in operation as expeditiously as possible. Acting under the authority conferred on me by Congress, I have, by Executive proclamation, promulgated the following schedule of tolls for ships passing through the canal, based upon the thorough report of Emory R. Johnson, special commissioner on traffic and tolls:

1. On merchant vessels carrying passengers or cargo, $1.20 per net vessel ton—each 100 cubic feet—of actual earning capacity.
2. On vessels in ballast without passengers or cargo, 40 percent less than the rate of tolls for vessels with passengers or cargo.
3. Upon naval vessels, other than transports, colliers, hospital ships, and supply ships, 50 cents per displacement ton.
4. Upon Army and Navy transports, colliers, hospital ships, and supply ships, $1.20 per net ton, the vessels to be measured by the same rules as are employed in determining the net tonnage of merchant vessels.

Rules for the determination of the tonnage upon which toll charges are based are now in course of preparation and will be promulgated in due season.

Panama Canal Treaty

The proclamation which I have issued in respect to the Panama Canal tolls is in accord with the Panama Canal act passed by this Congress August 24, 1912. We have been advised that the British Government has prepared a protest against the act and its enforcement in so far as it relieves from the payment of tolls American ships engaged in the American coastwise trade on the ground that it violates British rights under the Hay-Pauncefote treaty concerning the Panama Canal. When the protest is presented, it will be promptly considered and an effort made to reach a satisfactory adjustment of any differences there may be between the two Governments.

Workmen's Compensation Act

The promulgation of an efficient workmen's compensation act, adapted to the particular conditions of the zone, is awaiting adequate appropriation by

Congress for the payment of claims arising thereunder. I urge that speedy provision be made in order that we may install upon the zone a system of settling claims for injuries in best accord with modern humane, social, and industrial theories.

Promotion for Colonel Goethals

As the completion of the canal grows nearer, and as the wonderful executive work of Colonel Goethals becomes more conspicuous in the eyes of the country and of the world, it seems to me wise and proper to make provision by law for such reward to him as may be commensurate with the service that he has rendered to his country. I suggest that this reward take the form of an appointment of Colonel Goethals as a major general in the Army of the United States, and that the law authorizing such appointment be accompanied with a provision permitting his designation as Chief of Engineers upon the retirement of the present incumbent of that office.

Navy Department

The Navy of the United States is in a greater state of efficiency and is more powerful than it has ever been before, but in the emulation which exists between different countries in respect to the increase of naval and military armaments this condition is not a permanent one. In view of the many improvements and increases by foreign Governments the slightest halt on our part in respect to new construction throws us back and reduces us from a naval power of the first rank and places us among the nations of the second rank. In the past 15 years the Navy has expanded rapidly and yet far less rapidly than our country. From now on reduced expenditures in the Navy means reduced military strength. The world's history has shown the importance of sea power both for adequate defense and for the support of important and definite policies.

I had the pleasure of attending this autumn a mobilization of the Atlantic Fleet, and was glad to observe and note the preparedness of the fleet for instant action. The review brought before the President and the Secretary of the Navy a greater and more powerful collection of vessels than had ever been gathered in American waters. The condition of the fleet and of the officers and enlisted men and of the equipment of the vessels entitled those in authority to the greatest credit.

I again commend to Congress the giving of legislative sanction to the appointment of the naval aids to the Secretary of the Navy. These aids and the council of aids appointed by the Secretary of the Navy to assist him in the conduct of his department have proven to be of the highest utility. They have furnished an executive committee of the most skilled naval experts, who have coordinated the action of the various bureaus in the Navy, and by their advice have enabled the Secretary to give an administration at the same time economical and most efficient. Never before has the United States had a Navy that compared in efficiency with its present one, but never before have the requirements with respect to naval warfare been higher and more exacting than now. A year ago Congress refused to appropriate for more than one battleship. In this I think a great mistake of policy was made, and I urgently recommend that this Congress make up for the mistake of the last session by appropriations authorizing the construction of three battleships, in addition to destroyers, fuel ships, and the other auxiliary vessels as shown in the building program of the general board. We are confronted by a condition in respect to the navies of the world which requires us, if we would maintain our Navy as an insurance of peace, to augment our naval force by at least two battleships a year and by battle cruisers, gunboats, torpedo destroyers, and submarine boats in a proper proportion. We have no desire for war. We would go as far as any nation in the world to avoid war, but we are a world power. Our population, our wealth, our definite policies, our responsibilities in the Pacific and the Atlantic, our defense of the Panama Canal, together with our enormous world trade and our missionary outposts on the frontiers of civilization, require us to recognize our position as one of the foremost in the family of nations, and to clothe ourselves with sufficient naval power to give force to our reasonable demands, and to give weight to our influence in those directions of progress that a powerful Christian nation should advocate.

I observe that the Secretary of the Navy devotes some space to a change in the disciplinary system in vogue in that branch of the service. I think there is nothing quite so unsatisfactory to either the Army or the Navy as the severe punishments necessarily inflicted by court-martial for desertions and purely military offenses, and I am glad to hear that the British have solved this important and difficult matter in a satisfactory way. I commend to the consideration of Congress the details of the new disciplinary system, and recommend that laws be passed putting the same into force both in the Army and the Navy.

I invite the attention of Congress to that part of the report of the Secretary of the Navy in which he recommends the formation of a naval reserve by the organization of the ex-sailors of the Navy.

I repeat my recommendation made last year that proper provision should be made for the rank of the commander in chief of the squadrons and fleets of the Navy. The inconvenience attending the necessary precedence that most foreign admirals have over our own whenever they meet in official functions ought to be avoided. It impairs the prestige of our Navy and is a defect that can be very easily removed.

Department of Justice

This department has been very active in the enforcement of the law. It has been better organized and with a larger force than ever before in the history of the Government. The prosecutions which have been successfully concluded and which are now pending testify to the effectiveness of the departmental work.

The prosecution of trusts under the Sherman antitrust law has gone on without restraint or diminution, and decrees similar to those entered in the Standard Oil and the Tobacco cases have been entered in other suits, like the suits against the Powder Trust and the Bathtub Trust. I am very strongly convinced that a steady, consistent course in this regard, with a continuing of Supreme Court decisions upon new phases of the trust question not already finally decided is going to offer a solution of this much-discussed and troublesome issue in a quiet, calm, and judicial way, without any radical legislation changing the governmental policy in regard to combinations now denounced by the Sherman antitrust law. I have already recommended as an aid in this matter legislation which would declare unlawful certain well-known phases of unfair competition in interstate trade, and I have also advocated voluntary national incorporation for the larger industrial enterprises, with provision for a closer supervision by the Bureau of Corporations, or a board appointed for the purpose, so as to make more certain compliance with the antitrust law on the one hand and to give greater security to the stockholders against possible prosecutions on the other. I believe, however, that the orderly course of litigation in the courts and the regular prosecution of trusts charged with the violation of the anti-trust law is producing among business men a clearer and clearer perception of the line of distinction between business that is to be encouraged and business that is to be condemned, and that in this quiet way the question of trusts can be settled and competition retained as an economic force to secure reasonableness in prices and freedom and independence in trade.

Reform of Court Procedure

I am glad to bring to the attention of Congress the fact that the Supreme Court has radically altered the equity rules governing the procedure on the equity side of all Federal courts, and though, as these changes have not been yet put in practice so as to enable us to state from actual results what the reform will accomplish, they are of such a character that we can reasonably prophesy that they will greatly reduce the time and cost of litigation in such courts. The court has adopted many of the shorter methods of the present English procedure, and while it may take a little while for the profession to accustom itself to these methods, it is certain greatly to facilitate litigation. The action of the Supreme Court has been so drastic and so full of appreciation of the necessity for a great reform in court procedure that I have no hesitation in following up this action with a recommendation which I foreshadowed in my message of three years ago, that the sections of the statute governing the procedure in the Federal courts on the common-law side should be so amended as to give to the Supreme Court the same right to make rules of procedure in common law as they have, since the beginning of the court, exercised in equity. I do not doubt that a full consideration of the subject will enable the court while giving effect to the substantial differences in right and remedy between the system of common law and the system of equity so to unite the two procedures into the form of one civil action and to shorten the procedure in such civil action as to furnish a model to all the State courts exercising concurrent jurisdiction with the Federal courts of first instance.

Under the statute now in force the common-law procedure in each

Federal court is made to conform to the procedure in the State in which the court is held. In these days, when we should be making progress in court procedure, such a conformity statute makes the Federal method too dependent upon the action of State legislatures. I can but think it a great opportunity for Congress to intrust to the highest tribunal in this country, evidently imbued with a strong spirit in favor of a reform of procedure, the power to frame a model code of procedure, which, while preserving all that is valuable and necessary of the rights and remedies at common law and in equity, shall lessen the burden of the poor litigant to a minimum in the expedition and cheapness with which his cause can be fought or defended through Federal courts to final judgment.

Workman's Compensation Act

The workman's compensation act reported by the special commission appointed by Congress and the Executive, which passed the Senate and is now pending in the House, the passage of which I have in previous messages urged upon Congress, I venture again to call to its attention. The opposition to it which developed in the Senate, but which was overcome by a majority in that body, seemed to me to grow out rather of a misapprehension of its effect than of opposition to its principle. I say again that I think no act can have better effect directly upon the relations between the employer and employee than this act applying to railroads and common carriers of an interstate character, and I am sure that the passage of the act would greatly relieve the courts of the heaviest burden of litigation that they have, and would enable them to dispatch other business with a speed never before attained in courts of justice in this country.

Part III

[Concerning the work of the Departments of the Post Office,
Interior, Agriculture, and Commerce and Labor and
District of Columbia]

The White House, December 19, 1912

To the Senate and House of Representatives:

This is the third of a series of messages in which I have brought to the
attention of the Congress the important transactions of the Government
in each of its departments during the last year and have discussed needed
reforms.

Heads of Departments Should Have Seats
on the Floor of Congress

I recommend the adoption of legislation which shall make it the duty of
heads of departments—the members of the President's Cabinet—at convenient times to attend the session of the House and the Senate, which
shall provide seats for them in each House, and give them the opportunity
to take part in all discussions and to answer questions of which they have
had due notice. The rigid holding apart of the executive and the legislative
branches of this Government has not worked for the great advantage of
either. There has been much lost motion in the machinery, due to the lack

of cooperation and interchange of views face to face between the representatives of the Executive and the Members of the two legislative branches of the Government. It was never intended that they should be separated in the sense of not being in constant effective touch and relationship to each other. The legislative and the executive each performs its own appropriate function, but these functions must be coordinated. Time and time again debates have arisen in each House upon issues which the information of a particular department head would have enabled him, if present, to end at once by a simple explanation or statement. Time and time again a forceful and earnest presentation of facts and arguments by the representative of the Executive whose duty it is to enforce the law would have brought about a useful reform by amendment, which in the absence of such a statement has failed of passage. I do not think I am mistaken in saying that the presence of the members of the Cabinet on the floor of each House would greatly contribute to the enactment of beneficial legislation. Nor would this in any degree deprive either the legislative or the executive of the independence which separation of the two branches has been intended to promote. It would only facilitate their cooperation in the public interest.

On the other hand, I am sure that the necessity and duty imposed upon department heads of appearing in each House and in answer to searching questions, of rendering upon their feet an account of what they have done, or what has been done by the administration, will spur each member of the Cabinet to closer attention to the details of his department, to greater familiarity with its needs, and to greater care to avoid the just criticism which the answers brought out in questions put and discussions arising between the Members of either House and the members of the Cabinet may properly evoke.

Objection is made that the members of the administration having no vote could exercise no power on the floor of the House, and could not assume that attitude of authority and control which the English parliamentary Government have and which enables them to meet the responsibilities the English system thrusts upon them. I agree that in certain respects it would be more satisfactory if members of the Cabinet could at the same time be Members of both Houses, with voting power, but this is impossible under our system; and while a lack of this feature may detract from the influence of the department chiefs, it will not prevent the good results which I have described above both in the matter of legislation and in the matter of administration. The enactment of such a law would be quite within the power of Congress without constitutional amendment, and it has such possibilities of usefulness that we might well make the experiment, and if we are disappointed the misstep can be easily retraced by a repeal of the enabling legislation.

This is not a new proposition. In the House of Representatives, in the Thirty-eighth Congress, the proposition was referred to a select committee of seven Members. The committee made an extensive report, and urged the adoption of the reform. The report showed that our history had not been without illustration of the necessity and the examples of the practice by pointing out that in early days Secretaries were repeatedly called to the presence of either House for consultation, advice, and information. It also referred to remarks of Mr. Justice Story in his Commentaries on the Constitution, in which he urgently presented the wisdom of such a change. This report is to be found in Volume I of the Reports of Committees of the First Session of the Thirty-eighth Congress, April 6, 1864.

Again, on February 4, 1881, a select committee of the Senate recommended the passage of a similar bill, and made a report, in which, while approving the separation of the three branches, the executive, legislative, and judicial, they point out as a reason for the proposed change that, although having a separate existence, the branches are "to cooperate, each with the other, as the different members of the human body must cooperate, with each other in order to form the figure and perform the duties of a perfect man."

The report concluded as follows:

> This system will require the selection of the strongest men to be heads of departments and will require them to be well equipped with the knowledge of their offices. It will also require the strongest men to be the leaders of Congress and participate in debate. It will bring these strong men in contact, perhaps into conflict, to advance the public weal, and thus stimulate their abilities and their efforts, and will thus assuredly result to the good of the country.
>
> If it should appear by actual experience that the heads of departments in fact have not time to perform the additional duty imposed on them by this bill, the force in their offices should be increased or the duties

devolving on them personally should be diminished. An undersecretary should be appointed to whom could be confided that routine of administration which requires only order and accuracy. The principal officers could then confine their attention to those duties which require wise discretion and intellectual activity. Thus they would have abundance of time for their duties under this bill. Indeed, your committee believes that the public interest would be subserved if the Secretaries were relieved of the harassing cares of distributing clerkships and closely supervising the mere machinery of the departments. Your committee believes that the adoption of this bill and the effective execution of its provisions will be the first step toward a sound civil-service reform which will secure a larger wisdom in the adoption of policies and a better system in their execution.

(Signed) W. B. Allison
D. W. Voorhees
J. G. Blaine
M. C. Butler
John J. Ingalls
O. H. Platt
J. T. Farley

It would be difficult to mention the names of higher authority in the practical knowledge of our Government than those which are appended to this report.

Postal Savings Bank System

The Postal Savings Bank System has been extended so that it now includes 4,004 fourth-class post offices, as well as 645 branch offices and stations in the larger cities. There are now 12,812 depositories at which patrons of the system may open accounts. The number of depositors is 300,000 and the amount of their deposits is approximately $28,000,000, not including $1,314,140 which has been withdrawn by depositors for the purpose of buying postal savings bonds. Experience demonstrates the value of dispensing with the pass-book and introducing in its place a certificate of deposit. The gross income of the postal savings system for the fiscal year ending June 30, 1913, will amount to $700,000 and the interest payable to depositors to $300,000. The cost of supplies, equipment, and salaries is $700,000. It thus appears that the system lacks $300,000 a year of paying interest and expenses. It is estimated, however, that when the deposits have reached the sum of $50,000,000, which at the present rate they soon will do, the system will be self-sustaining. By law the postal savings funds deposited at each post office are required to be redeposited in local banks. State and national banks to the number of 7,357 have qualified as depositories for these funds. Such deposits are secured by bonds aggregating $54,000,000. Of this amount, $37,000,000 represent municipal bonds.

Parcel Post

In several messages I have favored and recommended the adoption of a system of parcel post. In the postal appropriation act of last year a general system was provided and its installation was directed by the first of January. This has entailed upon the Post Office Department a great deal of very heavy labor, but the Postmaster General informs me that on the date selected, to wit, the first of January, near at hand, the department will be in readiness to meet successfully the requirements of the public.

Classification of Postmasters

A trial, during the past three years, of the system of classifying fourth-class postmasters in that part of the country lying between the Mississippi River on the west, Canada on the north, the Atlantic Ocean on the east, and Mason and Dixon's line on the south has been sufficiently satisfactory to justify the postal authorities in recommending the extension of the order to include all the fourth-class postmasters in the country. In September, 1912, upon the suggestion of the Postmaster General, I directed him to prepare an order which should put the system in effect, except in Alaska, Guam, Hawaii, Puerto Rico, and Samoa. Under date of October 15 I issued such an order which affected 36,000 postmasters. By the order the post offices were divided into groups A and B. Group A includes all postmasters whose compensation is $500 or more, and group B those whose compensation is less than that sum. Different methods are pursued in the selection of the postmasters for group A and group B. Criticism has been made of this order on the ground that the motive for it was political. Nothing could be further from the truth. The order was made before the election and in the interest of efficient public service. I have several times requested Congress to give me authority to put first-, second-, and third-class postmasters, and all other local officers, including internal-revenue officers, customs officers, United States marshals, and the local agents of the other departments under the classification of the civil-service law by taking away the necessity for confirming such appointments by the Senate. I deeply regret the failure of Congress to follow these recommendations.

Compensation to Railways for Carrying Mails

It is expected that the establishment of a parcel post on January first will largely increase the amount of mail matter to be transported by the railways, and Congress should be prompt to provide a way by which they may receive the additional compensation to which they will be entitled. The Postmaster General urges that the department's plan for a complete readjustment of the system of paying the railways for carrying the mails be adopted, substituting space for weight as the principal factor in fixing compensation. Under this plan it will be possible to determine without delay what additional payment should be made on account of the parcel post. The Postmaster General's recommendation is based on the results of a far-reaching investigation begun early in the administration with the object of determining what it costs the railways to carry the mails. The statistics obtained during the course of the inquiry show that while many of the railways, and particularly the large systems, were making profits from mail transportations, certain of the lines were actually carrying the mails at a loss. As a result of the investigation the department, after giving the subject careful consideration, decided to urge the abandonment of the present plan of fixing compensation on the basis of the weight of the mails carried, a plan that has proved to be exceedingly expensive and in other respects unsatisfactory. Under the method proposed the railway companies will annually submit to the department reports showing what it costs them to carry the mails, and this cost will be apportioned on the basis of the car space engaged, payment to be allowed at the rate thus determined in amounts that will cover the cost and a reasonable profit. If a railway is not satisfied with the manner in which the department apportions the cost in fixing compensation, it is to have the right, under the new plan, of appealing to the Interstate Commerce Commission. This feature of the proposed law would seem to insure a fair treatment of the railways. It is hoped that Congress will give the matter immediate attention and that the method of compensation recommended by the department or some other suitable plan will be promptly authorized.

Department of the Interior

The Interior Department, in the problems of administration included within its jurisdiction, presents more difficult questions than any other. This has been due perhaps to temporary causes of a political character, but more especially to the inherent difficulty in the performance of some of the functions which are assigned to it. Its chief duty is the guardianship of the public domain and the disposition of that domain to private ownership under homestead, mining, and other laws, by which patents from the Government to the individual are authorized on certain conditions. During the last decade the public seemed to become suddenly aware that a very large part of its domain had passed from its control into private ownership, under laws not well adapted to modern conditions, and also that in the doing of this the provisions of existing law and regulations adopted in accordance with law had not been strictly observed, and that in the transfer of title much fraud had intervened, to the pecuniary benefit of dishonest persons. There arose thereupon a demand for conservation of the public domain, its protection against fraudulent diminution, and the preservation of that part of it from private acquisition which it seemed necessary to keep for future public use. The movement, excellent in the intention which prompted it, and useful in its results, has nevertheless had some bad effects, which the western country has recently been feeling and in respect of which there is danger of a reaction toward older abuses unless we can attain the golden mean, which consists in the prevention of the mere exploitation of the public domain for private purposes while at the same time facilitating its development for the benefit of the local public.

The land laws need complete revision to secure proper conservation on the one hand of land that ought to be kept in public use and, on the other hand, prompt disposition of those lands which ought to be disposed in private ownership or turned over to private use by properly guarded leases. In addition to this there are not enough officials in our Land Department with legal knowledge sufficient promptly to make the decisions which are called for. The whole land-laws system should be reorganized, and not until it is reorganized, will decisions be made as promptly as they ought, or will men who have earned title to public land under the statute receive their patents within a reasonably short period. The present administration has done what it could in this regard, but the necessity for reform and change by a revision of the laws and an increase and reorganization of the force remains, and I submit to Congress the wisdom of a full examination of this subject, in order that a very large and important part of our people in the West may be relieved from a just cause of irritation.

I invite your attention to the discussion by the Secretary of the Interior of the need for legislation with respect to mining claims, leases of coal lands in this country and in Alaska, and for similar disposition of oil, phosphate, and potash lands, and also to his discussion of the proper use to be made of water-power sites held by the Government. Many of these lands are now being withheld from use by the public under the general withdrawal act which was passed by the last Congress. That act was not for the purpose of disposing of the question, but it was for the purpose of preserving the lands until the question could be solved. I earnestly urge that the matter is of the highest importance to our western fellow citizens and ought to command the immediate attention of the legislative branch of the Government.

Another function which the Interior Department has to perform is that of the guardianship of Indians. In spite of everything which has been said in criticism of the policy of our Government toward the Indians, the amount of wealth which is now held by it for these wards per capita shows that the Government has been generous; but the management of so large an estate, with the great variety of circumstances that surround each tribe and each case, calls for the exercise of the highest business discretion, and the machinery provided in the Indian Bureau for the discharge of this function is entirely inadequate. The position of Indian commissioner demands the exercise of business ability of the first order, and it is difficult to secure such talent for the salary provided.

The condition of health of the Indian and the prevalence in the tribes of curable diseases has been exploited recently in the press. In a message to Congress at its last session I brought this subject to its attention and invited a special appropriation, in order that our facilities for overcoming diseases among the Indians might be properly increased, but no action was then taken by Congress on the subject, nor has such appropriation been made since.

The commission appointed by authority of the Congress to report on proper method of securing railroad development in Alaska is formulating its report, and I expect to have an opportunity before the end of this session to submit its recommendations.

Department of Agriculture

The far-reaching utility of the educational system carried on by the Department of Agriculture for the benefit of the farmers of our country calls for no elaboration. Each year there is a growth in the variety of facts which it brings out for the benefit of the farmer, and each year confirms the wisdom of the expenditure of the appropriations made for that department.

Pure-Food Law

The Department of Agriculture is charged with the execution of the pure-food law. The passage of this encountered much opposition from manufacturers and others who feared the effect upon their business of the enforcement of its provisions. The opposition aroused the just indignation of the public, and led to an intense sympathy with the severe and rigid enforcement of the provisions of the new law. It had to deal in many instances with the question whether or not products of large business enterprises, in the form of food preparations, were deleterious to the public health; and while in a great majority of instances this issue was easily determinable, there were not a few cases in which it was hard to draw the line between a useful and a harmful food preparation. In cases like this when a decision involved the destruction of great business enterprises representing the investment of large capital and the expenditure of great energy and ability, the danger of serious injustice was very considerable in the enforcement of a new law under the spur of great public indignation. The public officials charged with executing the law might do injustice in heated controversy through unconscious pride of opinion and obstinacy of conclusion. For this reason President Roosevelt felt justified in creating a board of experts, known as the Remsen Board, to whom in cases of much importance an appeal might be taken and a review had of a decision of the Bureau of Chemistry in the Agricultural Department. I heartily agree that it was wise to create this board in order that injustice might not be done. The questions which arise are not generally those involving palpable injury to health, but they are upon the narrow and doubtful line in respect of which it is better to be in some error not dangerous than to be radically destructive. I think that the time has come for Congress to recognize the necessity for some such tribunal of appeal and to make specific statutory provision for it. While we are struggling to suppress an evil of great proportions like that of impure food, we must provide machinery in the law itself to prevent its becoming an instrument of oppression, and we ought to enable those whose business is threatened with annihilation to have some tribunal and some form of appeal in which they have a complete day in court.

Agricultural Credits

I referred in my first message to the question of improving the system of agricultural credits. The Secretary of Agriculture has made an investigation into the matter of credits in this country, and I commend a consideration of the information which through his agents he has been able to collect. It does not in any way minimize the importance of the proposal, but it gives more accurate information upon some of the phases of the question than we have heretofore had.

Department of Commerce and Labor

I commend to Congress an examination of the report of the Secretary of Commerce and Labor, and especially that part in which he discusses the office of the Bureau of Corporations, the value to commerce of a proposed trade commission, and the steps which he has taken to secure the organization of a national chamber of commerce. I heartily commend his view that the plan of a trade commission which looks to the fixing of prices is altogether impractical and ought not for a moment to be considered as a possible solution of the trust question.

The trust question in the enforcement of the Sherman antitrust law is gradually solving itself, is maintaining the principle and restoring the practice of competition, and if the law is quietly but firmly enforced, business will adjust itself to the statutory requirements, and the unrest in commercial circles provoked by the trust discussion will disappear.

Panama-Pacific International Exposition

In conformity with a joint resolution of Congress, an Executive proclamation was issued last February, inviting the nations of the world to participate in the Panama-Pacific International Exposition to be held at San Francisco to celebrate the construction of the Panama Canal. A sympathetic response was immediately forthcoming, and several nations have already selected the sites for their buildings. In furtherance of my invitation, a special commission visited European countries during the past summer, and received assurance of hearty cooperation in the task of bringing together a universal industrial, military, and naval display on an unprecedented scale. It is evident that the exposition will be an accurate mirror of the world's activities as they appear 400 years after the date of the discovery of the Pacific Ocean.

It is the duty of the United States to make the nations welcome at San Francisco and to facilitate such acquaintance between them and ourselves as will promote the expansion of commerce and familiarize the world with the new trade route through the Panama Canal. The action of the State governments and individuals assures a comprehensive exhibit of the resources of this country and of the progress of the people. This participation by State and individuals should be supplemented by an adequate showing of the varied and unique activities of the National Government. The United States can not with good grace invite foreign governments to erect buildings and make expensive exhibits while itself refusing to participate. Nor would it be wise to forego the opportunity to join with other nations in the inspiring interchange of ideas tending to promote intercourse, friendship, and commerce. It is the duty of the Government to foster and build up commerce through the canal, just as it was the duty of the Government to construct it.

I earnestly recommend the appropriation at this session of such a sum as will enable the United States to construct a suitable building, install a governmental exhibit, and otherwise participate in the Panama-Pacific International Exposition in a manner commensurate with the dignity of a nation whose guests are to be the people of the world. I recommend also such legislation as will facilitate the entry of material intended for exhibition and protect foreign exhibitors against infringement of patents and the unauthorized copying of patterns and designs. All aliens sent to San Francisco to construct and care for foreign buildings and exhibits should be admitted without restraint or embarrassment.

The District of Columbia and the City of Washington

The city of Washington is a beautiful city, with a population of 352,936, of whom 98,667 are colored. The annual municipal budget is about $14,000,000. The presence of the National Capital and other governmental structures constitutes the chief beauty and interest of the city. The public grounds are extensive, and the opportunities for improving the city and making it still more attractive are very great. Under a plan adopted some years ago, one half the cost of running the city is paid by taxation upon the property, real and personal, of the citizens and residents, and the other half is borne by the General Government. The city is expanding at a remarkable rate, and this can only be accounted for by the coming here from other parts of the country of well-to-do people who, having finished their business careers elsewhere, build and make this their permanent place of residence.

On the whole, the city as a municipality is very well governed. It is well lighted, the water supply is good, the streets are well paved, the police force is well disciplined, crime is not flagrant, and while it has purlieus and centers of vice, like other large cities, they are not exploited, they do not exercise any influence or control in the government of the city, and they are suppressed in as far as it has been found practicable. Municipal graft is inconsiderable. There are interior courts in the city that are noisome and centers of disease and the refuge of criminals, but Congress has begun to clean these out, and progress has been made in the case of the most notorious of these, which is known as "Willow Tree Alley." This movement should continue.

The mortality for the past year was at the rate of 17.80 per 1,000 of both races; among the whites it was 14.61 per thousand, and among the blacks 26.12 per thousand. These are the lowest mortality rates ever recorded in the District.

One of the most crying needs in the government of the District is a tribunal or public authority for the purpose of supervising the corporations engaged in the operation of public utilities. Such a bill is pending in Congress and ought to pass. Washington should show itself under the direction of Congress to be a city with a model form of government, but as long as such authority over public utilities is withheld from the municipal government, it must always be defective.

Without undue criticism of the present street railway accommodations, it can be truly said that under the spur of a public utilities commission they might be substantially improved.

While the school system of Washington perhaps might be bettered in the economy of its management and the distribution of its buildings, its usefulness has nevertheless greatly increased in recent years, and it now offers excellent facilities for primary and secondary education.

From time to time there is considerable agitation in Washington in favor of granting the citizens of the city the franchise and constituting an elective government. I am strongly opposed to this change. The history of Washington discloses a number of experiments of this kind, which have always been abandoned as unsatisfactory. The truth is this is a city governed by a popular body, to wit, the Congress of the United States, selected from the people of the United States, who own Washington. The people who come here to live do so with the knowledge of the origin of the city and the restrictions, and therefore voluntarily give up the privilege of living in a municipality governed by popular vote. Washington is so unique in its origin and in its use for housing and localizing the sovereignty of the Nation that the people who live here must regard its peculiar character and must be content to subject themselves to the control of a body selected by all the people of the Nation. I agree that there are certain inconveniences growing out of the government of a city by a national legislature like Congress, and it would perhaps be possible to lessen these by the delegation by Congress to the District Commissioners of greater legislative power for the enactment of local laws than they now possess, especially those of a police character.

Every loyal American has a personal pride in the beauty of Washington and in its development and growth. There is no one with a proper appreciation of our Capital City who would favor a niggardly policy in respect to expenditures from the National Treasury to add to the attractiveness of this city, which belongs to every citizen of the entire country, and which no citizen visits without a sense of pride of ownership. We have had restored by a Commission of Fine Arts, at the instance of a committee of the Senate, the original plan of the French engineer L'Enfant for the city of Washington, and we know with great certainty the course which the improvement of Washington should take. Why should there be delay in making this improvement in so far as it involves the extension of the parking system and the construction of greatly needed public buildings? Appropriate buildings for the State Department, the Department of Justice, and the Department of Commerce and Labor have been projected, plans have been approved, and nothing is wanting but the appropriations for the beginning and completion of the structures. A hall of archives is also badly needed, but nothing has been done toward its construction, although the land for it has long been bought and paid for. Plans have been made for the union of Potomac Park with the valley of Rock Creek and Rock Creek Park, and the necessity for the connection between the Soldiers' Home and Rock Creek Park calls for no comment. I ask again why there should be delay in carrying out these plans. We have the money in the Treasury, the plans are national in their scope, and the improvement should be treated as a national project. The plan will find a hearty approval throughout the country. I am quite sure, from the information which I have, that, at comparatively small expense, from that part of the District of Columbia which was retroceded to Virginia, the portion including the Arlington estate, Fort Myer, and the palisades of the Potomac can be acquired by purchase and the jurisdiction of the State of Virginia over this land ceded to the Nation. This ought to be done.

The construction of the Lincoln Memorial and of a memorial bridge from the base of the Lincoln Monument to Arlington would be an appropriate and symbolic expression of the union of the North and the South at the Capital of the Nation. I urge upon Congress the appointment of a commission to undertake these national improvements, and to submit a plan for their execution; and when the plan has been submitted and approved, and the work carried out, Washington will really become what it ought to be—the most beautiful city in the world.

17

Special Message

[On fur seals]
The White House, January 8, 1913

To the Senate and House of Representatives:

At the last session of Congress an act was adopted to give effect to the fur-seal treaty of July 7, 1911, between Great Britain, Japan, Russia, and the United States, in which act was incorporated a provision establishing a five-year period during which the killing of seals upon the Pribilof Islands is prohibited. Prior to the passage of this act, I pointed out in my message to Congress, on August 14 last, the inadvisability of adopting legislation the effect of which was to require this Government to suspend the killing of surplus male seals on land before it was actually proved by the test of experience and scientific investigation that such suspension of killing was necessary for the protection and preservation of the seal herd. I also pointed out in that message that the other Governments interested might justly complain if this Government by prohibiting all land killing should deprive them of their expected share of the skins taken on land, unless we can show by satisfactory evidence that this course was adopted as the result of changed conditions justifying a change in our previous attitude on the subject. As was then anticipated, the other parties interested have now objected to the suspension thus imposed on the ground that it is contrary to the spirit, if not the letter, of the treaty, inasmuch as under existing conditions a substantial number of male seals not required for breeding purposes can be killed annually without detriment to the reproductive capacity of the herd. The same objection was raised by the other Governments interested under this convention while the bill was awaiting my signature, after its passage by Congress, but I refrained from vetoing it because at that time several thousand sealskins had already been taken on the islands and were ready for distribution in accordance with the requirements of the treaty, so that the suspension of land killing would not actually become effective until the following year, and I was satisfied that the information resulting from a study of the condition of the herd during the past summer would put this Government in possession of facts which would either lead to the amendment of the act at this session of Congress, or enable this Government to justify a temporary suspension of land killing; and apart from this particular provision, the act was needed to give effect to our treaty obligations.

It now appears that under the operation of the fur-seal convention during the past year the condition and size of the herd has improved to an extent which seems to indicate that there is now no necessity, and therefore no justification, for the suspension of all land killing of male seals, as required by the act under consideration.

Last season's reports from the officials in charge on the Pribilof Islands show that the herd which the year before contained at the highest estimate not more than 140,000 seals, now numbers upward of 215,000 by actual count, showing in one season an increase of at least 75,000 seals. This increase is largely due to the protection afforded by the treaty to the breeding female seals, which last summer numbered nearly 82,000, many thousands of which, except for the treaty, would have been slaughtered by pelagic sealers, and as every breeding female adds one pup to the herd each year, over 81,000 new pups were added last season. Moreover, instead of losing 10,000 or 15,000 of these pups through starvation as heretofore on account of the slaughter of the nursing mothers by pelagic sealers, this summer by actual count the number of dead pups found on the rookeries was only 1,060.

It is evident from these reports that there has been a very remarkable increase in the size of the herd in one season under the operation of this convention and that a large part of this increase consists of female seals, upon which the future increase of the herd depends.

The present condition of the herd shows that there will be about 100,000 breeding female seals in the herd next summer, each one of which will produce one pup, and in the following year the female pups born last summer, amounting in accordance with the laws of nature to one-half of the total number of the year's pups, will pass into the breeding class, subject to losses from natural mortality, thus adding a possible 40,000 more, which would bring the total up in the neighborhood of 140,000 breeding female seals; and so on from year to year the reproductive strength of the herd will increase in almost geometrical progression, so that we can confidently count on having the present size of the herd doubled and trebled within a very short period.

All that is required to fulfill these expectations is to protect absolutely the female seals and set aside an adequate number of male seals for breeding purposes. The protection and preservation of the herd does not require the protection and preservation of the surplus male seals not needed for breeding purposes. Owing to the polygamous habits of the seals, the increase in the number of these surplus bachelor seals can in no conceivable way increase the birth rate or the reproductive capacity of the herd. Seals of this class contribute nothing to the welfare of the herd, and in some ways they are a distinct detriment as a disturbing element on the rookeries and as consumers of food, which is bound to become scarcer as the size of the herd increases. These nonbreeding males, therefore, are of no value as members of the herd except to furnish skins for the market in place of those heretofore taken by pelagic sealers, and in this connection it should be noted that the value of their skins for commercial purposes diminishes after they are 4 years old and ceases altogether after the age of 5 or 6.

It is right and necessary that the killing of all seals in the herd other than the nonbreeding males should be absolutely prohibited not only for five years but forever. Land killing has been and always must be strictly limited by law to male seals, so that female seals would never be included in land killing in any event. Pelagic sealing, on the other hand, always has been chiefly directed against female seals, thus diminishing the size of the herd not merely by the number actually killed each year but also by an equal number of nursing pups killed by starvation and by the loss of the countless number of unborn pups which would have been added to the herd the following year and in succeeding years. Pelagic sealing has now been stopped, but it must be remembered that the United States alone was powerless to stop it. An international agreement was necessary for that purpose, and has at last been secured after difficult and protracted negotiations resulting in the present convention with Great Britain, Japan, and Russia, who have now joined with us in prohibiting pelagic sealing, and whose cooperation is necessary to make that prohibition effective. To secure such an agreement has been the aim of the United States throughout the entire period covered by the fur-seal controversy, and from the point of view of the United States this prohibition against pelagic sealing is the most important feature of the present convention. In order, however, to secure its adoption by Great Britain and Japan it was necessary for the United States to agree to give each of them a share of the proceeds of the annual increase of the American herd with the assurance, as an inducement, that a large annual increase available for commercial purposes would result from the abandonment of pelagic sealing. As stated in my former message to Congress on this subject:

> Ever since the question of land killing of seals was subjected to scientific investigation, soon after the fur-seal controversy arose, nearly 25 years ago, this Government has invariably insisted throughout the protracted and almost continuous diplomatic negotiations which have ensued for the settlement of this controversy that the progressive diminution of the herd was due to the killing of seals at sea, and that if pelagic sealing was discontinued the polygamous habits of the seals would make it possible to kill annually on land a large number of surplus males without detriment to the reproductive capacity of the herd and without interfering with the normal growth of the size of the herd. The position thus taken by the United States has always been put forward and relied on by the United States in urging that an international agreement should be entered into prohibiting pelagic sealing; and it is obvious that one of the considerations which induced Great Britain and Japan to enter into this convention prohibiting their subjects from pelagic sealing was the expectation that the position thus taken by the United States was well founded and that the skins falling to the share of those Governments from the land killing of seals, as provided for in this convention, would compensate them for abandoning the taking of sealskins at sea.

It was well understood by all the parties in entering into this convention that the result aimed at was to increase the annual reproductive capacity of the herd so that a larger number of sealskins might be taken each year for commercial purposes without injury to the welfare of the herd.

It is evident from these considerations that the United States is in honor bound under this convention to permit the killing annually for commercial purposes of male seals not required as a reserve for breeding before they have passed beyond the age when their skins cease to have a commercial value.

The question of how many male seals should be reserved each year for breeding purposes can readily be determined. In the act under consideration, as it passed the House and before it was amended in the Senate, there was a provision that hereafter only 3-year-old males shall be killed, and that there shall be reserved from among the finest and most perfect seals of that age not fewer than 2,000 in 1913, 2,500 in 1914, 3,000 in 1915, 3,500 in 1916, and 4,000 each year from 1917 to 1921, inclusive, and 5,000 each year thereafter during the continuance of the convention. These figures were arrived at after full and careful investigation by the House Committee on Foreign Affairs and it appears from the committee reports accompanying this act that these figures were intended to be and were regarded as large enough to be on the safe side. It would be more appropriate and convenient to leave the decision of this question to the Secretary of Commerce and Labor, subject to the limitation, which might properly be imposed, that each year before any commercial killing is done there should be marked and set aside or reserved from among the finest and best of the males of 3 years of age such number as is necessary, in his judgment, to provide an ample breeding reserve of males. In any event it is evident that the determination of the number of male seals to be reserved each year for this purpose will present no difficulty; and in this connection it should be noted, as stated in my former message on this subject, that "since the fur-seal business has been taken over by the Government and no private interests are now concerned in making a profit out of it, there is no urgent necessity for imposing by legislation stringent limitations upon land killing."

The only provision in the convention authorizing the United States to limit or suspend land killing is the reservation in Article X that nothing therein contained shall restrict the right of the United States at any time and from time to time to suspend altogether the taking of sealskins on its islands and to impose such restrictions and regulations upon the total number of skins to be taken in any season, and the manner and times and places of taking them, "as may be necessary to protect and preserve the seal herd or increase its number." It is clear from the terms of the convention that the right thus reserved to the United States to regulate or suspend land killing is not an arbitrary right, but can be exercised only when to necessary protect or preserve or increase the herd. It is also clear that this provision must be read in connection with the main purpose of the convention, and that the right reserved should be exercised in aid of that purpose. It has already been shown that the result aimed at by this convention was to increase the annual reproductive capacity of the herd, so that a larger number of sealskins might be taken each year for commercial purposes without injury to the welfare of the herd. It follows, therefore, that when a limitation or suspension of land killing would interfere with, rather than promote, this purpose of the convention there would then be not only no necessity but no justification for such limitation or suspension.

The argument has been advanced that in addition to the right thus reserved the convention recognized an absolute right in the United States arbitrarily to suspend all land killing, because, according to this argument, another clause of the convention fixes a measure of damages to be paid each year to the other parties whenever the United States prohibits all land killing. The clause referred to is found in Article XI, which provides that in case the United States shall absolutely prohibit all land killing of seals, then it shall pay to Great Britain and Japan each the sum of $10,000 annually in lieu of their share of skins during the years when no killing is allowed. It is evident, however, from an examination of the other provisions of the same clause of the convention that these $10,000 payments cannot be, and were not intended to be, regarded as a measure of damages, because Great Britain and Japan are required to repay them to the United States with interest at 4 percent out of the proceeds of their share of the skins taken whenever land killing is resumed. A payment which is subsequently to be refunded clearly is not a measure of damages. Moreover, even if this provision could be regarded as fixing a measure of damages, that in itself would not justify the United States in arbitrarily imposing those damages upon Great Britain and Japan. These provisions requiring the $10,000 payments to be made when land killing is suspended and to be refunded when killing is resumed clearly have an ulterior purpose; otherwise they are wholly unnecessary, for the same result would have been accomplished with much greater simplicity by omitting them altogether. The ulterior purpose becomes perfectly clear when we consider that under the laws in force when the treaty was made it was within the power of the Secretary of Commerce and Labor to suspend land killing altogether whenever in his opinion the welfare of the herd required such action. The evident purpose, therefore, of this requirement for making substantial payments when land killing was suspended, was to prevent the suspension of land killing by executive action unless Congress was prepared to appropriate the money necessary for making such payments. It was undoubtedly assumed that the necessity for adopting legislation appropriating the money to make these payments would lead to a careful investigation of whether or not the actual condition of the herd warranted a total suspension of land killing, and that the appropriation would not be made unless the investigation produced satisfactory evidence that such suspension of killing was absolutely necessary within the requirements of the treaty.

In view of the present condition of the herd and the very marked increase in its size and particularly in the number of female seals, which has resulted from the operation of this convention during a single year, and which, as above shown, is to be attributed almost wholly to the protection afforded by the prohibition against pelagic sealing, I recommend to Congress the immediate consideration of whether or not the complete suspension of land killing imposed by this act is now necessary for the protection and preservation of the herd, and for increasing its number within the meaning and for the purposes of the convention. If no actual necessity is found for such suspension then it is not justified under the convention, and the act should be amended accordingly.

As stated in my annual message to Congress in December last, it is important that in case there is any uncertainty as to the real necessity for suspending all land killing, this Government should yield on that point rather than give the slightest ground for the charge that we have been in any way remiss in observing our treaty obligations. I also wish to impress upon Congress that, as stated in my former message on this subject, it is essential in dealing with it not only to fulfill the obligations imposed upon the United States by the letter and the spirit of the convention, but also to consider the interests of the other parties to the convention, for their cooperation is necessary to make it an effective and permanent settlement of the fur-seal controversy.

18

Special Message

[Transmitting the report on the transportation question
in the Territory of Alaska, etc.]
The White House, February 6, 1913

To the Senate and House of Representatives:
In accordance with the provisions of section 18 of an act of Congress
approved August 24, 1912, I appointed a commission

> to conduct an examination into the transportation question in the Terri-
> tory of Alaska: to examine railroad routes from the seaboard to the coal
> fields and to the interior and navigable waterways; to secure surveys and
> other information with respect to railroads, including cost of construc-
> tion and operation; to obtain information in respect to the coal fields
> and their proximity to railroad routes; and to make report of the facts
> to Congress on or before the first day of December, nineteen hundred
> and twelve, or as soon thereafter as may be practicable, together with
> their conclusions and recommendations in respect to the best and most
> available routes for railroads in Alaska which will develop the country
> and the resources thereof for the use of the people of the United States.

Under the requirements of the act, this commission consisted of "an
officer of the Engineer Corps of the United States Army, a geologist in
charge of Alaska surveys, an officer in the Engineer Corps of the United

States Navy, and a civil engineer who has had practical experience in railroad construction and has not been connected with any railroad enterprise in said Territory."

The date when the act was passed was late in the summer season, thus allowing a very limited time for the preparation of a report for presentation at the present session of Congress. Nevertheless, within a week after the act was approved the commission had been appointed, as follows: Maj. Jay J. Morrow, Corps of Engineers, United States Army, chairman; Alfred H. Brooks, geologist in charge of Division of Alaskan Mineral Resources, Geological Survey, vice chairman; Civil Engineer Leonard M. Cox, United States Navy. Colin M. Ingersoll, consulting railroad engineer, New York, New York. This commission has transmitted to me a report, which is herewith submitted to Congress in accordance with the provisions of the act. An examination of this report discloses that the following are among the more important of the findings of the commission:

The Territory of Alaska contains large undeveloped mineral resources, extensive tracts of agricultural and grazing lands, and the climate of a large part of the Territory is favorable to permanent settlement and industrial development. The report contains much specific information and many interesting details with regard to these resources. It finds that they can be developed and utilized only by the construction of railways which shall connect tidewater on the Pacific Ocean with the two great inland waterways, the Yukon and the Kuskokwim Rivers. The resources of the inland region and especially of these great river basins are almost undeveloped because of lack of transportation facilities. The Yukon and Kuskokwim Rivers system include some 5,000 miles of navigable water, but these are open to commerce only about three months in the year. Moreover, the mouths of these two rivers on Bering Sea lie some 2,500 miles from Puget Sound, thus involving a long and circuitous route from the Pacific Coast States. The transportation of freight to the mouths of these rivers and thence upstream will always be so expensive and confined to so limited a season as to forbid any large industrial advancement for the great inland region now entirely dependent on these circuitous avenues of approach.

From these considerations the commission finds that railway connections with open ports on the Pacific are not only justified, but imperative if the fertile regions of inland Alaska and its mineral resources are to be utilized; but that with such railway connections a large region will be opened up to the homesteader, the prospector, and the miner. So far as the limited time available has permitted the commission has investigated, and in its report describes all of the railway routes which have been suggested for reaching the interior, including the ocean terminals of these routes. The relative advantages and disadvantages of these routes are compared. The principal result of this comparison may be stated to be that railroad development in Alaska should proceed first by means of two independent railroad systems, hereafter to be connected and supplemented as may be justified by future development. One of these lines should connect the valley of the Yukon and its tributary, the Tanana, with tidewater; and the other should be devoted to the development and needs of the Kuskokwim and the Susitna.

The best available route for the first railway system is that which leads from Cordova by way of Chitina to Fairbanks; and the best available route for the second is that which leads from Seward around Cook Inlet to the Iditarod. The first should be connected with the Bering coal field and the second with the Matanuska coal field. Other routes and terminals are discussed, but are found not to have the importance or availability for the development of the Territory possessed by the two mentioned. Thus, the route extending inland from Haines, in southeastern Alaska, has value for local development, though chiefly on the Canadian side of the boundary, but the distance to Fairbanks is found to be too great to permit of its being used as a trunk line to the Yukon waters. The route from Iliamna Bay also has value for local use, but is too far to the southwest to permit of its use as a trunk line into the interior. The proposed terminals at Katalla and Controller Bay are found to be very expensive both as to construction and maintenance, besides furnishing very inferior harbors. The route inland from Valdez is at a disadvantage because it would not serve any of the coal fields, although as hereafter noted Valdez is regarded by the commission as an important alternative terminal in the possible future development of the Chitina-Fairbanks route.

The investigations of the commission indicate that the route from Cordova by way of Chitina to Fairbanks would furnish the best trunk line to the Yukon and Tanana waters: (1) Because Cordova has distinct advantages as a harbor; (2) because this route requires the shortest actual amount of construction, but chiefly (3) because the better grades possible on this route should give the lowest freight rates into the Tanana Valley. The Copper River & Northwestern Railroad is now constructed from Cordova to Chitina and thence up the Chitina River. The commission recommends the building of a railway from Chitina to Fairbanks, 313 miles, estimated to cost $13,971,000, with the provision that if this railway is built by other interests than those controlling the Copper River & Northwestern Railroad, and if an equitable traffic arrangement can not be made with it, connection should be made with Valdez by the Thompson Pass route, 101 miles, estimated to cost $6,101,479.

The commission finds that Cordova offers the best present ocean terminal for the Bering River coal. The commission also points out that it would not be economical to haul the Matanuska coal to either Valdez or Cordova, and that therefore the logical outlet for that field is Seward. If commercial development of these two fields should disclose that the quality of the coal is the same in both, the Bering River field would have the advantage of greater proximity to open tidewater. A branch line from the Copper River Railway to the Bering River field, a distance of 38 miles, at an estimated cost of $2,054,000, is recommended to afford an outlet for the coal on Prince William Sound and into the Copper River Valley and the region where there is at present the largest market for Alaska coal.

The commission finds that a railway from Chitina to Fairbanks will not solve the transportation problem of Alaska, because it will not give access to the Matanuska coal field, the fertile lands and mineral wealth of the lower Susitna, or the great Kuskokwim basin. This province properly belongs to an independent railway system based on the harbor at Seward. The commission recommends a railway from Kern Creek, the present inland terminal of the Alaska Northern Railway, to the Susitna River (distance, 115 miles; estimated cost, $5,209,000), with a branch line to the Matanuska coal field (distance, 38 miles; estimated cost, $1,618,000); and an extension of the main line through the Alaska Range to the Kuskokwin River (distance, 229 miles; estimated cost, $12,760,000).

The entire railways thus recommended will constitute two independent systems involving 733 miles of new construction at a cost of $35,000,000. Eventually these systems will be tied together and there will be earlier demands for branch and local lines as the country develops. One of these systems will find an outlet to the coast over the Copper River & Northwestern Railroad; the other over the Alaska Northern. If these new lines are constructed by others than those financially interested in these two railroads respectively, satisfactory traffic arrangements would have to be made with them. If the new railways recommended should be constructed by the Government, the question is necessarily presented as to whether the Government should acquire the whole or any part of the existing lines, or either of them, or should endeavor to make appropriate traffic agreements. Much would depend upon whether the Government would operate its own railroads or would make operating agreements with those operating existing lines. The commission has not discussed these questions for the reason pointed out in its report that the act of Congress omits questions of this sort from those upon which the commission was instructed to report.

The report of the commission contains the following statement:

Its instructions from Congress do not contemplate that any recommendation should be made as to how railroads in Alaska should be constructed, i.e., by private corporate ownership or by one of the many forms in use whereby Government assistance is rendered. The commission disavows any intention of making such recommendations, believing that Congress, in its wisdom, desired to reserve to itself the solution of that problem; but it has been impossible to form any estimates of costs of operation without some assumption as to the interest rate on the capital required for construction. This interest rate would obviously differ in two cases—construction by Government or bond guaranty, and construction by private capital. Moreover, were construction carried on by private capital unassisted, the necessity of earning sufficient income to pay operating expenses and interest on bonded indebtedness might make it the duty of the directors of the corporation to impose rates on traffic that would seriously retard the development which the Territory so greatly needs.

The commission has therefore been forced to base its studies upon two hypotheses, viz.: That the capital necessary for construction is obtained at 6 percent interest, assumed as possible if construction is carried out by private corporate ownership unassisted; and that capital is obtained at 3 percent interest, assumed as possible if the construction is done either by

the Government itself or by private capital with bonded indebtedness guaranteed both as to principal and interest.

On similar grounds the commission did not feel justified in discussing
the use of the Panama Canal machinery and equipment or in including in
its estimates the effect of such use; but a list of the machinery and equipment available at Panama is given in an appendix.

Upon the assumption that the railroad from Chitina to Fairbanks is
built by private capital, eliminating promotion profit, but assuming the
necessity of earning 6 percent on the capital invested, it is the judgment of
the commission that on estimated available traffic the road could be operated from Cordova to Fairbanks without loss at a passenger rate of 7 cents
per mile and an average freight rate of 8 cents per ton-mile. This would
mean a through freight rate of $36.94 per ton from Cordova to Fairbanks
and a through passenger rate of $31.15. It is the opinion of the commission
that "an average freight rate exceeding 5 cents per ton-mile and passenger
rate in excess of 6 cents per mile would defeat the immediate object of the
railroad, namely, the expeditious development of the interior of Alaska,
and, furthermore, would introduce the question as to whether or not the
Seattle-Cordova-Fairbanks freight route would be able to compete with
the present all-water route via the Yukon River system, except on shipments in which the time element is of such importance as to warrant the
payment of a higher freight rate."

To meet the requirements of expeditious development and water competition the estimate of the commission involves a through freight rate
from Cordova to Fairbanks at $22.25 per ton, and a through passenger rate
of $26.70. The report further says: "Were the road to be constructed by
the Government, or by private corporate ownership with a Government
guaranty of principal and interest on bonded indebtedness, the capital required should be obtained at a much lower rate of interest, thus materially
reducing the annual expenditures."

Using 3 percent on the investment as fixed charges, and omitting mileage tax of $100, on the assumption that this tax would not be levied in the
case of a Government owned or aided road, the commission estimates that
the road would pay on the basis of a passenger rate of 6 cents per mile, and
a freight rate of 5.49 cents per ton-mile, making the average through freight
rate from Cordova to Fairbanks $24.43 per ton and the through passenger

rate $26.70. I give these figures as illustrations. The report contains similar estimates of freight and passenger rates and traffic for the road recommended from Seward to the Kuskokwim.

After recommending the construction of the two principal systems and their extensions already mentioned, the commission states in conclusion that it "is unanimously of the opinion that this development should be undertaken at once, and prosecuted with vigor; that it can not be accomplished without providing the railroads herein recommended under some system which will insure low transportation charges and the consequent rapid settlement of this new land and the utilization of its great resources."

The necessary inference from the entire report is that in the judgment of the commission its recommendations can certainly be carried out only if the Government builds or guarantees the construction costs of the railroads recommended. If the Government is to guarantee the principal and interest of the construction bonds, it seems clear that it should own the roads, the cost of which it really pays. This is true whether the Government itself should operate the roads or should provide for their operation by lease or operating agreement. I am very much opposed to Government operation, but I believe that Government ownership with private operation under lease is the proper solution of the difficulties here presented.

I urge the prompt and earnest consideration of this report and its recommendations.

19

Veto Message

[Transmitting to the House of Representatives, without approval,
"An act making appropriations for the sundry civil expenses
of the Government for the fiscal year ending June 30, 1914,
and for other purposes."]
The White House, March 4, 1913

To the House of Representatives:

I return without my approval the bill H.R. 28775, being "An act making appropriations for the sundry civil expenses of the Government for the fiscal year ending June 30, 1914, and for other purposes."

My reasons for failing to approve this important appropriation bill are found in a provision which has been added to that appropriating $300,000 for the enforcement of the antitrust laws in the following language:

> *Provided, however,* That no part of this money shall be spent in the prosecution of any organization or individual for entering into any combination or agreement having in view the increasing of wages, shortening of hours or bettering the condition of labor, or for any act done in furtherance thereof not in itself unlawful; *Provided further,* That no part of this appropriation shall be expended for the prosecution of producers of farm products and associations of farmers who cooperate and organize in an effort to and for the purpose to obtain and maintain a fair and reasonable price for their products.

This provision is class legislation of the most vicious sort. If it were enacted as substantive law and not merely as a qualification upon the use of moneys appropriated for the enforcement of the law, no one, I take it, would doubt its unconstitutionality. A similar provision in the laws of the State of Illinois was declared by the Supreme Court to be an invasion of the guaranty of the equal protection of the laws contained in the fourteenth amendment of the Constitution of the United States in the case of *Connelly v. Union Sewer Pipe Co.* (184 U.S., 540), although the only exception in that instance from the illegality of organizations and combinations, etc., declared by that statute, was one which exempted agriculturists and live stock raisers in respect of their products or live stock in hand from the operation of the law leaving them free to combine to do that which, if done by others, would be a crime against the State.

The proviso is subtly worded so as in a measure to conceal its full effect by providing that no part of the money appropriated shall be spent in the prosecution of any organization or individual "for entering into any combination or agreement *having in view* the increasing of wages, shortening of hours, or bettering the condition of labor, etc." So that any organization formed with the beneficent purpose described in the proviso might later engage in a conspiracy to destroy by force, violence, or unfair means any employer or employees who failed to conform with its requirements, and yet because of its originally avowed lawful purpose it would be exempt from prosecution so far as prosecution depended upon the moneys appropriated by this act, no matter how wicked, how cruel, how deliberate the acts of which it was guilty. So, too, by the following sentence in the act, such an organization would be protected from prosecution "for any act done in furtherance" of "the increasing of wages, shortening of hours, or bettering the condition of labor," not in itself unlawful. But under the law of criminal conspiracy acts lawful in themselves may become the weapons whereby an unlawful purpose is carried out and accomplished. (*Shawnee Compressed Coal v. Anderson*, 209 U.S., 423–34; *Aikens v. Wisconsin*, 195 U.S., 194–206; *Swift v. United States*, 196 U.S., 375–96; *United States v. Reading Company*, Dec. 16, 1912.)

The further proviso that the appropriation shall not be used in the prosecution of producers of farm products and associations of farmers who cooperate and organize in an effort to obtain and maintain a fair and reasonable price for their products is apparently designed to encourage or, at least, to discourage the prosecutions of organizations having for their purpose the artificial enhancement of the prices of food products, and thus to avoid the effect of the construction given to the antitrust law in the case of *United States v. Patten,* decided January 6, 1913.

At a time when there is widespread complaint of the high cost of living it certainly would be anomalous to put on the statute books of the United States an act in effect preventing the prosecution of combinations of producers of farm products for the purpose of artificially controlling prices; and the evil is not removed, although it may be masked, by referring to the purpose of the organization as "to obtain and maintain *a fair and reasonable price* for their products."

An amendment almost in the language of this proviso, so far as it refers to organizations for the increasing of wages, etc., was introduced in the Sixty-first Congress, passed the House, was rejected in the Senate, and after a very full discussion in the House failed of enactment. Representative Madison, speaking in favor of the amendment which struck out the proviso, characterized it as an attempt "to write into the law so far as this particular measure is concerned, a legalization of the secondary boycott. The laws of this country," he pointed out, "are liberal to the workingman. He can strike, he can agree to strike, he can act under a leader in a strike, and he can apply the direct boycott; but when it comes to going further and so acting as to impede and obstruct the natural and lawful course of trade in this country, then the law says he shall stop. And all in the world that this antitrust act does is to apply to him that simple and proper rule that he, too, as well as the creators of trusts and monopolies, shall not obstruct the natural and ordinary course of trade in the United States of America." "I believe," he added, "in the high aims, motives, and patriotism of the American workingmen and do not believe that rightly understanding this amendment they would ask us to write it into the law of this Republic." (Congressional Record, p. 8850, Sixty-first Cong., 2d sess.)

It is because I am unwilling to be a party to writing such a provision into the laws of this Republic that I am unable to give my assent to a bill which contains this provision.